BROKEN HORSES

BROKEN HORSES

A MEMOIR

. . . .

BRANDI CARLILE

CROWN
NEW YORK

Published in the United States by Crown, an imprint of Random House,
a division of Penguin Random House LLC, New York.

CROWN and the Crown colophon are registered trademarks of
Penguin Random House LLC.

Owing to limitations of space, permissions credits can
be found following the Acknowledgments.

Library of Congress Cataloging-in-Publication Data
Names: Carlile, Brandi, author.
Title: Broken horses / Brandi Carlile.
Description: New York: Crown, 2021.
Identifiers: LCCN 2021004334 (print) | LCCN 2021004335 (ebook) |
ISBN 9780593237243 (hardcover) | ISBN 9780593237250 (ebook)
Subjects: LCSH: Carlile, Brandi. | Singers—United States—Biography.
Classification: LCC ML420.C25555 A3 2021 (print) |
LCC ML420.C25555 (ebook) | DDC 782.42164/092 [B]—dc23
LC record available at https://lccn.loc.gov/2021004334
LC ebook record available at https://lccn.loc.gov/2021004335

PRINTED IN THE UNITED STATES OF AMERICA ON ACID–FREE PAPER

crownpublishing.com

2 4 6 8 9 7 5 3 1

First Edition

Book design by Elizabeth Rendfleisch

I'd like to dedicate this book to my family:

The Carliles for our sacred bond and struggle.

Its incarnation that is my very own family—my Catherine, and our girls, Evangeline and Elijah.

Most of all the family of fellow misfits on the island of the misfit toys. Anyone who's been rejected by this realm and its interpretation of your faith, but never by your Creator. To the repulsed, rejected, reformed, reaffirmed, the redeemed.

Your immeasurable worth precedes you.

PROLOGUE

I'm in bed with my wife, Catherine, and our two little girls with their sweet-smelling heads snuggled between us. We are drinking our morning coffee and continuing a five-day discussion about what I should name this book. "Heroes and Songs?" Too reductive and music-y. "The End of Being Alone?" Too depressing. "Mainstream Kid?" Too insignificant. "The Story?" Really?

Then I hear Evangeline's quiet voice ask: "Mama, remember when you were poor, how could you afford horses?"

Me: "I couldn't, I was given broken ones."

Evangeline: "You should name your book 'Broken Horses.'"

BROKEN HORSES

1.

....

MENINGITIS AND THE EARLY EDUCATION
OF AN EMPATH

The Carliles are nail-biters. I started biting my nails at three years old. Everyone told me that if I didn't keep my hands out of my mouth, I'd get sick.

I contracted meningococcal meningitis at age four.

We were living in Burien, Washington, in a single-wide trailer near the Sea-Tac Airport.

It was our third house since I was born. I'm the first born into my family and the first grandchild on both sides, contributing to my inflated sense of self-importance and burden of perceived responsibility. My life really starts here.

Before all that, though, my parents met at the Red Lion Hotel. My mother was a hostess and my father was a breakfast prep cook. My dad is very intelligent and intense, with a sick sense of humor. He's one of six siblings raised dirt-poor on a dirt floor by a single mom in south Seattle. He's got a father, too, but he and my grandmother divorced very young, and like many of the men on the Carlile side very rarely speaks a word. There are some quiet men in my family but none as quiet as Grandpa Jerry . . . you can feel how much he loves you, but he probably won't ever say it. It almost seems like a genetic trait, this strange brand of anxiety and quiet intensity. He had a daughter later in life, bringing the number of Dad's siblings to seven.

My mother had a more comfortable childhood. She's one of three girls and like her mother has always been very charming and mischievous. She can read a room like no one else. She's vain. She loves music and art. If she's sunny and happy, then everyone she meets is too. Her enthusiasm can't be resisted. If she's not in a good space though, you're not going to be either.

To put it mildly, they're special . . . and sparkly and complicated. When they met, my mom was twenty and my dad was twenty-one. Mom's family had temporarily relocated to Colorado, so she moved straight in with the crazy Carlile family. When my mother got pregnant with me, she and my father decided to get married. Like so many people who married this young, they are still married . . . and in many ways, are still very young.

For this and many other reasons, we moved around a lot after I was born. Fourteen houses actually. And lots of different schools. It's deceiving because sometimes they were all in the same district. Beverly Park Elementary for kindergarten and then to Hill Top Elementary, from there to Cascade View to North Hill Elementary to Olympic Elementary and then back to Hill Top, then there was Rock Creek Elementary, Tahoma Junior High, Glacier Park. And that was all before high school.

I don't think there was ever a housing transition I didn't want to make. There was always an exciting and dramatic buildup to the moving. Sometimes we moved because of evictions and job changes, sometimes for good reasons, like a better housing opportunity or a step up in comfort thanks to some connection that my charismatic parents had made. Either way, due to my frequently changing scenery and the undercurrent of chaos that poverty often creates, I developed somewhat of a photographic memory. It appears in all of its vivid detail right around the age of two.

Bedrooms change, the color of the wallpaper, the smell of a hand-me-down couch, the hum of a rental unit's avocado-colored refrigerator. There's a washing machine that is frequently mistaken for an earthquake, or a friendly neighbor with a horse called Pepper, or someone who lets you hop their fence to retrieve your Frisbee. Different houses sometimes came with different pets and the loss or abandonment of the old ones at the old place. And of course, there were the feuds. . . . I remember every drunk neighbor. The busybodies and gossips, the liberals and the divorcees. I can recall the name of just about every landlord who evicted us and my parents' list of grievances against them. I also remember every helping hand. Every nonjudgmental influence over our family and the impact of such relationships on our lifestyle. More than all this I remember worrying quite a bit.

Most people live in their childhood homes for a while. It softens the edges on the memories and gives them a comforting wash, a kind of afterglow, set against routine and consistency. For kids like me for whom every experience is set against a different visual and intense circumstance, it's really easy to remember details of an early life. I see this now as a priceless gift . . . but it isn't one I'd give to my kids. They're going to have to get scrappy some other way 'cause I don't have the stomach for it anymore.

Burien is all concrete and strip malls now, but parts of it used to feel like the country.

The airport has since shut down most of the land our trailer was on when I got sick. I think it was in a fuel dump zone, or some FAA law changed and it became uninhabitable somehow.

My little brother, Jay, and I were Irish twins. He was irresistible, with blond hair and blue eyes, full of pure drama, charisma, and conviction from birth. At only eleven months and twenty-seven days older than him, I thought he was adorable—and he was mine. He was tougher than me. My parents had to implore me to stand up for myself physically with Jay, because while we didn't really fight in a mutual sense, he fought the hell out of me. I couldn't work out whether he was supposed to be my formidable foe or my protected baby brother. It's an odd age difference. I was getting ready to start kindergarten. My dad wanted me to be homeschooled, but he came up against too much resistance from the rest of the family . . . I understand both inclinations now. The one to keep your kid at home when they seem so small and underprepared and the one that urges us to overcome all that and send them anyway.

I was shy and quiet but very clever. I was good at rhyming, had an extensive vocabulary, and had already dreamed up some songs— *"Smile at the sun, smile at the sun, life is so much fun, when you smile at the sun."* I still hear the melodies. My parents had no experience with children but had been told by enough people that I was advanced. So when my grandmother on my dad's side heard from a neighbor about a program at the University of Washington for gifted children, she hipped my mom to it and I was enrolled at the age of four. I have memories of wearing a lead jacket and playing with children's toys . . . presumably whilst being X-rayed? Now it seems dubious to say the least, but let's chalk it up to the '80s.

I had been a colicky baby with some weird infancy health issues that I had grown out of, but my mother had never grown out of her irrational tendency to worry about me. My dad was well aware of this and didn't attempt to hide his annoyance. Every sneeze or childish complaint would send my mother rushing to the phone to dial "24 Nurse" or Poison Control.

My illness when it hit felt like an extra-dreamy flu to me. Nausea and vomiting, but also a sense of euphoria that I can only imagine must be what morphine is like. My mother's first call was to my dad. They had a fight. Mom had no car and he wasn't about to leave work for yet another fruitless night in the ER for strep throat or gas. She hung up and called 24 Nurse. The TV was on. I remember vividly what it felt like to sink into our brown floral couch feeling so heavy and relaxed I couldn't hold my head up or stay awake. Mom was describing the symptoms to the woman on the phone and after a couple of minutes, she appeared at the couch. "Does she need to be sitting up?" she asked as she propped me up on another pillow. That's when my mother asked me to try and touch my chin to my chest. The last thing I remember was my mother frantically shouting into the phone, "Her eyes are rolling back in her head!"

I wound up on the floor in the backseat of my parents' car. I don't know how I got there. There wasn't time for a car seat and I vaguely remember being so uncomfortable sitting up that I was whimpering and asking if I could get on the floor. I don't know why they didn't call an ambulance. Dad's work was very close, and I am guessing they didn't call an ambulance because deep down they still weren't sure if they could trust themselves about what was an emergency and what wasn't. I don't remember arriving at the hospital, but I'm told that my heart stopped forty-five minutes later.

Everything past the car ride and before coming out of my coma is abstract. A foggy awareness of a very disabled blond-haired little girl with meningitis exactly my age who would never wake up from her coma . . . voices, flashes of light, adult conversations overheard in a dream state but nothing that can be trusted in recollection.

I take that seriously.

It can be hard to understand the difference between what you remember and the things other people tell you about your childhood, but I have a theory that people who are beyond consciousness or in a coma enter an astral plane of perception—what they hear in that state is clear and stored forever. I think we enter this state many times in our lives. Sometimes when we dream, sometimes when we disassociate, most extremely if we cross over through a near-death experience. This state informs who we are in between two worlds . . . which is probably who we really are.

Adults experiencing trauma might not always think children can hear them in any situation. I imagine a coma magnifies this assumption. Things get frantic and are discussed in barely hushed tones. I remember terrified adults if I remember anything. Before meningitis, grandparents were just fun older people who loved and spoiled us. My parents were each other's sworn enemy and the final word in life . . . all-powerful keepers of the universe. My adorable brother hated me, plain and simple. Aunties and uncles were super fun and loving grown-up stoner friends without any tangible connection to my actual family that I could reasonably identify.

The first thing I remember about the day I woke from my coma is something about a sunrise. I've been fascinated with them for most of my life. Not enough to wake up early to enjoy them, but on those few occasions when I have, I've been reminded what a miracle it is that they happen every day, regardless of the one before.

The second thing I remember is that I was STARVING! The party really started when my maternal grandmother, Grandma Dolores, got there and I asked for a tomato (my favorite food). The room erupted into chaos, tears, and laughter and then the questions: "What's your name? How old are you? What's your favorite food? What's Grandma's dog's name and what color is he?" *Brandi, almost five, tomatoes, Aspen, black.* I remember my grandmother joyfully exclaiming, "I'm going out to get you whatever you want!" (I imagine this was to give my parents some space.) "It can be anything!" she said. I thought about it for only a split second because I knew exactly what to ask for. "A full-size Rainbow Brite doll," I said, "and a really big tomato."

I didn't know I'd been gone. What I did know was Poor Kid Survival 101: You gotta know what you want and don't hesitate to ask for it, or you won't get it. Be ready to seize *every* opportunity; everyone is a potential resource. Especially your grandma.

But as the sensation of awakening set in, I had a developing and disturbingly deeper understanding of who all these people really were. The picture would only get clearer as I got older. My grandparents were suddenly the extremely worried parents of MY young parents. My folks didn't seem very powerful anymore. I had now seen them both cry a lot and it sent a chill down my spine to know how little control they had over the outcome of this or anything else ever again.

My mother was relieved beyond words when I regained consciousness, full of joy and frailty. My dad was quiet and sheepish, he even seemed somehow shorter. His relief had softened him to me, and I wasn't sure how to feel about it. I was out of tolerance for needles, IVs, or anything else that pokes or stings, and my parents were suddenly powerless to protect me from them. They were submitting to the doctors with a gratitude and humility that now through the eyes of a thirty-nine-year-old mother is more than righteous. But at the time this was an awakening to life's subtle power structures . . . for me it came too early and in the wrong kind of package.

My aunts and uncles were so obviously my parents' siblings now. I had always been told this was so, but my understanding was childlike. I couldn't picture it. *Now* I could. It was even obvious which ones were older by who was comforting my parents and who was looking to them for comfort. My father's youngest sister, Aunt Nichole, was suddenly another child. She even looked different. She was just a "big girl" to me now.

These realizations led to me feeling somewhat guardianless. It isn't anyone's fault, but this awakening should come much later in life for a very important reason: I'm still untangling what it means to confront mortality and powerlessness.

Perhaps the deepest epiphany came one morning in the hospital after I woke up. The door to my room opened and my little towheaded brother bolted to my bed hysterically crying and telling me he loved me. It wasn't like a scene from a movie; it wasn't sweet. It was pain and stress. Proper trauma. He must have overheard conversations about the likelihood of me pulling through. And he might have had an awareness of the little girl next to me and what was being discussed around her prognosis. To me it meant two things: that he loved me and that he was a child—and in some ways, I wasn't anymore.

I remember the first time I worried about my mom. It was also the first memory I have of my constant companion—debilitating empathy (which is a fancy couple of words for guilt). I was still in the hospital and nearing my birthday. I had a Cabbage Patch Kid doll called

Emmy that I was really attached to. My mom had met some lady in an alleyway and paid cash for her on the toy black market the year these dolls were in high demand. Horrendous-looking little things, but they were a hot commodity in 1984. My incredible nurses understood how tired I'd grown of the IVs and they made me a little IV kit for Emmy. I was ecstatic about this development. All I had to do was undergo one procedure for which I had to be put under (probably my last spinal tap), and when I woke up my reward was supposed to be *constructing* the doll-sized IV.

For all the right reasons, my mother thought she'd surprise me and put the whole thing together so that when I woke up, I could immediately play with it. But when I woke up, I was disproportionately furious. There was *so little* I had control over in there. I just wanted to build something on my own and get a little power back over something that was happening to me against my will. So I acted like a normal five-year-old and threw a fit. My mother of course totally understood, but because I'd become so perceptive, I immediately noticed the exhaustion and defeat on her face. I remembered everything I'd just put her through and was struck down by how guilty I felt.

They had told me to stop biting my nails.

That moment bothered me until I was an adult . . . until I had my children and realized that these are completely normal childish moments of innocent selfishness. The idea that a child might carry around guilt or a sense of responsibility for us as parents is so unfair . . . but I worry about it a lot.

I had flatlined several times and awoken from a coma. There was talk of miracles and mysticism. Jesus was in sharp focus.

Some members of our family were very religious; some just casually, but almost everyone believed in God. Mom's side of the family were technically Catholic. The Carlile family was loosely Baptist— some devout, some of them fragmented and became Evangelical, some even Jehovah's Witnesses. We had one Greek atheist and a few agnostics. The Jonestown Massacre had broken my father's heart. He would soon be baptized Mormon and then become viscerally anti-

Mormon. Procter & Gamble were supposedly Satan-worshippers and it was all happening.

I survived. One day, Dad turned the TV dial to the Christian channel and broke the dial off the TV. I couldn't watch *ThunderCats* anymore. But everyone agreed that God kept me alive because He had a plan for me.

The grossly inflated sense of self-importance was official.

MOM AND DAD HOLDING ME
AS A BABY. MOM ROCKING A
FARRAH FAWCETT FEATHERED
MULLET. THEY WERE 20 AND 21.

MY 4TH BIRTHDAY 1985

TEEN AGED MOM AND DAD LOOKING
VERY COOL

OUR FAMILY PRE TIFFANY
JAY STILL HAS THAT BELLY

ME BEFORE I GOT SICK

ME PROTECTING JAY

MOM AND DADS SHOT GUN
WEDDING .. YES I ATTENDED

ME AND DAD. DAD LOOKING LIKE HE'S
IN THE DRIVE BY TRUCKERS

2.

....

THE NIGHT OF THE LIVING DEAD 1986

When I returned to the trailer we'd been living in after I was discharged from the hospital, it was 1986.

I was in love with Jesus at that age, but I didn't love church. I hated the "Vacation Bible School" my aunt and uncle took us to once a week. I always felt that Jesus wasn't there, and I never wanted to go but I always did. One day in the summer, we were at that church and smelled what our teacher decided was a dead dog, so after repeated prodding from the extremely bored Sunday-school kids, the *even more* extremely bored young Sunday-school teacher decided to just give up on poor old Jesus and let us look for it.

I remember being utterly terrified because I had convinced myself that the dead dog was actually a woman who'd fallen victim to the "Green River Killer," the second most prolific serial killer in U.S. history. I had overheard my parents talking about him at home on many occasions. He was the boogeyman if you lived in Seattle at the time, and we happened to live near Pac Highway, *right* in the heart of his hunting grounds. The era of the Green River Killer haunted many an '80s childhood. I just couldn't keep myself from looking. No one understood my change of heart, but I begged to go to the Bible school after that and spent all of my recesses walking along the edge of the sticker bushes searching for the corpse of a murdered woman.

Overhearing adult conversations was a theme in my childhood. I was privy to just about everything. My mother would notice that I was listening when she was talking to my dad and try to redirect or even end the discussion, only to be met with my father's defiant belief that we should hear everything and nothing should be "sugarcoated." Dad just happened to talk a lot about fascinating things.

I would find out many years later after noticing an uncanny resemblance between my father and serial killer Gary Ridgway in the book *The Riverman* that my mother was deeply concerned that my father *was* in fact the Green River Killer for about four years in the late '80s. I'm fighting strange laughter as I write this, which should tell you everything about the dysfunction, humor, drama, and humanity of my childhood.

The year 1986 was also when my baby sister, Tiffany, was born. My mother had to have a C-section. My parents were understandably distracted and maybe missed some of the signs of the serious anxiety that I was starting to show.

I had gone to my grandma Dolores's house for the afternoon one day, and she accidentally sat me down with my lunch in front of *Poltergeist* and walked away to continue vacuuming her house. She was horrified when she realized what it was that I was watching, but it was too late. "I just skimmed the channels until I saw a little girl on the TV and walked away!" I remember her frantically telling my mother. By the time she shut down the vacuum and noticed what was on, I had seen plenty.

Similarly, *Stand by Me* took years off my life. I loved that damn film, until the part where they find the body. "The kid wasn't sick. The kid wasn't sleeping. The kid was dead" ran through my mind like a blade for years. Not because the dead body was gross and scary . . . it was because it wasn't. It was just lifeless . . . over. I didn't want to believe a kid could die; I needed to know that every kid can be saved by a miracle and it all turns out okay. Otherwise I could die again for real. I still get a chill every time I hear the bass line to "Stand by Me." I couldn't stop listening to it when I was a kid.

Nothing disturbed me visually, though, quite as much as the adverts for *Night of the Living Dead*. They had colorized the film and the ads were always on everyone's goddamned TV! Why were the '80s so fucking scary for kids?! Bloody Mary and Freddy Krueger. Nightmare.

Profoundly, there was an episode of *The Twilight Zone* called "Little Girl Lost," where a six-year-old girl disappears into another dimension through the wall next to her bed. She can see her parents looking for her, but she can't get back. She was so little and having to come to terms with her aloneness . . . It's more sad than scary, but this was a particularly disturbing concept for me because of what I'd just been through. I couldn't explain it to my parents. I just didn't have the faculties to articulate my emotional isolation and fear. In fact, I wasn't able to articulate much at all.

My brain had been through a lot, and I found myself struggling to communicate even for my age level. I went back to the University of Washington for the advanced program one more time, but not again after that. I was apparently not "advanced" anymore. I struggled with what must have been situational dyslexia for most of my childhood. For the most part I grew out of it, but it comes back when I get nervous. I always thought of the yellow-haired girl with meningitis back at the children's hospital and how much worse it could have been for me.

I clearly remember being able to understand everything and feeling sort of existential in general, but I simply couldn't explain why I was so worried all the time. It wasn't so much a daytime problem; I still had a lot of fun . . . but fear is indelible and playdates aren't.

I was so scared at night. I often just said I was sick to get the attention I needed, because I couldn't deal with the complexities in my mind. I would stand in the hallway from the fear of my room, and cry out that I had a sore throat. I had a lot of sore throats, and I still get them when I'm stressed and can't communicate. I felt like that girl from *The Twilight Zone,* lost in another dimension watching myself live like a child but not really feeling like one.

The presentation of faith on my father's side of the family was big, eccentric, and had a vibe to it that can only be described as post-hippie. We traveled together in a big blue culty-looking bus to family reunions and on day trips. Someone was always smoking weed. There was always an underlying thread of faith and humility through everything we did. Church had many meanings to me in those days.

My dad was my favorite person to talk to about Jesus . . . life, death, heaven, hell, angels, and even demons. The same God that brought me so much comfort in quiet moments could also raise terrifying questions for me. Conversations about God were never enough. I would stop speaking and finish them in my head. My dad didn't *want* me to feel so afraid . . . he wanted me to have faith and feel protected, but sometimes the conversations got too complex and dark. I see so much of that same tendency in my older daughter that I'm really careful not to overestimate her ability to process darkness.

I knew I was supposed to pray when I was scared, and I did. I was always afraid that if I wasn't doing it right or wasn't saying the right thing, something bad could happen. I wondered if it was selfish to ask for peace, or to find something lost, or even to ask for a toy I wanted. I would feel guilty if my please-may-I's and thank-you's were too light on the latter. I know my dad was concerned about my tendency toward heavy thinking but, again, he didn't know how to "sugarcoat" . . . you can't *un-have* conversations with a six-year-old about demon possession.

I just wanted God to answer me. For real. I needed real-life assurances.

And those assurances came from the most unlikely source. I still fight a strange embarrassment in telling this story. Honestly, what I'm about to describe makes me feel a tad cringy and self-involved. The thing is, though . . . it happened. It was a gift. It's unexplainable and it wouldn't be right *not* to talk about it because it's one of only a few times in my life that the veil has been lifted.

When you know, you know.

I had a Teddy Ruxpin. Teddy was a stuffed animal with an animatronic mouth and a cassette player in the back. These toys were notorious for breaking, but the Teddy lullaby tapes actually had some amazing melodies on them! This might be one of my earliest melodic influences. I found that bear so comforting, and I still look for them sometimes on vintage toy sites like a total nerd.

Because Teddy had an actual cassette player built in, I was given a few other tapes: *Sesame Street* and a couple kids' church tapes with Christian cartoon characters mostly singing in goofy voices, teaching lessons, and performing innocent slapstick comedy. I memorized those tapes down to the second. I could impersonate every voice and I knew every word of every segment. When Teddy Ruxpin predictably broke one day, I was devastated. Not so much because of the bear but because those tapes had become my companions. They got me through my nights. Sure, I would lie awake until it was almost light, but at least I wasn't alone. I had the stories and music.

An auntie came to my rescue by giving me a clunky '80s cassette player to replace Teddy. Do you remember them? They're motorized, and when you run out of tape, the spring-loaded Play button POPS up with such a vengeance that you're sure the ribbon must have snapped. I jumped every time . . . this is why I learned to time it.

Over the next few weeks my routine was the same: I would rewind all the tapes with the light on and dread the moment the player had to be turned off; Mom would press Play and leave the room, leaving me lying in the *center* of my bed to avoid disappearing into the "wall dimension." There was the relative peacefulness of listening to the stories and the voices of the playful characters, but beyond the songs and skits I was even more familiar with the dead space. The in-betweens. Silence . . . counting . . . and then a wash of relief as the next segment started.

Finally, the last track would come and go. This would start the excruciating countdown. Waiting for the Play button to "jack-in-the-box" up on me. One, two, three, four, four and a hal . . . SNAP! At which point I would spring into action! Jump out of my bed and run as fast as I could across my room (being careful not to disappear into the floor dimension), flip the tape over, press Play, and leap back into (the center of) my bed.

The next side would start, and I'd be okay for another half hour.

But one night the button didn't pop up. I counted . . . and counted again. No pop. I was sure the tape recorder had broken and that I was definitely gonna get a sore throat. After a few deep breaths, I was preparing to run across the floor dimension to inspect my broken Zen machine, when something unusual happened. Real music started playing . . . not *Sesame Street* kid music, but big, gorgeous, angelic voices in multiple layers of complex harmony. It sounded like a hundred people or angels (I feel weird saying angels), but the lyrics were about unseen guardians and peace—it was absolutely epic. Finally, a proper use for that overused word! This was epic. My family listened to country music. This was a kind of otherworldly sound that we didn't even have access to.

When the music ended (and it was long), I got up slowly without any anxiety and rewound the tape. It played again. I could not *fathom* how beautiful it was. I snuck out and stood in the hallway wanting to wake my parents up, but I lost my nerve. I went calmly back to my room and rewound the tape. It was still there. I was bewildered but I wasn't scared anymore, and I went to sleep.

I woke up the next morning and ran to the tape recorder and pressed Play. It was still there. So out of place.

I was in love with that piece of music . . . but I was starting to suspect my parents. I didn't understand the mechanics of cassette-tape manufacturing and recording, but I knew there was a red button on my player and it said RECORD in bold letters. My parents were *obviously* trying to trick and embarrass me by putting a beautiful angelic song on my stupid kid tape so they could laugh at my six-year-old ignorance out of spite and cruelty . . . but I wasn't falling for it.

Yes. This was the way my mind worked.

All the time.

I played it for my mom, and she was mildly perplexed as to how it got there, if not a tad distracted. Dad too. They didn't really listen to me or the song and I couldn't explain it to them like I'm explaining it to you. I remember my mom shuffling out of my room before it was over: "Of course we didn't put it on there. You probably just hadn't heard it yet." My dad was a little better about it, but he didn't listen to it. He didn't try to explain it and didn't seem appalled at the thought that it might have come from somewhere spiritual. They both maintained for years (until I finally stopped asking them) that they had nothing to do with it.

Of course they didn't. Even if they were so inclined it would have been physically impossible. I've had to accept it for what it is and not feel dramatic explaining it.

I was answered. With real music. And it brought me peace. That's all.

This experience and a few others have also given me a faith that is as impervious to political extremism as it is to the whims of culture.

That tape was my comfort blanket or that one tattered stuffed animal that a child is fundamentally attached to. I must have lost it in one of our moves. I think things disappear when we don't need them anymore. I listened to that music every night. It was my proof that God is real.

Music is still my proof that God is real.

"STAND BY ME"

When the night has come
And the land is dark
And the moon is the only light we'll
see
No I won't be afraid, oh I won't be
afraid
Just as long as you stand, stand
by me

So darlin', darlin', stand by me
Oh stand by me
Oh stand
Stand by me, stand by me
If the sky that we look upon
Should tumble and fall
Or the mountain should crumble
to the sea
I won't cry, I won't cry, no I won't
shed a tear
Just as long as you stand, stand
by me

And darlin', darlin'
Stand by me, oh stand by me
Whoa, stand now
Stand by me, stand by me
Darlin', darlin', stand by me
Oh, stand by me
Oh, stand now
Stand by me, stand by me
Whenever you're in trouble, won't
you stand by me?
Oh, stand by me
Whoa, just stand now
Oh, stand, stand by me
When all of your friends have
gone

  —BEN E. KING , WRITTEN BY
   BEN E. KING, JERRY LEIBER,
   AND MIKE STOLLER

THE CARLILE BUS ... ME FRONT AND CENTER WHERE I LIKE TO BE. DAD
HOLDING A SLEEPING JAY. THIS IS GRANDMA CAROL AND THE GROWING
FAMILIES OF HER SIX CHILDREN

BIKES PERMS AND ACID WASH!
CHRISTMAS PRESENT FROM GRANDPA VERN
AND DO J

MOM'S DRESS UP DOLL 1986

3.

·········

THE LOSS OF A YODELING PATRIARCH

My mother lost her father to ALS (we all called it Lou Gehrig's disease) in 1989. I say it this way, instead of "I lost my grandfather," for two reasons. One is that my mother was still in her twenties when she lost her dad at fifty-one years old, and it was life-altering for our family. The second reason is that I was already starting to learn that what was happening to other people was more important than what was happening to me.

Before all that, though, we went camping, trout fishing, and even cut down our own Christmas tree once or twice. We went to the ocean in Westport and to pancake houses, we had cousins, cats, bikes, and family jam sessions at my great-grandparents' house. We didn't play or sing but we loved to listen. I can still remember sneaking upstairs to listen after we'd been put to bed in their strange old-person house, laying my head on the plastic-covered steps and falling asleep to my grandfather singing Jim Reeves.

Grandpa Vernon and Grandma Dolores were like movie stars to us.

They stood out from the wear and tear that coated the rest of our poor and struggling family.

My grandma Dolores was charm personified. You would go dizzy if you had to count how many times in any conversation she'd wink at you. She would walk me through her house and point out all of her "crystal" knickknacks and candy dishes. She said it was so that I'd know not to handle and break them, but I could tell it was that she was new to money and they made her proud. If she bought you a gift, she struggled to keep herself from telling you how much it was worth. She could also slay a dozen salmon in a day and follow it up with an evening of clam digging. As much as she loved to shine, I still remember her in a navy-blue puffy down mountain vest in front of a campfire. She could rarely laugh without snorting. My grandpa was a cigar salesman; he had blond hair, slight but straight shoulders, he was athletic and glamorous in a rugged sense. A worthy patriarch in every way, but on top of this, he was "the singer" in the family and he could yodel. From what I can remember, he could mostly only yodel up and not down, but it was really special either way. His brother, "Uncle Sonny," played guitar and banjo, and his mother, Florentine, played honky-tonk piano like a fucking riot! They used to have family concerts and even ran an illegal dance hall out of their home to earn extra money.

Great-Grandma Florentine died of Alzheimer's disease. Sometimes it was scary to be in her house because she was always carrying on about a masked intruder and I believed her. My folks told me that this kind of paranoia was common with her disease, but it sounded real to me. She was so innocent. And even though she forgot her sons and relived the death of Elvis daily, she could play piano like that until the moment she died.

Grandpa Vernon was a bit of a father figure to my dad as well. Dad was a city boy who rode a motorcycle and wore leather pants until Grandpa took him to cut wood. Most people think my dad is an actual "man-bear," who crawled out of a cave somewhere with a raccoon in his teeth. Few think of him as an overburdened, dirt-poor prep cook from Burien, even though that's the truth.

This is how influential Vern Miller was. Time spent with him could be transformational. People are often elevated to sainthood upon their death (especially an untimely one). I'm sure this *is* the case with my grandpa, but many of us have passed on and more than three decades later he's the only one that no one can talk about without tears.

ALS always seems to strike the people who take the best care of themselves. Grandpa Vernon was an avid jogger. He golfed, hunted, fished, and traveled. One day he went for a jog, became disoriented, and fell. He didn't think much of it until it happened again. When he went to the doctor, he was tested for Lyme disease, and it seemed like he had it for sure because of his years hunting and fishing in the fields and streams of northern Minnesota where he was raised. But his deterioration set in so quick that it became very clear that something more sinister was at play.

My earliest memories of music were of hearing him sing and thinking he was good enough to be famous. My mom was so enamored with him and he'd try to get her to sing, but she was too shy. When he was diagnosed with ALS, we knew we'd only have him for a year. His illness moved so quickly. He somehow tried to make it fun for us. His attitude was remarkable. He told jokes about his failing body, gave us wheelchair rides, and laughed constantly. He was so affectionate it was uncomfortable for me.

I didn't understand why at the time, but I hated being called "pretty." Grandpa Vernon would tell me I was pretty from the time I walked in the door to the time I left. I told my mom on the ride home one night that it bothered me and asked why he did it. She said that he only ever had three daughters, who very much appreciated being called pretty. Fighting tears, she explained that we would lose him soon and he wanted me to remember that he loved me—calling me pretty over and over again was his way of saying something so much that it stuck. She suggested I tell him privately that I loved him so he would know, and so that he might see that I had my *own* way of showing it.

The next time I saw him, I waited until the room was loud with chatter so no one would notice me. I climbed up on his lap and nervously whispered, "I love you," into his ear. He looked at me and burst out laughing. I'll never forget it. Suddenly the room went silent and everyone in the family was watching. "Alright . . . what do you want?" he said with a chuckle. His eyes were twinkling, but it absolutely broke my heart. I jumped off of his wheelchair and ran away to hide until it was time to leave. I was utterly humiliated.

Of course, I understand now that he could only relate to me in the context of his cheeky daughters and the era in which they were raised. No one, including me, really understood how sensitive and serious I was. I was probably a mystery to him then. But I feel him often now and I know he's been with me all this time.

As a salesman, there was no one more convincing than Grandpa Vernon. But even he couldn't coax my mother out of her paralyzing anxiety around her voice. She loved to sing (still does), but she was a very young mother to three children and living significantly beneath the poverty line. These are stressful day-to-day realities. Singing and vocalizing in general create X-ray levels of emotional exposure. You may open your mouth and not know what's going to come out. It's like taking those first few steps on a broken leg when the cast comes off. Still broken, my mother made the boldest decision of her life to that point when she talked a group of musicians and studio owners into helping her record a song for her father just days before he died. It was Judy Collins's version of "Amazing Grace." He was thrilled.

They played it at his funeral, which was very long and very Catholic. It was the first time I heard the phrase *The Lord is my shepherd; I shall not want*. It stuck with me. That collection of words fed something in me that shouldn't have been sustained.

In the weeks following her father's death, my mother mustered the strength to put on one of his singing tapes. One side wouldn't play, so she flipped it over. The other side started exactly at the chorus of a Hank Snow song, and loud and clear she heard her dad belting the lyrics to "I Don't Hurt Anymore."

I think God quite clearly has a preference for analog tape.

Mom chose to sing after that. She fought depression with Prozac and a lot of time sleeping, but she *really* started to win when she fought with her voice. With some of the money Grandpa left, Grandma Dolores helped Mom buy a small PA system and put a band together. Grandma called herself Mom's "manager" and held auditions in her basement. Some of my favorite childhood memories involve Mom's bands, Nightshift and Inside Track. There were logos, T-shirts, banners, and glamour shots, but most memorable were the musicians who surrounded my mom, a parade of good-natured, paternal men who gave great bear hugs. They always had the time to learn a song on guitar for an eight-year-old girl who wanted to sing Tanya Tucker songs.

Meanwhile, Grandma Dolores developed a penchant for blue topaz, sequins, and cowboy hats.

Grief is weird.

We became COUNTRY. It was the era of line dancing and western shirts. There were urban-western-wear stores in every strip mall. I developed a Southern accent that I still have to this day. It's been a part of me for so long that it's no longer an affectation. "Country isn't Southern, it's Western!" is a Pacific Northwest slogan I've always been fond of . . . I do love a Pacific Coast cowboy.

This was the world we were living in right before we left the city. Dad hated how Burien was rapidly developing, and even with the sudden influx of Garth Brooks fanaticism, it wasn't feeling country to him in the way he needed. Our parents decided that they wanted to raise us in the woods. We moved our family of five into a run-down single-wide mobile home up on top of a mountain in a tiny, zero-stoplight town called Ravensdale.

I remember going to see the house for the first time. It was so far up a winding dirt road that it reminded me of being in the forest with Grandpa Vernon and good times with Dad cutting down a Christmas tree. It felt like scenes from summer camp movies and adventures and *The Goonies*. My brother and I were in love with it right away. We took off into the woods following some deer tracks and terrified our mother. It was the beginning of a lifelong penchant for building fires and living in the wilderness.

The Carliles had begun to change their identity.

It was heaven.

"I DON'T HURT ANYMORE"

It don't hurt anymore
All my teardrops are dried
No more walkin' the floor
With that burnin' inside

Just to think it could be
Time has opened the door
And at last I am free
I don't hurt anymore.

No use to deny I wanted to die
The day you said we were through

But now that I find you're out of
my mind
I can't believe that it's true

I've forgotten somehow ·
That I cared so before
And it's wonderful now
I don't hurt anymore.
    —HANK SNOW, WRITTEN BY JACK
      ROLLINS AND DON ROBERTSON

THE MILLER FAMILY BAND OF RADIO AND TV FAME!
UNCLE SONNY PLAYING THE GUITAR I NOW TOUR WITH,
AND MY TEEN AGED GRAND PARENTS LOCKED IN A
SLOW DANCE.

GRANDPA VERNON AND
HIS ACCORDION

THE MILLER FAMILY JAM SESSIONS GREAT GRANDPA
ON BANJO, GRANDPA VERN SINGING AND PLAYING
SPOONS, GREAT GRANDMA FLORENTINE ON PIANO
THIS IS WHERE THE MUSIC STARTED.

GRANDPA VERNON WITH MOM

MY MOTHER WANTED THIS PHOTO TAKEN RIGHT AFTER
HER DAD DIED. GRIEF IS WEIRD. SHE WAS NOT YET 30
I REMEMBER THIS AS A SAD DAY. I COULDN'T UNDERSTAND
WHY SHE WANTED TO DO IT.

4.

....

A COAT OF MANY COLORS

As my mom's band developed into a proper bar band, the music became a little more serious. She had notebooks filled with lyrics and the song structures of the late-'80s country divas. It was around this time that Mom took me to my first concert. We saw the Judds at the Puyallup Fair in Washington State. We absolutely loved the Judds; they would become our second and third concerts as well. I believe the Judds were one of the first important influences on my connection with my mother. I knew subconsciously that I wasn't feminine or lighthearted enough for her . . . but I could sing, and I loved music as much as she did. That was our language.

We heard about a small theater holding auditions for *The Northwest Grand Ole Opry Show*. We were very familiar with the Grand Ole Opry in Nashville and often fantasized about traveling south to see it. My mother had decided that she wanted to try out, so my siblings and I went to Mom's audition. Right before Mom took the stage, a little girl about nine years old strutted out in a yellow frilly dress and sang the shit out of Dolly Parton's "Coat of Many Colors." My mind was blown. This was the first time I realized that kids didn't have to wait until they were grown-ups to follow their dreams and start their lives. I didn't want to be a kid anymore anyway. I always said I did, but I was lying.

I wanted to be a singer.

My mother read my mind. She knew I had made the connection and that I no longer saw singing as something I wanted to do "when I grew up." We started talking about songs and singers all the time, correcting each other's misheard lyrics and complimenting each other's vocal choices. When she had band rehearsals, she was careful not to leave me out. The band would learn one of "my songs," and I'd get to sing at least once a practice.

Very shortly after all that I had my first audition at the Opry. It was just me singing, with my mom's friend Bill Stevenson playing guitar. No one got paid, these were just good people who wanted to play music for anyone in any way possible. It was a very powerful lesson for a young person to learn about what a privilege it is to get to play music even for free.

To my delight, I got a spot in the show and was instructed to practice my song, put together an outfit, and be at a Wednesday-night practice for the performances Friday and Saturday night.

I chose "Tennessee Flat Top Box," a song by Rosanne Cash and written by her father. It was a song about a poor but very talented little dark-haired boy in a south Texas border town (I always imagined him as Mexican) who believed that he could be a country star. He would play his guitar week after week in a tiny Texas cabaret for a crowd of adoring young girls until he disappeared, only to reemerge on the Hit Parade as a big star.

My first real moment onstage came that weekend. I was around eight or nine years old. It was right after Grandpa died. My outfit was mostly homemade, and funnily enough, it was very similar to the kind of thing I'd wear onstage now. Tight black jeans tucked into cowboy boots, a light-blue shirt tucked in with a homemade vest and bolo tie. My great-grandfather on Dad's side loved to find and polish turquoise in Arizona whenever he and my great-grandmother weren't wandering between bluegrass festivals in their motor home playing Dobro. He'd make us bolo ties and vests, hatbands and belt buckles. He made quite a few special things for us to wear onstage as a quiet way of showing his pride in our music. I topped off the whole outfit with a powder-blue cowboy hat that had been bedazzled the night before by my mother.

I still can't bring myself to go out onstage in ordinary clothes . . . I see it as a sign of disrespect to the audience and to the art of entertainment. It's not about having fancy clothes and being rich; it's about communicating to the crowd that you understand the evening is special for them.

The stage door was painted to look like the entrance to a castle, and the backstage had real vanity lights on the "ladies' side." The separation between the crowd and the backstage was bizarrely intoxicating. "Backstage" still has an allure to me. I think that's true for most people. Not everyone gets to be back there. It holds the secrets and it knows what the audience is about to experience when they don't. It's like the anticipation you feel when someone is about to open a really spectacular Christmas present that you put a lot of thought into.

The Opry had an announcer. I'll never forget the sound of my name as I was being called out onstage for the first time. You don't hear your full name for too many reasons when you're a kid. Attendance in school, maybe a stern warning from your parents, but it's not too often that your name is called out like an adult's to do something extraordinary. I still think about it sometimes when I'm introduced to the stage or if I accept an award. It's an honor to hear your name spoken in such a way.

"And now for her Northwest Grand Ole Opry debut, please put your hands together for Brrrandi Carlile!"

The lights created a glare in my glasses, and I couldn't see the crowd of 250 people, but I could *feel* them. I knew I had their affection and encouragement . . . The only way I can describe the way that I felt is "safe." I was making myself very vulnerable, but I trusted that part of human nature—the empathy and support that emerges when someone puts themselves out there. I knew I would always feel most at home in that tension and embrace. The song went too fast and the guitar player stumbled through every musical interlude (to be fair, "Tennessee Flat Top Box" is a tough song), but the applause at the end was the nail in the coffin of any other path I might have gone down in life. I never wanted to leave that stage. Or if I did, it would have been to step down into the audience and just sit with them for the rest of the evening. I wanted to be with the people who I suddenly believed understood me.

I was realizing early on in life that music, for me, was pure joy. For Mom, though, it was stressful and important. She was very proud of me and very supportive, but her own experience was tied up with grief for her father, stress from poverty, even body image. She wouldn't realize this fully until looking at her anxiety-ridden performance photographs years later. You can't hide much when you're onstage. People see you. They see your talent and your flaws, your clothes and your fear. Guilelessness is an imperative gift for any performer, and not everyone comes by it naturally.

My brother, Jay, may have made his debut that night too; I honestly don't remember. I was pretty preoccupied with myself . . . narcissism is such an embarrassing but necessary part of an artist's development. Jay was technically better than me. He regularly stunned our whole family with his superior voice and his ability to pick up and play any instrument. Even his comedic timing was extraordinary! He could play the spoons, guitar, and piano just from visits to family homes that had these things lying around. He could dance with old ladies at weddings and hold his own. He even introduced a new concept to the family called harmony. All this before he was even nine. I had to work much harder to keep up, but I *wanted* to work harder.

We all started thinking of him as "Little Vern." But Jay was different. Just like for Mom, live performance and music in general were incredibly stressful for him. He would frequently try to get out of participating in family performances to avoid the stress. This became a complicated part of our childhood relationship—I felt like I needed him more than he needed me. I enjoyed the healthy competition and the give-and-take of exchanging new musical skills and influences. But I felt like I was always having to beg him to play with me or even talk with me about music as much as I wanted to. It was confusing and hard for me to accept.

The Carlile family spent several years entrenched in the eccentric Northwest Grand Ole Opry community, and it was transformative for us. The shows just kept coming! There were variety shows and Christmas shows, the Opry and the "kids'" Opry, and so on.

One of my favorite performances happened unexpectedly when a celebrity came to the Opry one weekend: the legendary country singer Dottie West's daughter, who was a country star in her own right, Shelly West. She had a hit country song on the radio called "Jose Cuervo"—I called it "The Fightin' Song." My mom was scheduled to open for her on the big stage. The three of us—Jay, Tiffany, and me—were gonna join in during Mom's set. Coordinated outfits had been made for our guest appearance onstage. The problem was that on the day Shelly was set to arrive, she allegedly told the folks at the Opry that she didn't want another woman opening the show. To be fair, they both had the exact same haircut. This was one of my earliest glimpses into institutionalized female competitiveness.

I don't want to put words into Mom's mouth, but I'm gonna go out on a limb here and assume she was incredibly relieved and had probably made herself sick with nerves leading up to the show. She offered me up as her replacement, and I was going to get to sing multiple songs in a row! I basically got to sing every song I had ever learned that night, and we all got our picture taken with Shelly West.

Shelly sang her hit song about kissing cowboys and starting fights, and I watched with my mom from the back of the room near the soundboard. I was manic, explaining to my mom how incredibly possible it all was! The divide between the woman onstage who had a hit song on the radio and me wasn't really that great. We had just shared the same stage . . . and the audience wasn't clapping any louder for her than they did for me. Plus we were both in tiny Auburn, Washington, weren't we? My mom leaned down and whispered in my ear about something called a "composer." She told me that she had just met one and he had two "original" songs that he wanted her to sing.

This was an unsettling revelation. I had never thought about where songs come from. They came from the radio. You learn them, write them down in your notepad, ask a musician to learn the chords . . . and then you sing them. I thought they belonged to *all* of us. Now I was having to wrap my head around the concept that once someone records a song, it's only an "original" to them. Everyone else is just acting . . . I was dissatisfied with that. I knew I needed to find one of these composer people to write me an original, but I had no idea how.

My brother had a red acoustic guitar that someone had won for him at the fair—the kind of cheap toy you get by throwing darts at a balloon. He called it "Dead Fret" because all but two of the frets were dead, and if you pressed a string down almost anywhere on the neck it would buzz instead of making a note. With only the two top strings left intact, it was more like half of a bass guitar that you could play a grand total of six notes on.

I knew I would never find a composer, and I started to wonder if maybe I could just *be* one. I took the string off of a longbow and arrow set that my dad had and tied it around Dead Fret as a strap so that I could stand in front of the bathroom mirror with my hat on and imagine I was a guitar-playing composer and country star. I was sliding my thumb over each of the strings in time and back again in a lonesome cowboy pattern. I started to imagine I was in the old West, with a horse riding off into the sunset and sleeping in the desert by a campfire. I started singing and rhyming, keeping the pattern simple, and after a few minutes I'd written my "original" in the bathroom mirror. It was called "Ride On Out." In my mind I could even play the guitar.

I had closed the distance between me and Shelly West for good now. I was a composer and I could create my own originals. Nothing else could stop me . . . I just needed four more strings on Dead Fret.

Playing music with my family and singing for people in *any* circumstance was all I wanted to do. Anything I ever learned to do from that point forward, whether it was writing, playing instruments, or even singing karaoke, was only to facilitate my addiction to performing. Finding a way to get myself onstage was my endgame from morning until night.

The landslide came when I couldn't apply myself in school. I was dyslexic, and failing sixth grade. I'd already been to six schools and simply couldn't function in an academic setting. I struggled to get along with other kids and spent a lot of time worrying about being poor. I tried to make my singing the thing about me that would get me some attention and acceptance from my classmates. I was a mean, scrappy little trailer girl with the wrong clothes and a very sensitive soul that I was hiding behind a bravado that I had developed performing onstage. I'm only just now starting to blame the Tanya Tucker songs. She was always one of my favorites because she was so tough. Dolly and Reba, too, these badass bombshells with their teased mullets and camel toes.

School was an alternate reality. It didn't matter to me. My dad had made me hate it as an institution with his diatribes about communism . . . I had chosen music anyway.

Being tough was starting to become painfully important to me. I wasn't sure what any of it meant, but my need to be perceived as confident and strong was starting to consume me. This period is, to say the least, a fragile time in any child's life. Gender dysphoria as I understand it now is a natural concept during adolescence, but I had no language for it, only a growing sense of self that was starting to stretch beyond my situation—I was way too poor and way too awkward to want to make as much of a spectacle of myself as I was.

If only to ease the memory of some retrospective embarrassment, I wish sometimes that my station had stopped me or at least slowed me down. . . . but nothing did. I was determined to make an impression.

"I might've been born just plain white trash, but Fancy was my name."

"RIDE ON OUT"

I wanna ride on out I wanna hit the road
And when I take to the trails with a speedy mode
I will leave you behind in a dusty cloud
I want to hear nature's song in the quiet and loud
When the sun sinks behind the mountains high
I'm gonna sing my sad songs beneath a purple sky
I will fall asleep into my saddle deep
And wake on up to the morning sweet
I wanna ride on out I wanna hit the road.

    —BRANDI CARLILE

"JOSE CUERVO" (THE FIGHTIN' SONG)

Well, it's Sunday Mornin'
And the sun in shinin'
In my eye that is open
And my head is spinnin'
Was the life of the party
I can't stop grinnin'
I had too much tequila last night

Jose Cuervo, you are a friend of mine
I like to drink you with a little salt and lime
Did I kiss all the cowboys?
Did I shoot out the lights?
Did I dance on the bar?
Did I start a fight?

Now wait a minute
Things don't look too familiar
Who is this cowboy
Who's sleepin' beside me?
He's awful cute, but how'd I
Get his shirt on?
I had too much tequila last night

All those little shooters
How I love to drink 'em down
Come on, bartender
Let's have another round

Well, the music is playing
And my spirits are high
Tomorrow might be painful
But tonight we're gonna fly

Jose Cuervo, you are a friend of mine
I like to drink you with a little salt and lime
Every time we get together
I sure have a good time
You're my friend
You're the best
Mi amigo
(Tequila)
Jose Cuervo, you are a friend of mine
I like to drink you with a little salt and lime
Did I kiss all the cowboys?
Did I shoot out the lights?
Did I dance on the bar?
Did I start a fight?
Jose Cuervo, you are a friend of mine

    —SHELLY WEST, WRITTEN BY CINDY JORDAN

"TENNESSEE FLAT TOP BOX"

In a little cabaret
In a south Texas border town
Sat a boy and his guitar
And the people came from all
around
And all the girls
From there to Austin
Were slippin' away from home
And puttin' jewelry in hock to take
the trip
To go and listen
To the little dark-haired boy who
played the
Tennessee flat top box
And he would play

Well, he couldn't ride or wrangle
And he never cared to make a
dime
But give him his guitar
And he'd be happy all the time
And all the girls
From nine to ninety
Were snappin' fingers, tappin'
toes

And beggin' him: "Don't stop"
And hypnotized and fascinated
By the little dark-haired boy who
played the
Tennessee flat top box
And he would play

Then one day he was gone
And no one ever saw him 'round
He vanished like the breeze
They forgot him in the little town
But all the girls
Still dreamed about him
And hung around the cabaret
Until the doors were locked
And then one day
On the hit parade
Was a little dark-haired boy who
played the
Tennessee flat top box
And he would play
    —JOHNNY CASH, PERFORMED
      BY ROSANNE CASH

"COAT OF MANY COLORS"

Back through the years
I go wanderin' once again
Back to the seasons of my youth
I recall a box of rags that
someone gave us
And how my momma put the rags
to use
There were rags of many colors
Every piece was small
And I didn't have a coat
And it was way down in the fall
Momma sewed the rags together
Sewin' every piece with love
She made my coat of many colors
That I was so proud of

As she sewed, she told a story
From the Bible, she had read
About a coat of many colors
Joseph wore and then she said
Perhaps this coat will bring you
Good luck and happiness
And I just couldn't wait to wear it
And momma blessed it with a kiss

My coat of many colors
That my momma made for me
Made only from rags
But I wore it so proudly
Although we had no money
I was rich as I could be
In my coat of many colors
My momma made for me

So with patches on my britches
And holes in both my shoes
In my coat of many colors
I hurried off to school
Just to find the others laughing
And making fun of me
In my coat of many colors
My momma made for me

And oh, I couldn't understand it
For I felt I was rich
And I told 'em of the love
My momma sewed in every stitch
And I told 'em all the story
Momma told me while she sewed
And how my coat of many colors
Was worth more than all their
clothes

But they didn't understand it
And I tried to make them see
That one is only poor
Only if they choose to be
Now I know we had no money
But I was rich as I could be
In my coat of many colors
My momma made for me
Made just for me
   —DOLLY PARTON

TIFF, JAY, ME, MOM — AND THE HAIR SHE OBVIOUSLY
DID FOR ALL OF US. OUR CLOTHES WERE
HOME MADE.

ME, JAY AND TIFF RIGHT AFTER
LOSING GRANDPA

MY OLD AUTOGRAPH ON AN OLD OPRY PROGRAM FROM 1992 SUPPORT AND LOVE FROM ALL THE GROWN UP SINGERS

ME AND JAY IN A "PROMO PHOTO" MY GOD THAT HAIR!

MOM ON STAGE WITH HER KIDS. I WAS MISERABLE IN THAT THAT SKIRT. BEING PUT IN A DRESS WAS THE ONLY WAY TO BREAK MY CONFIDENCE. TIFFANY OF COURSE LOVED IT.

5.

....

HONKY CAT

My father had always had a drinking problem, but it was spiraling out of control living in the country. His whole family, even his kids, were playing music in bars several days a week, and he would come out and just drink. I don't think he knew exactly where he fit in. Things got pretty tense for me and my siblings. My little sister was almost six and starting to become very aware of how unstable our home life was getting. While Mom was still struggling with depression from losing her father and sleeping a lot of the time, my young dad was slipping into dangerous alcoholism.

My dad was a machinist at Boeing in the early '90s. He worked very hard, sometimes even covering the graveyard shift; then the union went on strike. Families of Boeing employees were really struggling during this time. Lots of people were laid off. My dad was and is profoundly anti-union and he crossed the picket line on principle. He struggled with his anger around this and we talked a lot about politics late into the night. At that point in my life I always agreed with everything he said. A very intense but intelligent man, he was an enormous influence on me. I became a bit arrogant and belligerent myself. I got into a lot of arguments with teachers. To this day, I hope that they could see through that veneer and forgive me.

The first wave of a fundamental shift in my worldview came at the beginning of sixth grade. It was my first year at a new school out in the country and I was wanting to start over. My parents explained to us that in our new town there would be lots of poor white kids at school and we'd have better luck making friends than we had in the city. Our teacher gave us the parameters of a book report, which would be a regular feature of our middle school and high school years. When I went to the library to pick out my book, I stumbled across one with a handsome boy on the cover who I thought looked like Edward Furlong or any one of the teen heartthrobs that I was supposed to be collecting photos of from *Seventeen* magazine. I was certainly curious. At one point I was so concerned with fitting in that I pasted a picture of child actor Jonathan Brandis on the front of my three-ring binder. (As one of my childhood friends still relishes in reminding me, I had written an apostrophe between the *i* and the *s* in his name.) Similarly, on some level I probably felt like walking around school with a cute boy on the cover of my new "book report" would make me feel cool. But the boy on this book cover had sadly passed away. His name was Ryan White. I knew I needed to understand more about him, so I checked out the book.

Until this point, I had been taught that AIDS was a disease caused by homosexual men. I of course was told for most of my childhood by multiple sources that to be gay was a one-way ticket to hell. Homosexuality and suicide were the "unforgivables," and I believed this wholeheartedly. Thank God for books and libraries . . . and school.

Ryan White had died at the age of eighteen. He contracted HIV through a blood transfusion before he was a teenager. I had never even heard of a hemophiliac. When he was diagnosed in 1984 and given six months to live, he was ostracized by his community and forbidden to return to school. No one understood what HIV was and how it was contracted. From what I gathered by talking about it around home, people in my town and family were certainly no *less* ignorant.

The homophobia was staggering. I had a teen Baptist study Bible that famously stated in its footnotes that "AIDS was God's way of punishing homosexuals and when other people get it, it's meant as a reminder of how much evil there is in the world."

The foot soldiers of religious homophobia targeted Ryan White and tried to make him into their poster child for anti-gay rhetoric. But his wisdom was already beyond his years and he wasn't having it. In fact, his friendship with a gay British rock-'n'-roll singer had shifted my perspective in a tectonic way. I was irreversibly shook.

When the boy died, this singer, Elton John, played a song called "Skyline Pigeon" at his funeral. The words were right there in the book I'd checked out of the library. The lyrics were written by Elton John's longtime friend and collaborator Bernie Taupin. This was poetry like I had never imagined before, far beyond the kind of dimension I would have heard in a country song. It flew off the page. You could step right into it like a diorama or a Velvet Elvis. People can stand in a gallery and stare at an abstract painting forever. I never understood that . . . I just didn't get it, and I wondered if I had the intelligence necessary to appreciate high art. But I could have read the lyrics of that song for hours. It was like staring into a fire or at the stars. This is when I really knew I was going to write. Those lyrics led me to the King County Library to find that song and embark on my very first independent and non-country musical journey of discovery.

Needless to say, I found way more than music.

I would go back to the library again and again to look for books and music pertaining to Elton John. I found *Tumbleweed Connection, Here and There*, and a duets album. I asked for all Elton John and Bernie Taupin–related birthday and Christmas gifts, cut out newspaper clippings, and collected vinyl records from thrift stores. Before long, my walls were completely covered with photos and lyrics. I found a biography by a guy called Philip Norman, and through that book I discovered Freddie and Queen, the Beatles, George Michael, David Bowie.

I wasn't a country singer anymore.

I shared a room and a bunk bed with my sweet little sister, Tiffany. She endured hours and hours of Elton John. In the top bunk I had a boom box and I'd program the CD to play Elton ballads overnight ALL night in the hopes that I'd become a genius by osmosis. I'd press the speaker to my ear and listen to "The Greatest Discovery," "Blues for Baby and Me," "Daniel," "Come Down in Time," and "Burn Down the Mission" until my alarm went off. Tiffany still dreams the music. No one else would have let me get away with that, only her.

Keep in mind that this is pre–*Lion King*. Elton's most recent album was 1992's *The One*. There was absolutely nothing about my fascination that was helping me blend into my Nirvana-era rural school scene. And soon enough my affinity for Elton John would become very public.

One of the interesting things we would do besides sing in bars and at the Northwest Grand Ole Opry, was to enter singing competitions. Mom won a lot of them, but I always lost. I was too awkward. These were really just pageants at the end of the day. Little girls in perfect dresses and updos ALWAYS singing Whitney Houston or Bette Midler. I just didn't fit. I couldn't walk right, and I liked weird songs that no one knew. The prizes were really big and serious too! Scholarships, thousands of dollars, record contracts—the kinds of things that really make your heart pound. I know it bothered my mom to see her frumpy daughter get up on that stage and lose to all those perfect pageant girls every single time. The truth is that we had no money for those things even if I could have pulled it off.

For one of these big contests in a serious auditorium I hatched a plan to help me stand out. By then, my Elton John obsession was getting absolutely insane and I had seen a man's white polyester suit at the Catholic church's clothing mission where our family got a lot of our clothes. I had seen footage of him performing "Honky Cat" in a white suit with glitter shoes and feather glasses and I decided THAT was going to be my act!

I told my mom, and her head just dropped. She knew right then and there that I wouldn't win . . . and that I was going to look like a freak, but she got me that suit. She stayed up late at night in the days leading up to the contest bedazzling it with yellow sequins and rhinestones that she'd bought at Michaels craft store. She used a hot-glue gun to adorn a pair of drugstore boat shoes with the letters "E.J." However, my favorite accoutrement was a twenty-inch pair of yellow-feathered glasses that she created from pipe cleaners and feathers. I felt AMAZING.

I lost. But she'd helped me *try* to win . . . and she helped me truly express myself in front of my peers for the first time.

Junior high school came on like a fever. I liked the freedom of walking from class to class, but it's easier to see who the loner kids are when you have to pick your own lunch table in the cafeteria. I remember just walking around with my drink, trying not to be noticed as someone who didn't have a place to sit. It was so out-of-body. You're just observing yourself at that age.

I spent a lot of time worrying about my brother and sister during that time. Because of the anxiety I used to get a lot of colds and sore throats back then and soon came down with a powerful case of mononucleosis. I couldn't return to school for most of that year. It was pretty fun to pal around with Mom and get special treatment, but I knew that school wasn't going to disappear simply because I was excused from it temporarily.

My doctor during that time had a mullet. She was butch and I absolutely loved her. I didn't understand why, but I knew that my mom thought she was a little gross. My dad knew I couldn't be a typical girl and he respected it. He took me fishing and gave me the same opportunities and consequences he gave my brother. Tiffany was treated more like a girl. He talked a lot to my brother and me about defending ourselves, and encouraged it maybe a bit too much. I'm not proud of it, but I found myself in a lot of physical fights as a young teen, especially after my long absence. My dad picked me up from the bus stop one day after a particularly tumultuous day at school and drove me to a fistfight. I told him that I had committed to fighting two boys at a lake in Ravensdale. Cousins. Rich, soccer-playing preppies. I told him that I was going whether he drove me or not. I remember him point-ing his truck toward the lake and muttering some misguided thing about how soon I wouldn't have to worry about this . . . how boys would want to date me and start being kinder as a result. He dropped me off and left. I knocked one of the boys into the lake and the other one didn't show. I wound up playing baseball with the same kids I'd been fighting for the rest of the afternoon. My mom could never quite understand these things, and to be fair, neither did I. School was bru-tal. My brother and I were being bullied and being bullies every day. The pecking order around this age is all-consuming, always avoiding embarrassment while trying to embarrass others . . . just trying to survive on fistfights and bravado, hiding and making a scene all in the same day.

Mom and Dad were in my corner in the best way that they knew *how* to be. I was coming home trying out new political beliefs and theories. I'm sure they sensed me trying to change, but they definitely had bigger fish to fry at that time. The scarcity we had always lived with had reached an all-time low. Dad lost his job at Boeing and we had to move again. We only ate because the food bank fed us. Or if Dad shot an elk. I still have vivid memories of tracking blood trails and wrapping prized cuts of meat in butcher paper just feet from the window Dad had taken the shot from. I don't like remembering that smell. I can't stomach wild game even in a Michelin-starred restaurant to this day. It's not that I wouldn't like the taste of it, I just don't like the way that smell makes me feel.

We had a lot of animal drama . . . or trauma, depending on what you're made of. Animals were ever present. Wild and domestic. Entire litters of kittens would die and, heartbroken, we'd bury them out in the woods . . . or they'd live and we'd excitedly wait for their eyes to open so we could raise them up and hustle them to people outside the grocery store once they were old enough. We had cats and dogs that would stumble in earless or covered in porcupine quills. I can re-member sitting on top of a Siberian Husky with a pair of pliers and pulling spines and quills from her face on more than one occasion. A lot of times the animals killed the other animals. I had a cat called Skitzy from age four to twenty-two. We didn't even feed her for swaths of her life; she was feral. I was the only one who could make any meaningful contact with her. She had buckshot embedded in her skin from someone . . . I still remember the sound of her scratching her way up the outside of the trailer to climb in the window and up to the top bunk of my bed. She'd make her way up to my face and groom my hair with her sandpaper tongue before settling in at the end of my bed to eat whatever creature she'd drug in with her. I would simply ignore the crackling sound of breaking bird or mouse bones drifting off to sleep . . . just happy that she was with me.

One of the hardest and most humiliating parts of my childhood was repeating seventh grade (at this point, my eighth school). The mono, the stress of living with my father's addiction, and our family's constant dance with chaos would make it impossible for me to finish my first attempt at seventh grade.

I felt like someone died when they told me I was being held back. I knew it was coming. I would not move on with my class (I had no friends anyway), I would be in the same grade as my little brother, and I would be switching schools again. I couldn't progress in math and I would also need special education classes just to get me to where I needed to be to start the year over.

As devastating as this turn of events felt to me at the time, it would turn out to be a total miracle. I would have never known the gifts that repeat year held for me: finding myself in the same grade as Jay and a curly haired little blond boy in a Colorado Rockies uniform who would become one of the great loves of my life and the father of my children. I saw David from across the classroom on the first day and was immediately obsessed with him. He was very quiet and absolutely adorable. He looked like a little lamb, but I knew he would hate to hear that. I made friends with him and his best buddy, Michael. The three of us were inseparable at school.

If I ever believed in an argument for synchronicity or past-life phenomena, it would be because of David. How can you explain looking at someone and seeing past and future generations? Family from before and the family to come. I would run from the bus and straight to the phone to call him after only seeing him thirty minutes prior: 432-9900. Some numbers you just never forget.

"HONKY CAT"

When I look back, boy, I must have
been green
Bopping in the country, fishing in a
stream
Looking for an answer, trying to
find a sign
Until I saw your city lights, honey, I
was blind

They said, get back, honky cat
Better get back to the woods
Well, I quit those days and my
redneck ways
And, oh, the change is gonna do
me good

You better get back, honky cat
Living in the city ain't where it's at
It's like trying to find gold in a
silver mine
It's like trying to drink whiskey
from a bottle of wine

Well, I read some books, and I
read some magazines
About those high-class ladies
down in New Orleans
And all the folks back home, well,
said I was a fool
They said, oh, believe in the Lord
is the golden rule

They said, get back, honky cat
Better get back to the woods
Well, I quit those days and my
redneck ways

And, ooh ooh ooh ooh, oh, change
is gonna do me good

They said, get back, honky cat
Better get back to the woods
Well, I quit those days and my
redneck ways
And, oh oh oh oh, oh, change is
gonna do me good

They said, stay at home, boy, you
gotta tend the farm
Living in the city, boy, is going to
break your heart
But how can you stay when your
heart says no?
How can you stop when your feet
say go?

You better get back, honky cat
Better get back to the woods
Well, I quit those days and my
redneck ways
And, ooh ooh ooh ooh, oh, the
change is gonna do me good

You better get back, honky cat
Living in the city ain't where it's at
It's like trying to find gold in a
silver mine
It's like trying to drink whiskey, oh,
from a bottle of wine
  —ELTON JOHN AND BERNIE
    TAUPIN

"SKYLINE PIGEON"
Turn me loose from your hands
Let me fly to distant lands
Over green fields, trees and
mountains
Flowers and forest fountains
Home along the lanes of the
skyway

For this dark and lonely room
Projects a shadow cast in gloom
And my eyes are mirrors
Of the world outside
Thinking of the ways
That the wind can turn the tide
And these shadows turn
From purple into grey

For just a skyline pigeon
Dreaming of the open
Waiting for the day
That he can spread his wings
And fly away again

Fly away, skyline pigeon fly
Towards the dreams
You've left so very far behind

Fly away, skyline pigeon fly
Towards the dreams
You've left so very far behind

Let me wake up in the morning
To the smell of new mowed hay
To laugh and cry, to live and die
In the brightness of my day

I wanna hear the pealing bells
Of distant churches sing
But most of all please free me
from
This aching metal ring
And open out this cage towards
the sun

For just this skyline pigeon
Dreaming of the open
Waiting for the day
That he can spread his wings
And fly away again

Fly away, skyline pigeon fly
Towards the dreams
You've left so very far behind

Fly away, skyline pigeon fly
Towards the dreams
You've left so very
So very far behind
      —ELTON JOHN AND BERNIE
        TAUPIN

WESTPORT, STARTING TO FEEL LIKE ME

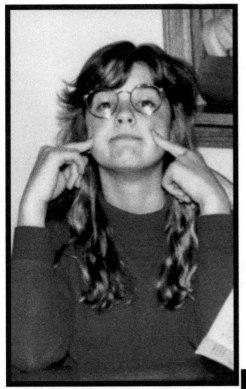

HAMMER PANTS AND BIRTHDAY
PARTIES IN RAVENSDALE AT
OUR SINGLE WIDE TRAILER.
THE ONE I'M ALWAYS HIDING
OUT IN, IN MY DREAMS

WHAT I LOOKED LIKE WHEN MOM
LEFT ME THE HELL ALONE

THE CARLILE FAMILY PHOTO IN DADS
"COWBOY HAT" PHASE

6.

....

ELVIS AND THE GAY '90S

I t was 1997. My father was out of work, but he had gotten sober and we were spending a lot of time together. Mom's music was slowing down and Dad was obsessively writing political letters to the newspaper and expressing himself. He was in AA working the steps and was very candid and open about his struggle with alcohol, and our family felt pretty tight.

We were comedically disrespectful to our parents. We'd developed a kind of a vulgar, dry, Bart Simpson–style rapport. We were lazily lounging around the Nintendo in the fall when Dad hollered at us to go outside and "sort garbage" for the burn barrel. I must have shot back some off-color retort when my mother shouted from the other room that "he's your father" in an attempt at demanding respect, to which I replied that I'd like to take a DNA test to prove it. It was during this strange moment of dark humor and tension that he revealed to us kids that he had another daughter living in Oregon. He casually said something like, "Actually, I do have another kid. . . ." He'd never met her. He was asked to leave her alone so that she could grow up separate from the scallywag Carlile family.

All I really heard was that I wasn't his firstborn child anymore and I was weirdly upset. He took me for a long walk on the Cedar River. I was embarrassed because I had cried, so we didn't really talk. Just watched the salmon.

The five of us Carliles were an arguably codependent but intimately connected family. The trailer was small. We got the power shut off a lot. There were animals everywhere. The friends who were allowed to come over loved the wildness of our house, but I remembered overhearing stories of my father's childhood and realized that, in some ways, history was repeating itself. We hung around some *rough* folks and our street smarts were well earned.

Some days I believed that my childhood was a dream and some days I was sure it was a nightmare. We had an abundance of complicated freedom. I'd hike in the woods in groups of kids and alone, looking for abandoned mine shafts and coal miners' graves. If we found a pond, we'd build a raft . . . I got my last ever spanking for that raft. I ran into a bear one day and threw a can of hairspray at him. My sister and I even saw one of our feral dogs kill a deer one afternoon when we were out for a walk . . . she just locked onto its neck and swung there until the deer stopped moving. There were pig roasts and overnight parties, where my parents' friends would pepper the yard with colorful tents; we had a potentially deadly rope swing and fought paintball wars that lasted through the weekend. It was in the midst of all this wildness that I would meet my first broken horse.

You may have heard the word "broke" as it pertains to tamed horses. That is not what I mean. To be "broke," a horse must allow a person to believe that it is afraid enough to be conquered, tamed, and ridden. It's never true. They don't break. I've never been thrown, kicked, or stepped on by a wild horse . . . they've always been "broke." Horse people never say a horse is broken even when it would seem to make sense . . .

"Can I ride him?"

"No! He ain't broke yet."

I mean *actually* broken in some obvious way. An apparent flaw that would suggest that the animal can no longer serve his man-made, human-serving purpose. Work.

He was a retired racehorse with a broken leg called Drummer.

Drummer was a quarter horse. He was over sixteen hands tall, a term I would proudly use when describing him to people—it was "horse terminology." He went down during a race one day and instead of being euthanized, he was given to the jockey. That's how he found his way to me. I had dreamed of having a horse my whole life. I drew them on every surface and fantasized nonstop about being a "horse person." I even had a recurring dream about having a horse that could talk with me at night but never in the daytime.

Spoiler alert: I'm still not a "horse person." I never got there. As much as I adore horses, I never was a proper rider. I was too afraid after being thrown off repeatedly by a series of horses the "Dolls" had put me on. The Dolls are a part of my family that's comprised mainly of crazy-ass jockeys. Five feet tall and full of piss. I mean this affectionately, of course . . . but dang! My favorite second cousin, Connie Doll, is one such jockey, and she got Drummer for me. I was never brave enough to ride in front of people for fear of embarrassment. If you can believe it, the physical pain of being injured by a twelve-hundred-pound animal didn't bother me a bit, but I don't do humiliation. I would slip outside alone and tie a rope around Drummer's halter, lead him to a stump, and jump onto his back. He was a gentle giant and he would just saunter back into his pen before I'd have to jump off to avoid the roof of his crumbling stall, *but I was riding*. He was naughty for sure, but he was remarkably protective of me. The day I got him, he had blood poisoning and an infection from a massive tear between his leg and his chest from being tangled in barbed wire. It was my job to give him shots of antibiotics and change his gauze. I would clean off the pus with hydrogen peroxide and his whole body would shake and twitch, but he would never have hurt me. I was too young to do all that, and I probably didn't do that good of a job, but it bonded us forever.

There was a girl just through the woods who rode horses for real. Her name was Bri, and I couldn't stop thinking about her. I kept telling her about my horse and what a great rider I was until she eventually invited me and Drummer for a ride. She couldn't have lived much more than a quarter mile away and could have easily ridden to my house, but I didn't really want her to see how we lived, so I was going to have to ride to her. I'd never really made an attempt to properly ride Drummer before, but I was determined to try. I didn't ask anyone, I just led Drummer to the edge of the woods and used a different stump to climb onto his back. He stood perfectly still. I think he sensed my bravery and the fact that we were taking a risk.

The woods were thick. You can't see through woods in western Washington at all. Trails are made by humans or animals; everything else belongs to the underbrush. The leaves were wet and it was raining, so I had my hood up, blocking my peripheral vision. I gave Drummer a light kick and he started obediently making his way through the nettles with his ears perked straight forward. I closed my eyes, leaned all the way down, and pressed my head against his neck. I put all my faith in his sense of direction and that I knew he'd never buck. We rode like that for probably five minutes before I felt his skin start to twitch. It was random at first, and if it hadn't been raining, I'd have thought it was flies. But when his ears pinned back, I knew from the time I'd spent treating his wound that he was fighting the urge to spook and throw me. I pulled back on his lead rope and he stopped. Sensing that something strange was happening all around me, with one hand clutching Drummer's mane, I pulled off my hood. As I looked around the forest and clocked my surroundings, I froze, overwhelmed with emotion and excitement: Drummer and I had managed to assimilate by accident into a massive herd of elk. Maybe they didn't notice us at first because of the rain and because I was bent all the way down. Maybe they just didn't see us as a threat. When they

finally did notice, they calmly scattered and trotted off in every direction. I still think about what an unusual privilege it was to be in the
middle of that herd out there in the rain. We didn't make it to Bri's
house. Drummer made the decision to turn around and steadily take
us both home.

Later that year, Connie came and got Drummer. She wanted to
further rehabilitate him and had just gotten herself into a place with a
pasture. Looking back on it now, we probably weren't taking the best
care of him. I realize now that in some quiet way that actually he was
taking care of me. I was devastated. I would go and visit him whenever I could get my folks to drive me, but it was probably only a handful of times. Soon after he left, he got a brain tumor and Connie shot
him. I found out after the fact standing outside of the Black Diamond
Eagles Club on karaoke night. Some parts of my childhood are a bit
brutal and that was one of them. I wished I could have said goodbye
to that big ol' guardian angel, and I'm still not over it.

Meanwhile, at some point after my failed singing competition/
pageant career, I had started to develop a friendship with another, far
more successful, contestant. Amber Lee was the eight-year-old who
strolled out onto the Northwest Grand Ole Opry stage in her yellow
dress and had me believing by the end of her Dolly Parton song that I
was destined to be a child star. Needless to say, even years down the
road I was enamored with her. We started hanging out at karaoke bars
with our parents, and I was immediately obsessed with her and her
father, who was an Elvis impersonator. I was spending weekends at
her house in the summer of '96 and Elvis was in the basement rehears-
ing with his band. I heard a song I recognized from the Opry and I
suggested to Amber that we go down and sing a harmony behind him
just in case he'd want to invite us to sing on a microphone (always
hustling). He loved it, and it became a thing. I started teaching Amber
harmony, courtesy of Jay Carlile, and she'd help me fix my hair.

Singing for her dad was my first real musical job—twenty-five
bucks a show. We were booked almost every weekend. I was unwit-
tingly learning about harmony and backing vocals from the Jordan-

aires and learning about fronting a band from someone trying to impersonate the man who invented rock stardom. You couldn't pay for that education . . . not that I could have paid for any education at that point.

I returned from Amber's house late one night with a head full of confusing feelings. The rest of my family was asleep, but I saw a VHS tape of the movie *Philadelphia* sitting on the kitchen counter ready to be returned to the video store, and I snuck it into the VCR. The film and its music galvanized my respect for the plight of LGBTQ people in a deep and personal way that I was inching ever closer to understanding. I had been reading that Elton John biography that introduced me to Queen, U2, George Michael, the Beatles, and David Bowie. The music I was seeking out and becoming attached to was becoming my home and my emotional support system.

It was around that time that someone slipped the *Philadelphia* soundtrack into my stocking at Christmas and also I discovered the Indigo Girls. I can't say enough about them. The Indigos were huge for me. They had androgynous music and images. They were singing love songs and using same-gender pronouns. That should have felt normal, but to me it was radical. I felt like I knew them . . . and I couldn't understand why. Whatever it was, it was in their voices. They sounded like they were resisting something . . . I couldn't make sense of it at the time, but I knew that somehow I was in that fight too.

It was that same Christmas that my parents managed to buy me a Casio keyboard. It couldn't have been easy for them. I had been looking at it in the Toys "R" Us catalog for months and I knew it cost $80 . . . I couldn't even imagine actually owning one. Even the keyboard stand was twenty bucks! But there it was on Christmas morning out of the box all set up on the stand with a bow on it. It was my prized possession and I set it up between two broken garage-sale speakers, each five feet tall, so I could pretend it was an actual PA. I had learned to play every song from the *Philadelphia* soundtrack by ear before winter ended.

Whenever I wasn't spending time with Amber, I was with David. (I never could spend a day alone, then or now, and I have never once been single.) I had a deep and enduring crush on David and he didn't give a shit about my awkward eccentricity, or my passion for music, for that matter. David and I played video games, horse, and flag football. I wore his Green Bay Packers jacket at school every day because I loved the way he smelled. We sometimes made a plan to sneak a kiss on the school bus at the end of the day, and I'd look forward to it all day long. I wasn't attracted to him sexually, but to be honest, I was too innocent in that way to really understand what that even meant.

The Ellen DeGeneres coming-out episode was the beginning and the end of any confusion I was having around my sexuality. Ellen was obviously gay but hadn't come out yet. I loved her so much and my dad did too. We never talked about her sexuality, but we lounged around the TV in the evenings and watched her show together quite a bit, both of us recoiling from embarrassment when she'd start rambling and digging herself into those famous Ellen holes. There was a buildup to her coming out and it was all over the news. I recorded the episode on a VHS tape marked "David's baseball game" that I still have.

I needed to admit to myself that I was becoming very attracted to women. I thought about it all the time. It wasn't that it was gross to me, but it freaked me out. I would imagine holding and kissing other girls, but I would always fantasize that I was someone else. Just some blank-faced character who wasn't me so that I personally could still be "not gay." At first, this character had a different hair color, different skin and clothes, and most importantly, they were nongendered. But before too long I was having to accept this character as a woman. Day by day and moment by moment, that character was starting to feel more and more *like me* until it just was. That's when I finally felt right and I knew that what I was feeling was real.

I knew that when Ellen said she was gay on national television that I was, too, and it was time to tell my parents. It didn't happen all at once, so I don't really have a coming-out *story* for you. . . . I wish I did, but I guess it was clumsier and less beautiful than that; honestly it was a series of awkward little chats and avoidances. But maybe there are too many "coming-out stories" and not enough of us talking about an uncomfortable and awkward . . . emergence. Ellen gave me the language and an inroad to a dialogue with my family. It was the first mile of a very long road toward all of us understanding what any of that meant. I was, simply put, the only gay person I had ever met. Even I didn't accept me yet. . . . Should I cut my hair? Am I a vegetarian now?

David didn't care. We continued to sleep in the same bed and hold hands. Even when I cut off all my hair, we stayed the same. The first time I said the words it was to Amber Lee. I told her on my sixteenth birthday. It was awkward and hard for her. She already knew, and she still loved me and wanted to accept me, but she began to phase me out as her friend. She had a very religious boyfriend and was feeling conflicted. Then her dad fired me—he said that my sexuality made the bass player uncomfortable.

I had lost my first job. The worst part was being told that because I was gay, I couldn't do that music anymore. That was the one rejection I couldn't take.

I was drawn back to church at this point because it had brought me such comfort as a young child, and I was fundamentally unsettled. All was not right with my soul.

It's probably safe to say that again I didn't find mercy there.

"PHILADELPHIA"

Sometimes I think that I know
What love's all about
And when I see the light
I know I'll be all right.

I've got my friends in the world,
I had my friends
When we were boys and girls
And the secrets came unfurled.

City of brotherly love
Place I call home
Don't turn your back on me
I don't want to be alone
Love lasts forever.

Someone is talking to me,
Calling my name
Tell me I'm not to blame
I won't be ashamed of love.

Philadelphia,
City of brotherly love.
Brotherly love.

Sometimes I think that I know
What love's all about
And when I see the light
I know I'll be all right.
    —NEIL YOUNG

"I DON'T WANT TO TALK ABOUT IT"

I can tell by your eyes
That you've probably been crying
forever
And the stars in the sky
Don't mean nothing to you they're
a mirror

I don't wanna talk about it
How you broke my heart
If I stay here just a little bit longer
If I stay here won't you listen to my
heart
My heart

If I stand all alone
Will the shadow hide the color of
my heart
Will they be blue for the tears,
black for the nights we spent
apart

The stars in the sky don't mean
nothin' to you
They're a mirror

I don't wanna talk about it
How you broke my heart
Oh if I stay, if I stay here
Won't you listen to my heart
I don't wanna talk about it
How you broke my heart
If I stay, if I stay here just a little
bit longer
If I stay here won't you listen to my
heart
If I stand all alone
Will the shadows hide the colors
of my heart
    —WRITTEN BY DANNY WHITTEN/
      CRAZY HORSE MUSIC,
      PERFORMED BY THE INDIGO
      GIRLS

"HAPPY"

I don't hang around that place no
more
I'm tired of wearing circles in the
floor
And I don't carry myself very well
I've gotten so much braver,
Can you tell?

I'm happy, can't you see?
I'm alright, but I miss you, Amber
Lee

And I line my secrets up all one by
one

I put 'em all away when I was
done
And I would really love to hear
your voice sometime
To close a little distance in my
mind

Where have you been all these
years?
And how could you just
disappear?
And when did you stop missing
me?
            —BRANDI CARLILE

ME RIDING MY HORSE DRUMMER
AROUND AGE 12 - HE WAS HUGE!

ME AND MY BELOVED DRUMMER

7.

··········

THAT YEAR

was SO gay by the end of 1997. I started to have relationships with girls in secret at school and creepy relationships with much older women in my band/work life. I had found a group of friends who accepted me, and my brother, Jay, and I were inseparable. He wasn't crazy about my sexuality, but we each individually thought that the other was a total dickhead anyway, so it didn't really matter. We are both quite judgmental by nature.

Then Dad fell off the wagon and we got evicted from the trailer on the hill. I still dream about that place all the time. I think it's the most time we spent in a house and although it was only a mystical moment in a complex and meaningful childhood, it has sustained itself in my memory through all my transitions.

In my dream, we're all adults but we're squatting there. It'd been abandoned for years, but we're always fixing it up and salvaging useful bits of garbage, like the Boxcar Children. We are hanging Christmas lights and cooking on a fire while hiding out from "Jack Heckenlively," the evil landlord who will toss us out on our asses if he catches us there. I'm in the top bunk of my old bed, with Tiffany below me and Jay on the other side of the wall. No money, no wife or kids. Feeling nervous but somehow so comfortable, like all is right with the world. Back where my animals are buried and I'm totally free . . . I'm equal to my family members. Nothing is separating us.

WE LEFT THE trailer on my sixteenth birthday, and it was profound.

Jay and I moved into the detached garage of a trailer in a Maple Valley trailer park. The two of us were sharing a room for the first time, and I loved it. I would lie in bed and laugh all night because Jay is fucking FUNNY—Chris Farley funny . . . and humble and accident-prone. We'd stay out late and come home to our garage and wash our spiky hair in a washing machine with powdered detergent. The guy who owned the trailer was sharing it with the rest of our family and he slept in a recliner in the living room. We never wanted to walk past him. If we had to pee, we'd do it in a cup and pour it outside. Everything was hilarious to us. That's how we were coping with it, like brothers.

We'd buy rolls of quarters and hang out with our mom, our dad, and Dad's best friend, Ron, to play poker for real money. Our family has always had a tense relationship with gambling, but in those days, and in contrast to everything else, it felt like the most wholesome thing in the world. If I was lucky the next day I'd be hauling several hundred dollars' worth of quarters to the Coinstar machine at the grocery store. It was on one of these nights that we'd meet Darren and Troy, a couple of brothers in their thirties who were learning to play instruments. They were practicing in a shed off a trailer down the street on Lake Sawyer. Jay and I fell head-over-heels in love with them and joined their band. We called it "The Shed."

We didn't really want to drink, but we could have if we wanted to. We were high on possibility, and the adult surroundings we were being accepted into were truly extraordinary for kids our age. It felt really weird to go back to school after that.

In high school, we had a small group of best friends. Band geeks and rejects: a bass player called Brian Seeley, who was extremely gifted and had a penchant for Jaco Pastorius; Sean Morrissey, a gorgeous jazz drummer with a genius vocabulary; and Blair Barnes, a lanky blue-eyed comedian who had been severely bullied in junior high but was developing quite the fan club for his unpredictable quirkiness—the kind not often found in kids . . . something you'd see in an *SNL* cast member who also understands string theory. The older guys from the Shed began to hang out with us and our limited number of school friends. I know how weird that sounds now, but at the time, we sort of formed one big band. These guys would all spend the night at my house on the living-room floor and I'd stay at theirs. Grown men, just hanging out constantly with a crazy sixteen-year-old girl who looked exactly like a sixteen-year-old boy. It still cracks me up to remember how strange it all was.

School was the only thing left in my life that I felt helpless about. I hated it. It was the last place standing that still made me feel like a child. I had removed all other infantilizing institutions from my life in an effort to feel like I could control my surroundings. I was out of the closet at school. The only gay person. My brother and I were different kids there. Jay began to struggle with paralyzing anxiety and agoraphobia. He developed crippling stomach problems and had to stop playing in the band for a while. I was skipping many of my classes for fear of the embarrassment of my classmates watching me walk into the special-education classes.

We were both smart. We were both failing.

Shortly after the Shed started getting serious, my family moved out of the trailer park and into a different part of Ravensdale. Dad started a new job in construction, and he was instantly very talented at it, but his drinking was the worst anyone had seen it. Tiffany was finally old enough to really understand how complicated our lives were. We got along, and I have always felt like a second mother to her. I'm not as good of a friend to Tiffany as I should be because I still can't move past that responsibility.

Jay and I dropped out of high school together on Valentine's Day in 1998. It was our sophomore year. We became very depressed. We picked up an unlabeled box of VHS tapes at a garage sale and watched old movies, sharing a twin bed for months. Our anxiety had stunted us, and we had disappointed our parents. Neither of them had finished high school either, and the resignation stung us all . . . Just another stain.

We kept talking about going to Crown College and being cops (hilarious), but we were punk-asses too. I don't know why this stands out in my mind but one of our many low points came when Tiffany was about to start junior high. She was extremely nervous and had meticulously laid her clothes out and packed her backpack. Another new school was no big deal, but this was a new school district altogether. She knew no one, and junior high is terrifying in any case. Sometime around three A.M., we thought it'd be funny to wake her up and make her breakfast so that she'd get ready to go to school only to find out that it was a prank and have to go back to bed again. She kept asking us why we were being so nice to her. It was awful! She laughed, but my dad woke up and called us losers, said that we should be ashamed of ourselves. And let me tell you—we were. Just the thought of being so mean now is unthinkable. So often parents seem to pull back when those awful teen years hit just from the unpleasantness of it . . . but it's so rudderless. It's when we need parenting the most. After all the mess that Dad had gotten us into and even as the one person in our family probably least worthy of respect at that point, Dad telling me that I was a loser and that I should be ashamed of myself was exactly what I needed to hear. I had dropped out of school. I had to pull it together and get back on my feet.

Artists I love never seem to reveal themselves later in life as a person who struggled to get by in their youth *and also* a person who is a narcissistic, insufferable asshole at times. I just personally find it liberating to tell you this because it's true. I can't be seen as an angel in these times or any times, although I wish it were so. I have been lost, racist, religious, brutal, and broken before. I hurt people as much as I've been hurt.

I began working as a barista at a curbside coffee stand, a sample lady at a grocery store, and as a roofing laborer whenever I could. The young guys in the band would sometimes get hired and work alongside me. Not Blair though. He was way too smart for our kid jobs.

The band became my North Star. I was sad about my life and feeling really conflicted about school, but I wasn't worried. I was absolutely going to be famous, and when I closed my eyes I fantasized constantly about all the things I would buy my family. Mostly four-wheelers and huge houses. Speaking of houses, we had to move into a new one in the fall that year. I had my own room for the very first time, and this house had a great big barn, oil heat, a big yard—and rats. Everyone on that road had rats. Tons of rats. The dump across the street had closed and thousands of rats had scattered and infested the houses across the street—at least, that's how I remember it. It was hard to get comfortable living with them. That was a RED LINE for my mother! She was horrified. We liked that house a lot but never could get used to those damn rats.

Because of the barn, our parents had worked out a horse-boarding situation with their friends, and then horses turned into cows. There was an auction in a nearby town and animals were cheap. We knew some people making good money raising and selling cows, and you could pick these calves up for twenty to thirty bucks, so I got to attend these auctions from time to time. No one told us that the calves really like to just up and die on you . . . but they did.

As a little girl I loved the story of the ponies of Chincoteague, and I had always romanticized the idea of buying a horse of my own. Once you have a horse, you never forget the way they smell, or how reassuring it is to look one in the eye and hug his neck.

I was at the auction with my mom's friend and a big wad of roofing cash when they opened the gate and three squirrelly little foals ran into the ring. That's the first time I laid eyes on my second broken horse. He was an unpapered Arab. Absolutely worthless in his world and not destined for much of a life. He was a bay with no socks and a matted and filthy jet-black tail. His mane had been rubbed off and he was covered in bug bites. Having no plan and knowing full well that it'd be less than a hot second until we got thrown out of the rat house with the barn, I raised my paddle and bought that mangey little horse for $75 anyway.

I took him home in the back of a pickup like a dog. He was tiny. I could push him right over and I did. He was my world. I played with him all the time. He healed me from the trauma of losing Drummer (twice), and I was actually pretty good with him, for a seventeen-year-old. I called him Sovereign after my mom brought home a guitar of the same name that she found in the bushes outside a casino. Just like him it was deep red and flawed in the best way. I had no idea that of all the impulsive decisions I made as a teenager, buying that horse would be the most impactful by far. I would have that responsibility with me until I was nearly forty. He was the gift of burden that gave me my work ethic.

I had a lot of freedom, and my band and my brother were a band of brothers for me in a way I'll never forget. I had a couch in my room, and there was always some wayward dude on it. Blair, Sean, and Brian were mainstays. The grown-ups in the band were starting to get some understandable resistance from their wives. Apparently hanging out with teenagers wasn't winning them any family points. But their disapproval was nothing that we couldn't handle.

At one point, the young part of the group contemplated stealing a car. We wanted to play a show in Spokane, and no one had a car that would make it there on this particular weekend. One of us had access to a key to a brand-new car parked on a lot in town, so Blair suggested we go get it and take off to eastern Washington, and then scrap it once we got to Spokane. It's the kind of thing that all kids talk about around a campfire before coming to their senses. Of course, we came to ours . . . some kids don't. But our funny, sweet friend Blair was getting kind of dark . . . no one said it out loud, but sometimes it felt scary.

I was still trying relentlessly during that time to drag Jay out of the house and to band practice, karaoke, road trips, and camping in eastern Washington. Sometimes he'd come! But he struggled.

One New Year's Eve, we decided to break into Sean's dad's house for a party. I call it breaking in, but really Sean had a key . . . he probably even had permission, but we enjoyed feeling like we were living on the edge. It was nothing crazy, just some band geeks with cupcakes and wine coolers. We liked to use his dad's hot tub.

It was the first and last time we decided not to invite Blair. He was getting really intense. We all had new girlfriends and we didn't want him to make the evening feel crazy. He was behaving more and more erratically and always ramping up our sense of adventure past where any of us felt comfortable. To top it all off, he was doing it stone-cold sober!

Instead, Blair's parents took him to a fancy New Year's Eve dinner in Bellevue at a nice hotel. The next morning, he got into a taxi and went back to the same hotel, where he jumped out of a window and killed himself.

The shock and guilt were unbearable.

I transformed these feelings into visceral teenage Baptist judgment and condemnation. Monkey see, monkey do.

One of the older brothers in my band gave me a guitar. I dove into it with everything that was left of me . . . I lost all track of time after that.

"THAT YEAR"
I must have been sleeping, I must
have been drinking
I haven't been dreaming about
you for years
There was a sharp turn and a
sunburn,
I was too cool for high school that
year.

It must have been New Year's
No one invited you, you took
things too far
But I missed you, and your antics
You were lonesome and blue-
eyed and so special to us.

You should have taken a long
break
Instead of a long drop from a high
place
Ten years I never spoke your name
Now it feels good to say it you're
my friend again

He said he forgave you, I said I
hated you,
He was the bigger man, I was
sixteen
All the innocence it took for you
To finally make the yearbook that
year

You could have taken some time
away
Instead of a long drop, instead of
a leap of faith
Ten years I never spoke your name
Now it feels good to say that
you're my friend again

I was angry, I was a Baptist

I was a daughter, I was wrong.
    —BRANDI CARLILE

"FARE THEE WELL"

Fare thee well my bright star
I watched your taillights blaze into
nothingness
But you were long gone before I
ever got to you
Before you blazed past this
address
And now I think of having loved
and having lost
But never know what it feels like
to never love
Who can say what's better when
my heart's become the cost
A mere token of a brighter jewel
sent from above

Fare thee well my bright star
The vanity of youth the color of
your eyes
And maybe if I'd fanned the
blazing fire of your day-to-day
Or if I'd been older, I'd been wise
Too thick the heat of those long
summer evenings
For a cool evening I began to
yearn

But you could only feed upon the
things which feed a fire
Waiting to see if I would burn

Fare thee well my bright star
It was a brief brilliant miracle dive
That which I looked up to and I
clung to for dear life
Had to burn itself up just to make
itself alive
And I caught you then in your
moment of glory
Your last dramatic scene against
a night sky stage
With a memory so clear that it's
as if you're still before me
My once in a lifetime star of an
age

So fare thee well my bright star
Last night the tongues of fire
circled me around
And this strange season of pain
will come to pass
When the healing hands of
autumn cool me down
    —INDIGO GIRLS

RIGHT AFTER I BROKE MY MOTHERS
HEART AND CUT MY HAIR

ME AND SOVEREIGN WITH THE LOCAL PUNKS

MY BAND WHEN I WAS A BOY.

8.

....

BAPTISTS ARE MEAN

It was July and the adolescent boys' swim trunks I was wearing under my baggy "poor-kid" jeans were uncomfortable as I shuffled north on Coal Street toward the town's only Baptist church for my big day. I never knew what kind of swimsuit I was supposed to wear. I avoided pools in favor of floating the river because I felt like I was under less pressure to wear a "proper" swimsuit. I didn't want to wear a bikini, and board shorts felt just a little too butch. So I settled on my drummer friend Sean's tightest trunks and a sports bra. I was supposed to feel vulnerable anyway. Baptism isn't a bandstand.

It had been a few years since the beginning of my spiritual transition. I was drawn back to church when I came out of the closet as both a comfort and out of fear. Church made sense of things: Blair, sex, money, and desire. The church camp that I had attended at my brother's request had made a massive impression on me. But even still, it took me a long time to collect enough nerve to take the step I was about to take.

The Evangelicals and the Baptists have a special brand of homogeneous teen religion, and it all starts at "church camp." It has all the things a regular camp has: food, games, music, exhilarating independence, and an overall togetherness that feels somehow less intimidating than trying to fit in at school. Sometimes it's a weekend, sometimes it's an all-day trip, but there's always an agenda—which is more often than not teenage salvation. Sure, there are advantages to adolescent piety, but in my experience, these standards of purity cannot be sustained in the modern age. At best, they inevitably lead to real shame, and at worst, self-destruction—and that's if you're NOT gay.

We were motivated holistically by hormones, and we were obviously in desperate need of a spiky-haired, ultra-hip youth pastor to show us how we could stop living for ourselves and join the rock club. Electric guitars, swimming pools, girls, and Capri Sun juice boxes for anyone who wants to self-consciously approach the altar and be saved in front of their tearful peers, their eyes shut tight with outstretched hands, singing a Christian power ballad: *"Open my eyes to your heart, Lord."*

Even in the years that followed, every time I stood up at church, I felt an overwhelming urge to cry. I never understood why at the time. The pastors were all used to it; people feel the spirit and they are overcome. This time, though, I was ready. I had been in spiritual training with Pastor Steve all week. Baptism was going to be no big deal. My younger brother and sister had already been baptized; I was just a late-bloomer.

To my immense relief, my anxious meditations were interrupted by the familiar sound of Sheryl Crow coming in louder and clearer by the second. I knew if I turned around, I'd see my girlfriend's red 1995 Jetta approaching at the brutally enforced Black Diamond speed limit of twenty-five miles per hour. "All I Wanna Do Is Have Some Fun" felt audacious and foreign in contrast to the thoughts I was having. I was waxing philosophical about duty and rebirth. I didn't want her to stop the car; I didn't want to talk. She caught my eye and smiled; she knew why I wanted to walk to the church.

I met Jessica at the grocery store where I was working. I was instantly enamored with her. She worked in the photo department and was a photographer. I used being a musician to my advantage and asked her to take some photos of "my band" that quickly turned into one-on-one photo shoots—and you can guess how that went. I still see the insecure photos sometimes and they make me smile because the affection I have for her is so clearly written on my face. I was in the process of moving in with her, effectively dragging my seventeen-year-old self and my now-eight-hundred-pound horse into her life like a sledgehammer. I didn't even have a bank account or a driver's license. Also, I told her I was eighteen.

She was my first real girlfriend, and my whole family absolutely loved her. She was a Mormon and understood the complicated dance I was doing with organized religion. She wasn't a fan of my church, but not because it wasn't liberal enough; she just felt like the rug was about to be pulled out from under me. I had already been discouraged from participating in musical worship because of my "spiritual state of mind," but I assumed that just meant that I needed to be baptized . . . Then they were going to let me sing.

Jay was out of town for the weekend with his near-future fiancée. Things were getting tense between us and it felt like it was connected to the church. There was a community there and they adored him—me, not so much. But again, as soon as I was baptized, I was sure . . .

Most of my family and my "occasional" friends were all there sitting in folding chairs, but I was too nervous to chat. I was nervous about my swimsuit, nervous about having my head dunked (control freaks always are), and nervous about the crying thing. I wanted people to think I was cool, just like the rest of the kids who got dunked in the holy water and high-fived—only to return immediately to rolling around in the backseat of cars and drinking too many wine coolers. Baptism was the final step in my journey to community and self-acceptance. It was going to make me the same as everyone else, or at the very least, a fellow purchaser of the same brand of fire insurance.

I got to the church and was greeted outside the building by an unusually manic and smiling Pastor Steve. There was another kid participating in the ceremony, James—he was only thirteen and he was ready to give his life to the Lord . . . again. He'd been baptized Catholic but that doesn't count to the Baptists—full submersion or afterlife combustion. Pastor Steve took us into the back room together and asked if we had our swimsuits on. I was mortified, but I answered yes. The next question tickled me. I was actually grateful to the good pastor for making a joke and breaking the ice.

"Do you currently practice black magic or witchcraft?"

I knew I'd laughed too loud when he didn't smile. "Uh, no," I mumbled, feeling my face get hot. All at once I knew what was coming next . . . He looked like it was killing him to ask. He already knew the answer: I was the only person out of the closet in Black Diamond and three towns over in every direction.

"Do you practice homosexuality?"

I was a student of all the parts in the Bible that pertained to me. I hated the word "homosexual." I felt it didn't belong there and always wondered why we let them pin it on us. I pontificated often in uncertain terror about the nuanced and cultural meaning of the actual words "Malakois" and "Arsenokoitai"—in my opinion two of the most mischaracterized words in the Bible, often used to condemn and cast their misleading net over queer people for centuries. Two of the broadest brushes ever to paint a painful picture.

"I don't care for that word," I said calmly. "I'm only being who I was born to be."

Pastor Steve was sweating profusely and looked as if he was reading straight from the script of a graphic porno film. "I know," he said, "but I have to ask these two questions, and if you can't repent, I can't baptize you."

My heart sank like a stone from the weight of the imminent embarrassment. "What about this week?" I asked. "You know me, and you know my girlfriend. You let me go through the training program. You know I'm gay."

He went hoarse. "I know . . . I'm so sorry."

The lapsed Catholic kid in the corner had stripped. It would have been such comic relief, if only I could have seen the humor in a half-naked preteen boy being forced into a conversation about homosexuality and witchcraft whilst standing in his underwear.

I said, "Okay," and I bolted.

Everyone I loved was a blur as I ran out of the church. Not everyone "agreed with my lifestyle" (the most common dismissal of gay people in the '90s), but they all wanted me to have my moment with the Lord and feel supported. My mom and dad didn't care for church and avoided it at almost all costs. So, when I got to my parents' house, they were just putting out their cigarettes and leaving for the spectacle—always late. I told my mom what had happened and ran up to my room. My dad said he was going to go beat up Pastor Steve. He was pacing and ranting as he repeated his mantra—he'd been telling me all year, "Baptists are mean," but I never really agreed. "I'm gonna kick that guy's ass," he said. I knew it wasn't true and I knew that Pastor Steve was beating himself up worse than anything my dad would have done to him.

Looking back on it now, I see grace everywhere. There was grace in the outrage my public rejection incited in my family and in that tiny town. I hadn't fully seen it until then. That's how real "heart change" is made. Consciousness that shifts not as the result of triumph, but of sacrifice, even sometimes humiliation. That's where the mercy creeps in.

It's not a cry that you hear at night
It's not somebody who's seen the light
It's a cold and it's a broken
Hallelujah

Everyone hated Pastor Steve after that. He called and called and called. I never spoke to him again. But I wasn't mad at him. I didn't feel "wronged" yet because I still felt wrong.

I was nowhere near ready to be forgiven. The whole ordeal would have meant nothing to me spiritually. It was a checklist for conformity. I wasn't upset with Pastor Steve for not baptizing me . . . I was upset because I knew that *I* wouldn't have baptized me.

I fell asleep listening to Jeff Buckley sing "Hallelujah" every night after that for weeks. I was becoming more and more awake, more certain that I had been looking for my salvation in all the wrong places. My obsession with "Hallelujah" had begun to transform itself into a fantasy future life full of concert stages and deep and meaningful relationships with friends. Having never taken a plane ride, there was also a burning desire welling up inside me to see the rest of America.

I would take the leap, move out of my parents' home, and find salvation where the rest of the misfits and the rejects find it.

Through twisted, joyful, sexual, weird, and wonderful music.

"HALLELUJAH"

Well, I've heard there was a secret chord
That David played and it pleased the Lord
But you don't really care for music, do you?
Well, it goes like this
The fourth, the fifth, the minor fall and the major lift
The baffled king composing
Hallelujah
Hallelujah

Well, your faith was strong but you needed proof
You saw her bathing on the roof
Her beauty and the moonlight overthrew ya
She tied you to her kitchen chair
And she broke your throne and she cut your hair
And from your lips she drew the
Hallelujah
Hallelujah

Darling, I've been here before
I've seen this room and I've walked this floor
You know, I used to live alone before I knew ya

And I've seen your flag on the marble arch
And love is not a victory march
It's a cold and it's a broken
Hallelujah
Hallelujah

There was a time when you let me know
What's really going on below
But now you never show that to me, do ya
But remember when I moved in you
The holy dove was moving, too
And every breath we drew was
Hallelujah
Hallelujah

Maybe there's a God above
But all I've ever learned from love
Was how to shoot somebody who outdrew ya
It's not a cry that you hear at night
It's not somebody who's seen the light
It's a cold and it's a broken
Hallelujah
        —LEONARD COHEN

"EYE OF THE NEEDLE"

Twenty years of pushing pens
Of up the stairs and down again
I should've learned to style my
hair
I could never sleep at night
I've never mastered eating right
Distracted by the skin I wear

I'm alive in here somewhere
I can feel me twisting
I'm so far beyond my years
So don't be fooled by today

Please, just believe in me
Don't lose hope so easily
Because passing through the eye
of a needle
Isn't as easy as it sounds
For those like me

Nothing short of miracles
Can save a small and dying world
That offers no apologies
To lay their hopes and dreams to
sleep
But pray the Lord their gold to
keep
I still got a soul in me
Old predictability
And delusions of grandeur
I once was blind but now I see
They got everything for me but
grace

Please, just believe in me
Don't lose hope so easily
Passing through the eye of a
needle isn't as easy as it sounds
For those like me
    —BRANDI CARLILE

"IN MY OWN EYES"

Hold me down, lift me up
There's someone on the bedside
waiting there for me
I hear my name, turn around
There's gotta be a downside,
something I don't see
Around me

Hide me
Dying in the light of the room
Blind side please
I don't really want to be seen
In my own eyes

Something's wrong
Awake all night
'Cause I can feel the dark side
Closing in on me
Do you see me
As I see myself?
I promise there's a downside
Something you can't see

Lost in translation
Free to fall
One situation
Lose it all.
    —BRANDI CARLILE

ME AND JESSICA

ME STARTING TO STEP INTO MYSELF
WANTING TO FIND MY SWAGGER
BUT NO LONGER FEELING AS MALE.
GROWING MY HAIR OUT AND DIPPING MY
TOE INTO THE FUTURE

ME AND THE SHED SQUATTING CAMP
SITES AT LILITH FAIR THE GORGE

FIRST PHOTO SHOOT WITH JESSICA

JESSICA CHASE - THE MOST ADORABLE AND HILARIOUS
HUMAN ON EARTH "JEX"

9.

....

IRISH TWINS

My band, the Shed, was phasing out for me and I was talking to a music manager called Jim Crow (a horribly unfortunate name) about maybe managing me as Brandi Carlile. I don't really know what caused the shift. It could have simply been my age, my music, or it could have been something that was naturally happening in my relationship but I was starting to embrace my femininity in a way that I never had before. The Shed felt like a boy band to me. I was a boy in it. I didn't know if I could shift my gender energy and still fit in with those guys. I didn't believe any of them would understand.

I was getting pretty good at guitar, and I went downtown and got a busking permit so that I could play for tips in front of the flying fish at Pike Place Market in Seattle. I needed to play music by myself for the first time. I still didn't have a driver's license and was really afraid to get one. Jay and the Shed guys had driven me EVERYWHERE, but that was coming to an end. It was an hour to the city, and I was stranded and frustrated all the time.

My girlfriend Jessica had a full-time job. In addition to busking, I was still a part-time barista and a roofing laborer. The grocery-store job ended when the manager decided to move me and the other noticeable-looking lesbian I worked with to a store nearer the city, one that would have an easier time dealing with our "lifestyle." Obviously, I couldn't get there anymore without a ride and I had to quit.

I was tired of doing nonmusical work, but I needed to make a consistent living. The Shed was fun, but it was about practice; it was never going to be a job . . . Even Elvis had fired me. I hadn't heard from Amber Lee in a long time; not unlike my other childhood friends growing up alongside me in chaos, her life was extremely hard. She made the wise decision to get married at seventeen and get out. I was her maid of honor and then we lost touch for years. It was the last time I would wear a dress . . . until my own wedding.

Sovereign had become a massive responsibility. He left me with so few options that, in some ways, I felt like a young parent. Horses are a tad less time-consuming if you get lucky and have one without any problems, but they're actually more expensive. I had to work to afford hay, vet bills, and boarding. I couldn't live in apartment buildings or city houses with roommates; I had to live in the country and rent serious property with land, pay for hay and hauling, hire farriers to trim and shoe, and that's not including supplemental feed or equipment. Buying that horse was stupid, *but it made me a hustler.* Did I mention that I still didn't even really ride ride?

After lying awake all night one night trying to think of what I could pawn for hay, I had a groundbreaking thought: If I could amplify myself, I could go into local restaurants and ask them if I could sing one night a week for just food. I'd try to win over customers, and if the night I'd chosen to play started to consistently bring in more business, the restaurant had to start paying me. If they refused, at least I would have gotten to eat and jam! I'd move on happily.

It worked. I managed to scrape together and borrow enough money to buy a little PA system, and I teamed up with what I now believe was a brilliant but maybe a cocaine-fueled guitar player who knew how to run it. (Although he was thirty, he didn't have a driver's license either . . . my poor girlfriend.) I started playing six nights a week all over western Washington. Soon I was earning a real living and could finally feed my horse.

My brother played with me whenever he could. His harmonies and harmonica playing added more to our shows than anything else. We even got a shot at a record deal once. I remember when the guy at the label called me, I asked him what time it was where he was, even though we were on the same coast. I was nineteen! We were flown to L.A.; it was our first airplane ride. Jay and I thought our hotel room was the fanciest thing we'd ever seen. We were so proud to be there.

Quietly, we had grown very distant from each other though. Jay still went to the same Baptist church and spent all of his time in the church community. It was a demoralizing compromise—to love being with him as much as I did and know that he sided with them. I had to accept what he thought of me, and I did, but it never felt okay.

Not long after returning from L.A. something had changed for Jay. This was the moment that my brother decided to stop playing music with me, even privately or for fun with the family. It was the end of the laughter and the ease and the harmony. It wasn't a childhood fight; suddenly it was more like a divorce and it was very adult. I was so self-involved about it that I judged him like he was no doubt judging me and swore I'd never forgive him for it. Many of my early songs are about this rift.

I just couldn't understand it. My grandpa and his brother played music together. The Shed guys were brothers. We were a lifelong family band as far as I was concerned. The only thing I could think of that was different from any of that connective tissue and those sacred bonds was that I was a freak lesbian and must have just been hard to be with. I don't believe this anymore.

Time flew by and I started to gain real traction in my music. Record labels were getting more and more interested. I was trying to feel strong without Jay. I met a powerful producer and I was wearing cool clothes. I spent most of my money on guitars, hay, and poker. I didn't own a single guitar worth over $100, but I had about ten, give or take a few, any one of which may have been enjoying a temporary stay in the pawnshop at any given time. I had finally gotten my driver's license and was making payments on a 1993 Toyota SR5 pickup with a lift kit.

One late afternoon I was cooking tacos with my mom for a poker game when we got a call from the police that my brother had been in an accident. He wasn't responsive and it didn't look good. He was going to be airlifted to Harborview Medical Center. I remember driving on the wrong side of the road and honking, swerving around people and running red lights. I didn't even know where I was going, I was just looking for a helicopter. I finally saw it landing in a field near the elementary school and left my truck running in the road. I just ran. I could see them pushing him on a stretcher toward the helicopter and I was just running through the football field screaming, "I love you, Jay!" I was him at four years old . . . running to my bedside in the hospital. I felt unabashedly human and nothing mattered anymore except that he *knew* I loved him.

Jay barely made it through that. I won't even list everything that happened to his body. I set up a hospital bed in the living room of my house and took care of him alongside his now wife, Lia, until he was better. He got married in a wheelchair. I sang at their wedding and wrote him a song.

In my hurt, I'd forgotten that music was actually MY dream and had, in fact, always been a source of anxiety and stress to him. It wasn't his path—just like I knew what mine was, he knew what his wasn't.

He would make it up to me years later with the arrival of my first niece. The lightning strike that was Caroline.

"TURPENTINE"

I watch you grow away from me in photographs
And memories like spies
Salt betrays my eyes again
I started losing sleep and gaining weight
And wishing I was ten again
So I could be your friend again

These days we go to waste like wine
That's turned to turpentine
It's six AM and I'm all messed up
I didn't mean to waste your time
So I'll fall back in line
But I'm warning you we're growing up

I heard you found some pretty words to say
You found your little game to play
and there's no one allowed in
Then just when we believe we could be great
Reality it permeates
And conquers from within again

These days we go to waste like wine
That's turned to turpentine
It's six AM and I'm all messed up
I didn't mean to waste your time
So I'll fall back in line
But I'm warning you we're growing up
    —BRANDI CARLILE

"MY SONG"

Everything I do surrounds these pieces of my life that often change
Or maybe I've changed
Sometimes seeming happy can be self-destructive even when you're sane
Or you're insane
Don't bother waking me today

Here I am
I'm so young
I know I've been bitter
I've been jaded, I'm alone
Every day
I bite my tongue
If you only knew, my mind was full of razors
To cut you like a word if only sung
But this is my song
It is My Song

I live every day like they'll never be a last one till they're gone
And they're gone
I'm too proud to beg for your attention and your friendship and your time
So you can come and get it from now on

Here I am
I'm so young
I know I've been bitter, I've been jaded, I'm alone
Every day I bite my tongue
If you only knew my mind was full of razors
To cut you like a word if only sung
But this is My Song
    —BRANDI CARLILE

"WASTED"

If you had eyes like golden crowns
and diamonds in your fingertips
you'd waste it
If shining wisdom passed your lips
and traveled to the ears of God
you'd waste it
And so I hate that you're
overrated most revered and
celebrated because you'll waste it

Then again it's good to get a call
Now and then just to say hello
Have I said
I hate to see you go
I hate to see you go

But every time you close a door
and nothing opens in its place
you've wasted
And when you speak the words
you know to those who know the
words themselves
you're wasted
You're such a classic waste of
cool, so afraid to break the rules
in all the wrong places

Then again it's good to get a call
Now and then just to say hello
Have I said
I hate to see you go
I hate to see you go
    —BRANDI CARLILE

"HEART'S CONTENT"

Maybe you thought I hung the
moon
And maybe we thought we were
Johnny and June
Maybe we thought it was just us
two
Maybe we spoke too soon

We never lie
And we don't tell tales
We bite our tongues
And our fingernails
We fall in love and we don't fall
out
Maybe we speak too soon

Here's you and me and in
between
We draw a line but we can't see
where it's bent
We scratch our heads and rage
against the heart's content

Maybe we hurt who we love the
most

Maybe it's all we can stand
Maybe we walk through the world
as ghosts
Break my own heart before you
can

Maybe we know how the story
ends
Maybe it's not even about us
We both retreat to opposing
stands and the love lives on
without us

One thing I know for sure is love
will find a way

Here's you and me and in
between,
We draw a line but we can't see
where it's bent
We scratch our heads and rage
against the heart's content
        —BRANDI CARLILE

WE ORGANIZED OUR OWN PHOTO
SHOOT FOR MOMS CHRISTMAS
PRESENT

BRANDI AND JAYS FOREVER
DYNAMIC

FAM JAM WITH BLOND TIFFANY

SHED BAND PRACTICE

ME AND JAY

JAY AND RICK PARASHER ON OUR FIRST FLIGHT

ME AND LITTLE SOVEREIGN AT TWO YEARS OLD... THE ONLY TIME I EVER RODE HIM.

ME AND JAY DAYS BEFORE HIS ACCIDENT

ME AND JAY

ME AS AMBERS MAID OF HONOR, THE TRAUMA OF WEARING THAT
DRESS AT THIS POINT IN MY LIFE MAKES THIS DAY A BLUR
BUT WE'VE SINCE RE-UNITED AND I'D DO THE WHOLE THING AGAIN.

10.

ACTUAL TWINS

I had moved on and embraced so many other musical outlets, but in 1999, I finally let go of the Shed brothers in the interest of self-discovery. It was hard to say goodbye—they were heartbroken. They taught me so much and I still think about them all the time . . . but I was getting stuck out there in the country and I needed to grow up.

I borrowed enough money to make a demo in a legitimate studio in Seattle called London Bridge. I wanted some music to sell at my shows and I also wanted a record deal. I couldn't afford to work in the actual recording studio downstairs, but upstairs there was an attic room with a Pro Tools–ready computer and the London Bridge engineer Jon Plum occasionally took side projects upstairs. This is where I met Tim Hanseroth for the first time. He came to meet me after Jon suggested, at least for my recorded music, that I move past the eccentric guitar player without a driver's license that I'd been in a tense musical relationship with for the past couple years.

I knew of Tim and his twin brother, Phil, because they were kind of famous in Seattle. They could sell out the Showbox and they had a real record deal with their band, the Fighting Machinists, and were recording in the real studio downstairs. I was instantly enamored with Tim and shocked at how nice he was to me considering how "cool" they all were. We exchanged numbers and decided to keep in touch.

Seattle was a real music city for a time. Relics of the grunge scene, record labels were headquartered downtown like it was L.A. A year or so after I recorded at London Bridge and met the twins, I was running into walls. I would walk up and down the street, leaving demos on doorsteps in vain just to feel productive. In addition to my restaurant residencies, playing bars, and busking at Pike Place, I had been participating in an open-mic night at a place in the university district called the Rain Dancer. After doing well at an open mic one Tuesday night, the director started asking me to play more and more songs. Some nights I would just get up and play for forty-five minutes, and eventually it developed into another residency. When the director suggested that I put together a showcase evening, I immediately thought of the twins. Their band had broken up a year prior, and although they were still calling themselves the Fighting Machinists, they had started playing stripped-down gigs with a boom box for a drummer.

I booked all of the baby bands and called Tim Hanseroth. He agreed that he and his elusive brother, Phil, would play. I made posters and hung them all over Seattle and the show sold out! I covered the stage with Christmas lights and emceed the whole event. As the evening progressed toward the twins' highly anticipated set, it became more and more clear that they weren't going to show. They'd stood me up. I took the stage and played by myself for the remainder of the night, including a little-known song that the twins had written called "The Story." I heard it on a little EP I got from the Fighting Machinists email list. I was obviously very disappointed . . . but I wasn't about to give up on them.

One day out of the blue, Phil's wife at the time, Jamie, called me up and asked me to play at Sandel Park across the street from the twins' dad's house. They needed to raise money to keep the park open, and people were really starting to come and see me play. I was so determined to get close to those twins that I went, and we played together. I asked them if I could sing "The Story," and we limped through it. Soon after that Tim and I decided to start a band.

Phil was in a punk band called the New Black. He had blond spiked hair and he was very cute—they both were! But Phil wasn't very interested in joining our band. Looking back on it, I can see how it must have been weird for them after living their whole lives in tandem to that point—they had the same houses, same jobs at Kmart, then Home Depot, then Meta Marble & Granite, which is where they worked when we met.

Tim and I recruited our drummer, Scotty Mercado, from the Seattle grunge band Candlebox. I was living at Scotty's house at the time (after one of my many breakups with Jessica) along with a real estate agent turned virtuoso bass player named, of all things, Phil, who joined our band. Tim and I played our first show several months later at the Tractor. We played original songs (mostly mine) and covered Third Eye Blind. Phil came and I think he was impressed. He agreed to practice with us.

The twins and I hung out in Seattle one day when I went to have lunch at their work and we made a plan to get together in our band's rehearsal space in secret to see if we had any chemistry as a trio. Tim and I had been writing a song together for the first time, "Follow," and I had asked the twins' permission to sing another one of their songs, "Fall Apart Again" (which used to be called "Long Is the Day"). Out of necessity, that day Phil jumped up into a high-pitched Graham Nash–style harmony and we heard the complete chord of our three voices for the first time. I was in total disbelief . . . It was surreal. People say it takes time to cultivate a harmony blend that mystical, but I swear to God it was instantaneous in this case.

I was convinced.

Meanwhile, out in the hallway Other Phil's best friend had walked past our rehearsal door and heard us playing. He popped in to say hi to Other Phil and realized that Tim and I were practicing with Phil Hanseroth. . . . I wasn't even out to my car before Other Phil was calling me.

"Hello, Phil," I said with my voice full of shame.

"Hi, B," he said. "I know you and Tim are playing with his twin brother right now. I just got a new amp and I love being in the band, but you'd be stupid not to play with the twins. Those guys really should be together."

I always had a way of finding the kindest people to let down, and this was no exception. I felt simultaneously terrible and inspired by the way Other Phil reacted to the situation, and I vowed to be forgiving and insightful for the rest of my life in music. I've also never been afraid to move on. I have a horrible case of Catholic guilt about everything, except my music. I will step away from anything that prevents me and mine from evolving and moving forward. I've been called every name in the book and I'd do it again. This was not the case with Other Phil. He was genuinely wishing us well and setting himself aside. I still think about him.

"Thanks, Phil," I said. "I'm really excited and I love you, man."

"Good luck, B," he said.

I got into my pickup and went home with some serious tunnel vision. It was time for one last trip to the pawnshop, but I wouldn't be taking home any cash.

Over the next few days, I strung and reassembled all of my broken, shitty guitars that I'd been tinkering with and using as actual wall art. I loaded them all into the back of my Toyota and drove downtown to the Trading Musician. I remember the clerk laughing at me as I made trip after trip outside to bring the guitars into the shop. I traded them for two Shure Beta SM58 microphones and an EBow. I had saved two guitars.

I called the twins and asked them to come out to my new house in Ravensdale. I was living by myself for the first time. (It lasted about a month.) When they got there, I gave them each a microphone and I gave Tim the EBow and lent him one of my two remaining acoustics. I asked them to be in a band with me and told them that we would make it without any doubt. Tim said yes immediately; Phil was in but "still had to play with some other guys too."

I didn't tell them that I had to sell all my shit because I didn't want them to think I was poor. I still didn't have a bank account or even know how to get a credit card. It was just me and my horse and a lifted early-'90s pickup. They obviously knew I was poor.

After that the twins started doing my residencies with me—four-hour gigs with fifteen-minute breaks—they didn't eat the free food and they felt uncomfortable getting paid. They had good jobs, but it made me feel proud and in charge to pay them. They used to sneak cash back into my guitar cases and into the console of my truck.

Shortly after we officially became a band, there was an incident where I nearly killed the twins by poisoning. I admit I'm being dramatic, but that's the way I tell the story. I had a really cool, very small rehearsal space in south Seattle that I was renting at a place called Hush. It was a refurbished storage facility with soundproof little shoe boxes for garage bands without garages. One particularly hot day, I had a genius idea to cool our room down and impress the twins with my innovative problem-solving skills. So, I swung by the butcher shop and loaded my truck up with dry ice and fans. I set it up in the space and it really did cool down quickly, but we were only a couple songs in before everyone started stumbling outside to get sick. We still laugh at that. Thankfully, I've redeemed myself.

I never got over trying to win the twins' affection and loyalty. They are the kind of people that you feel lucky to know. If you get to actually do life with them, you never stop being grateful. They work HARD and make everyone smile while they're doing it.

We developed a wicked and inappropriate sense of humor together. The pranks and jokes we got up to still make me blush and even I feel uncomfortable about it at times. I still remember how it all started. We were recording a song together at London Bridge for the first time. It was "Until I Die." I was sitting on the couch next to Tim and he had his big, weird man-foot in flip-flops resting on my lap. Sticking out of the couch was the needle-sized ball end of a broken guitar string. I still don't know why, but I picked it up and stabbed his ankle with it. I didn't poke him; I *stabbed* him. I shocked myself and Tim screamed until a smile slowly spread across his face. I had passed some sort of psychotic test. It was as if I had just revealed to him that we spoke the same foreign language. It was such a small incident, considering the levels we wound up taking our behavior to, but that's when I knew it was ON.

We were completely inappropriate. We wrote terrible joke songs. (They loved Ween.) We were wild and we liked kid booze— Jägermeister, Goldschläger, and Rumple Minze. We used to wrestle and beat the living shit out of one another; we'd wear T-shirts and be covered in bruises. We'd trash hotel rooms and press our bare asses against any window, anytime, anywhere. We were horrible and we were *inseparable*. No one liked to be around us for very long. They'd always feel left out. No one was on our wavelength . . . we got matching tattoos.

The thing is, the twins were both married. They got married young within weeks of each other and their wives were friends. It was kid stuff, really, and no one was very happy, but when the three of us found each other it was such a new beginning . . . such a baptism that nothing from before could have survived. The details of their divorces are their story, but they also happened within weeks of each other. Jessica and I were history after meeting the twins. I wrote the song "Tragedy" about the loss of our youthful loves; I hated their wives for hurting them. I see it differently now, but to me, the twins can still do no wrong.

Most twins are a little bit psychic by nature, but this is especially true with the Hanseroths. Years later, they would tell me of recurring dreams they'd had since they were babies.

Tim's was of him and his brother at around four years old walking to the left and the right of a little brown-haired girl, each with an arm around her. Phil's was of two identical shapes orbiting a slightly different shape in perfect time and space, always settling on the right and left in tandem. He realized, looking at one of our stage plots one day that the three of us are the symbol from his dream.

Before that he thought it was a UFO.

"THE STORY"

All of these lines across my face
Tell you the story of who I am
So many stories of where I've
been
And how I got to where I am
But these stories don't mean
anything
When you've got no one to tell
them to
It's true . . . I was made for you

I climbed across the mountain
tops
Swam all across the ocean blue
I crossed all the lines and I broke
all the rules
But baby I broke them all for you
Because even when I was flat
broke
You made me feel like a million
bucks
You do
I was made for you

You see the smile that's on my
mouth
It's hiding the words that don't
come out
And all of my friends who think
that I'm blessed
They don't know my head is a
mess
No, they don't know who I really
am
And they don't know what I've
been through like you do
And I was made for you . . .

All of these lines across my face
Tell you the story of who I am
So many stories of where I've
been
And how I got to where I am
But these stories don't mean
anything
When you've got no one to tell
them to
It's true . . . I was made for you
              −BRANDI CARLILE

"FOLLOW"

Follow your heart and see where
it might take you
Don't let the world outside there
break you
They know not who you are inside
They have never felt your hell
Don't ever let them crack . . .

Hold out I know you feel it getting
cold out
Without the blanket for your soul
now
Before you know it you'll be frozen
You have to see this through
There's no one here but you

I feel the rain coming down
It reminds me of who I used to be
But now that's nothing more
Than a memory

Don't go, to sleep and cry because
tomorrow
If you let it it will swallow
You up and none of this will
matter
Matter anymore.
              −BRANDI CARLILE

"FALL APART AGAIN"

Long is the day, take it away
Hold it up and you don't let it fall
Devil's play, was yesterday
And I don't care about that at all

I just smile, once in awhile
Because I don't want the lines on
my face
I sit right here, holding the years
And I count all the stars in space

You fall apart again and you can
find a friend
Don't turn to someone else
because they won't
understand . . .

Self respect, goes unexpressed
I don't dream because I cannot
sleep
And I think the world of myself

But the world doesn't think much
of me
As long as the day is full of time
there will always be room for your
hand in mine

When you fall apart again and
you can find a friend
Don't turn to someone else 'cause
they won't understand I don't
want to hear you say that You
miss yesterday, if you don't like
what you see that means Nothing
to me

No one's home, I'm alone
With my music and my TV
And I still say that yesterday
Is best when left to sleep
        —BRANDI CARLILE

"PSYCHO BITCH"

You call me on my cell phone
You call me at home
You nutty ass bitch, why won't you
leave me alone?
We'll never be lovers we'll never
be friends
It's safe to say goodbye this is the
end

Psycho bitch stalking me
Get off my tit, bitch, leave me be
Psycho bitch stalking me
Hit the fucking road and set me
free

I can't even walk on down the
street
Without you walkin' on the back of
my feet
Who in the hell do you think you
are?
I found the shit that you left on my
car

Psycho bitch stalking me
Get off my tit, bitch, leave me be
Psycho bitch stalking me
Hit the fucking road and set me
free
        —PHIL AND TIM HANSEROTH

THE NIGHT I STABBED
TIM... A PROPOSAL.

PHIL THE BABE

TIM LOOKIN' HOT
SIDEBURNS

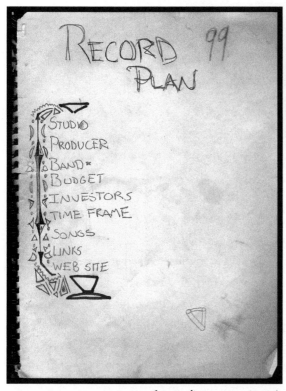

RECORD 99
PLAN

- STUDIO
- PRODUCER
- BAND *
- BUDGET
- INVESTORS
- TIME FRAME
- SONGS
- LINKS
- WEB SITE

PHIL BEATING ME WITH
A FLIP FLOP

MY OBVIOUSLY SUPER SOLID "RECORD PLAN"
FOR US. I'M SURE THEY RAN OUT AND QUIT
THEIR DAY JOB.

11.
. . . .

BRANDI CARLILE AND THE FAMILY NAME

I met a woman I was instantly enamored with at the end of my last relationship . . . or relationships—they were always overlapping, for both parties. I found out right away that lesbians hate leaving each other. We would draw out our breakups for a year or more, forcing each other to accept new relationships while the lines were still blurred.

She was a cop in Seattle named Kim. She was very cool and popular and also quite protective. We had a seventeen-year age difference and that was no problem for me at the time. In many ways, I was nowhere near finished growing up, but I was out in the world living as an adult and I was trying really hard. At the time Kim made me feel secure and focused.

We began dating. She accepted my horse and loved the twins. I was a broke, struggling musician, and she didn't care. I started staying most nights at her house in West Seattle, while also maintaining my rental house out in the country for Sovereign.

It was a big transitional time. The twins and I had started to gain traction around Seattle, and we hired a music manager who believed he could get us a record deal. We always used my name as the band name because of all my residencies and because of the following I had cultivated in the city. We were dreaming big, but we didn't foresee a time when confusing a few hundred Seattle fans with a different name would be a good idea.

Sometimes I regret that.

Aside from the fact that I don't have a particularly attractive name or a name that anyone wanted to wear on a T-shirt, it's strange when your name no longer belongs to you. The risk and reward reside with the name, so even though it's your name on the line, the process involves everyone. I was born to be with other people—creatively, spiritually, and in every other way you can imagine. Psychologically, I've had to work hard to dissociate the pressures, failures, and even the victories from my person. I haven't been Brandi Carlile since 1999 . . . but that is to say that I've really been Brandi Carlile since 1999. Are you confused? So am I.

What if Brandi Carlile decides to become a country singer? Then Tim and Phil are gonna have to be country singers too. What if Brandi Carlile's album absolutely tanks? Well, then Tim and Phil's band has a tough year. But Brandi Carlile has to drown out some serious internal demons. *Was it my voice? Was it my lyrics? Was I too honest? Is my body weird? Am I wearing the right clothes?*

The way our band agreement works is really pretty funny. If I decided to quit and rename myself Yusuf Carlile, the twins could tour and call themselves Brandi Carlile for the rest of their lives. I don't own that name anymore. There's so much in a name . . . but that one's taken. It's a family name now.

I'm grateful for all of that. I think it's helped me keep my feet on the ground. I've never lost myself to my ego, but I've definitely burdened myself with the weight of us all from time to time. It's a problem usually solved by a nice long dinner with the twins and our families.

We started recording our songs on a 4-track recorder in a filthy rehearsal space in Georgetown. I had let go of the shoe box at Hush where I nearly killed the twins, and we moved into their old Fighting Machinists room. There wasn't a clean surface in the place. Cigarettes everywhere, American flags draped over amps, broken equipment, and posters of naked people covering the holes in the walls.

I could have easily lived there.

We had written a handful of pretty good songs and covered a couple too. We made a little demo, and I had about five hundred of them pressed onto a CD at Disc Makers, which is a cool little warehouse operation that made CDs for indie bands only. It had "Shadow on the Wall," "Throw It All Away," "Tragedy," and "Hallelujah" on it.

The twins and I had also become friends with a local promoter and his wife. They often consulted on our career and helped us cultivate a live show. If a national act came through town and the opener got sick, they promised to call me. It happened twice, and both times were total game-changers.

Someone opening for Dave Matthews Band had gotten sick. There was a "beer garden side-stage opportunity" for us, but we'd have to rent our own PA system and get it three hours east to the Columbia River Gorge. The Gorge was my dream concert venue. I was obsessed with it after attending all three Lilith Fairs. This place WAS my coming-of-age story. That venue and those shows had motivated me beyond belief; I never stopped dreaming about them. I would show up a day in advance with my guitar and stay the whole weekend, stalking lesbian campsites for drum circles and Indigo Girls sing-alongs and serenading people in the general-admission line . . . It was a really great time to grow up experiencing successful women in that way. The Gorge is one of those vortices for me.

Dave's Gorge shows were a cultural phenomenon for us in high school, and still are. People come from all over the country to watch DMB rock the sun to sleep in that beautiful canyon. This was BIG for us. We went for it. We spent $1,500 to rent a U-Haul and a PA. We had to sleep in the U-Haul as well . . . but it was so worth it.

During our sound check on the first day, I was singing and noticed a little golf cart winding its way up the road from the main stage. As it got closer, I realized it was actually Dave Matthews himself. It made me nervous, but when you are walking around looking for your big break day and night, you're ready to seize the moment . . . *I want a full-sized Rainbow Brite and a giant tomato!*

I laid *into* it. You would have thought I was Axl Rose the way I turned up the heat on that beer-garden sound check! Dave made sure I watched him very deliberately buy our little demo CD. He held it up and winked at me. Then as quickly as it had arrived, the golf cart was gone. Suddenly it was all worth it. I was at the world's greatest venue doing what I loved, and Dave Matthews knew I existed.

Legend has it that he played his show and somehow got word to his booking agent, Chip Hooper, around midnight on the West Coast to tell him about us. Now, for an independent artist a booking agent is the Holy Grail. They put you on the road. A record deal puts you in the studio, but the road was always calling me and there's really only one way for a wanderluster.

I heard from Chip's staff the following week . . . he was curious. I needed to get myself a show in San Francisco and try to get this guy out to watch! Our manager found us a show in a tiny café called Café du Nord, opening first of three for a woman called Vienna Teng. It was our first road trip, and it was exhilarating. We got halfway there only to find out that Chip wasn't coming but would send an assistant he'd just hired. Someone called Duffy.

We played a killer little show for about eighty people and then slept in Tim's van in the Mission. Duffy was impressed and told Chip to invite us for lunch. We drove from San Francisco to Monterey to meet one of the tallest, most boisterous characters I have ever met in the music business.

It was love at first sight. Chip was a soul mate for me immediately. He laughed at me and said, "I can't do shit with you! You're in a bar band . . . but I'll be your buddy and you can call me day or night." He made good on that promise and properly mentored a twenty-year-old lesbian bar singer with an accidental mullet. I called him on a lot of nights.

Lightning struck twice for me a year later when a young guitar player called Jonny Lang was coming through town to play the Paramount Theatre and needed an opener. With about three hours' notice, Tim and I (we hadn't found a way to integrate Phil on bass without drums yet) had loaded up our demos and our two guitars and headed to the unfathomably legendary Paramount. We had been walking underneath its marquee for our whole lives and wondering how it would feel to walk through its stage door. When we did, it just smelled like music and dreams. Even the sound check would have been enough to fuel me for months' worth of chowder-house gigs . . . but I got to play the real event, and it was packed.

We crushed the gig. I closed with "Hallelujah," alone on a darkened stage, and got my first standing ovation. It took my breath away. I was back at the Northwest Grand Ole Opry in my mind.

I didn't get to meet Jonny Lang that night, but in the audience by total coincidence was a young A&R scout from L.A. called Brendon Mendoza. He was born and raised in Seattle and was in town visiting his mother. He worked for a guy called Rick Rubin at American Recordings. (I knew Rick Rubin because he had produced some of our favorite musicians—I loved Johnny Cash, and the twins loved the Red Hot Chili Peppers.) He made his way backstage and asked us if we had any recorded music. We played it cool and handed him our demo, but when he left it was like a scene out of *Bill & Ted's Excellent Adventure*. We were jumping up and down and slapping each other in the stomach. We were pretty sure that this was going to lead us to our big break.

Our manager heard from American Recordings and Rick Rubin the following week. He wanted us to come to L.A. Our manager cleverly pushed it out a month and used the leverage from our American Recordings meeting to get us an admirable number of other showcases. We practiced like we were about to perform brain surgery with lasers . . . no mistakes were permitted, and our confidence was bullet-proof.

First, we traveled to New York City for the first time on a red-eye flight. We stayed in a TINY hotel together and walked for hours. September 11 had only happened two years prior, and we went down to see the rubble and the famous cross. Tim's hips got sore, so he put one arm around me and one around Phil, and we carried him through the last few blocks. The granite job was catching up to both of them physically. They were lifting slabs of rock and tile all day every day. They are machines, and if you ever saw the twins do a job, you'd understand that for the sake of their bodies they really needed to quit.

Every single label in New York passed on us. Columbia, Warner Bros., Atlantic, and Capitol—but we weren't discouraged. We went to Little Italy and ate lobsters and drank beer. We didn't blink . . . It was time to go to L.A.

I landed at LAX with a splitting headache and was starting to recognize, to my horror, that I was coming down with a wicked sinus infection. This would become a recurring theme throughout my career, becoming sick under pressure (until I was hypnotized . . .). We had three showcases the next day, and I was feeling like I could pull it off. The Rick Rubin showcase—the one I had my heart set on—was still forty-eight hours away.

Just like in New York City, the first three labels passed on us— Columbia on the West Coast, Epic, and an independently funded startup that eventually dissolved. Now, you gotta understand that by "passed," I mean they would stand straight up and leave while I was singing. No goodbye. Just a short wave and a glance back at their stupid little BlackBerrys. They had no idea how hard we'd worked.

This is not for the faint of heart. You need to have been booed, puked on, had your mic knocked into your teeth, and demoralized in almost every way to go to L.A. and get your heart broken like that. But I had gone through all those things and more.

I didn't yet know how to put on my makeup. I was wearing Gap jeans and trying to grow my hair out. The rejection was ROUGH. But my life until this point had prepared me for it.

The night before the Rick showcase, I went to a drugstore and stocked up on cough medicine. Now, even as a child I would immediately vomit upon taking that stuff, but I always thought it was just the taste. I was determined to keep it down this time—because I was an adult and because I couldn't be coughing during my big shot. So, I got in the shower (in case I puked) and took the medicine.

What I didn't know at the time is that I have a weird neuro allergy to the relaxant in almost all cough medicines and antinausea meds, which is why my body rejects them. A "paradoxical response," it's called. I began to twitch and went to bed. I had nightmares all night and crippling anxiety.

I woke the morning of the showcase tweaking and trying to put on my mascara. I took more cough medicine and headed to L.A.'s Swing House to sing for Rick Rubin.

I'm sure you can imagine how it went.

My face was in spasms, I couldn't remember the words or play my guitar, and Rick very sweetly stopped the showcase by asking, "Is there something going on that's making you not yourself today?" I fought the lump in my throat and told him I thought I might be having an allergic reaction to my cough medicine. He said to go ahead and go on home to get better and that he'd look forward to our paths crossing again.

I was obviously devastated and was certain that our paths *wouldn't* cross again. I understood the music business to be unapologetically ruthless at this point.

To my shock and surprise, Rick Rubin made good on his word and flew us back to L.A. the following month. We played one song, "Shadow on the Wall," and anticipating his leaving we rushed into the next intro and he held up his arms and stopped us. "That's an incredible song," he said quietly. "Can you please play it again?" We would play it three times before he let us move on to the next song. He asked us to play that one three times too. We were there for an hour. We played three songs nine times: "Shadow on the Wall," "Throw It All Away," and "The Story."

We had gotten our record deal. I couldn't wait to call Chip Hooper.

The deal was nowhere near done several months later and, in fact, quite in limbo. But Kim and I had decided to move in together and properly merge lives. I told her it had always been a dream of mine to live in a modest log cabin on a creek. After a day and a half of searching online, the first place we saw was just that.

There are some really strange coincidences surrounding the purchase of that house . . . things like arriving to the showing and noticing that there were pictures of my extended family members on the wall (the Dolls!). That would have been an odd enough coincidence. Then we discovered that we had pulled up in the owners' actual car that they had traded in years earlier. A quick comparison of serial numbers and the remnants of an old bumper sticker confirmed it. The owner was very recently widowed under mysterious circumstances. There was a strangeness about the house, and I was drawn to it instantly. I think it was haunted at first. There was a series of serious accidents and a heavy but irresistible vibe about the place. We bought it immediately, and twenty years later I still live there . . . it owns me. The twins moved me into that house with Kim on my twenty-first birthday, June 1.

A year went by and our record deal was falling apart. American Recordings was splitting with its parent company, and ownership was officially in question. But Rick's interest in me had lit a fuse in that town. Other labels were reaching out and wanted to talk to us.

We were BROKE. We had quit our residencies and restaurants thinking we had a record deal, so we went on tour with Hanson in Tim's barely running Ford Econoline van. We sold our own CDs for cash at the merch tables just to keep Tim's van on the road. Kim was basically supporting me, and the twins kept their day jobs.

Whenever we flew back from a gig, as our plane would begin its descent into Sea-Tac Airport, the twins would look out the window to see if there were trailers backed up in the loading bays of the granite warehouse. If there were, they'd go straight from the airport to unload slabs and tiles. They had an incredible boss whom they adored, a self-made Turkish guy called Atilla, who would continue to pay them while we toured even though he knew they would eventually leave. He is still one of our greatest mentors in business and in life.

We ran out of people to sell our demos to and we were tired of waiting, so we asked Rick's permission to record another EP in order to have something new to sell at shows and he obliged. He split our thirty songs right down the middle and explained that we could record an album of B-sides but to wait to record the really special songs once the deal was done. This is the premise of the album *Brandi Carlile*. We made our first album with borrowed money under the guiding hand of Rick Rubin.

It turned out to be more than just a collection of B-sides.

We got a gig opening for James Taylor in L.A. for an HIV benefit, and Rick came out to the gig. Unbeknownst to me, my manager had stacked the audience full of record label reps. There was only one way backstage in this venue, and it was a stage door that was basically *on* the stage. After my set, Rick climbed up ON STAGE during James's first song and walked through the stage door to come and see us . . . all the label reps saw that happen, and that was it. Everyone wanted to know what Rick was doing in those days—and even today. His record label was in limbo and although I never did end up being able to sign to American Recordings, his distinct interest in me as an artist had finally made us desirable to the record industry as a whole.

I signed to Columbia Records that year.

The man who gave me my first deal is Will Botwin, the president of Columbia Records. We flew to L.A., a tad beat-up and jaded, to do one final showcase. We played four songs. Phil was on the stage with us as a trio for the first time. When we finished, a really handsome guy stood up. Everyone looked at him to see what he would do, and I remember realizing that meant he was the boss. I waited for him to grab his BlackBerry and leave, but he slowly began to clap his hands. One by one, the rest of the group stood up and did the same thing. I was skeptical. I wanted to cry. He asked if we would mind playing a few more songs and he motioned for everyone to sit down.

That was it.

We signed to Columbia Records shortly after that. I never forgot the respect and kindness we were shown by Will and his friends. Years down the road with Columbia Records in both of our rearview mirrors, I asked Will to join my team and manage us . . . I still think about that showcase.

When someone believes in you while you're a work in progress, never forget them.

Columbia signed our album of "B-sides" and put us on the road.

We got a check from the record company and went to the guitar store. We each bought one guitar, and Tim financed our first new van. We would create fake rental invoices each time we went on tour and bill it back to the label for tour support. (This part of the story really cracks Will up.) I have no guilt about this! We worked our asses off and paid off our van in under ten years.

One night in San Francisco, we played a particularly spectacular show. We really gave it our all because Chip and Duffy were supposed to be in the audience. Our record deal was a dream come true, but we wanted a booking agent. We wanted to live our lives on the road. We knew we were still too small for Chip and Duffy, but we weren't going to give up, and this show was supposed to at least be a good start at convincing them we were serious. It was the first time Chip would see us as a real band of grown-up professionals.

We were the opening band that night, and the PA system unfortunately cut out for almost ten of the thirty minutes we had to win over this audience. We stood around for a few minutes until finally I had an idea. After noticing that the whole audience had laughed at a joke I thought I was making just to Phil, I walked to the front of the stage and started singing without a microphone. The twins' harmonies were coming in loud and clear, and we had no problem filling that place up with voices. The audience response was overwhelming.

When we got backstage, Chip and Duffy were already there. Chip stretched out his enormous hand and said, "Can I be your agent?" After all those nights and long chats and all the great advice, I had made it far enough into his world to shake his hand and stand beside him as a musical ally. It wasn't charity, it wasn't affection. I was good enough. For THIS reason, he wanted to work with me as much as I wanted to work with him.

He always told me I'd play the 22,000-capacity Gorge someday . . . I never believed him.

A few hours later, we were trying to roll out of San Francisco late at night to beat the traffic. We stopped about a half hour outside of the city so that I could use the bathroom. The twins parked the van on the far side of a dark parking lot, and I went inside. The clerk was decidedly sketchy, but I asked where the bathroom was, and he handed me a giant wooden spoon with a key on it. He then directed me outside and around the building. I always hated those outside toilets. When I came out of the bathroom, the twins were standing outside the door in front of the clerk with a bicycle chain and a crowbar. The clerk didn't see the van, and the twins watched him come outside and look around before following me toward the bathroom . . . They were skinny, but they were bald, covered in tattoos, and scary. I saw the country and a lot of the world in my twenties under the watchful eye of brothers like that. I'm a lucky girl.

We were made for the road. Our shenanigans were as out of control as ever and we rarely spoke outside of the context of humor—the sicker the better.

We all went home and started to prepare emotionally for this next phase in our lives. Phil got divorced and moved into my barn. He wrote a song about my log cabin: "Have You Ever."

My house was getting weirder and weirder. I was sure there was a ghost. My brother broke his leg on the Fourth of July in my garden while my dad was chasing him with a roman candle. It was bad. We all went to the emergency room. I picked up my brother and the beloved family dog a few days later to look after him while his wife, Lia, was at work and help him recover. It was a very hot day . . . and in my struggle to get him out of the car and into the house, I had a regrettable lapse in judgment and I accidentally killed the dog. She was so quiet I forgot she was even in the car.

It was one of the most traumatic moments of my life, and as I recovered my faculties, I kept thinking, *I need to explain to the twins that this will never be funny to me.* It sounds like an odd thought, I know! But they were my whole life, and all we did was fuck with each other.

I needed to take our friendship past all that and to the next level. It was an all-hands-on-deck deep family hurt that required us to stay together in my living room for a few days. Mom, Dad, Tiffany, Jay, Lia, and Kim. We all took turns cooking and just tried to find some peace. I didn't talk to the twins for a week and when I did, I asked them to never laugh or tease me about it.

Of course, they never did.

That was the beginning of the REAL intimacy and respect for one another that we have today. Our friendship grew up that day.

"HAVE YOU EVER"

Have you ever wandered lonely
through the woods?
And everything there feels just as
it should
You're part of the life there
You're part of something good
If you ever wandered through the
woods

If you've ever wandered lonely
through the woods

Have you ever stared into a starry
sky?
Lying on your back you're asking
why
What's the purpose I wonder who
am I

If you've ever stared into a starry
sky

Have you ever stared into a starry
sky

Have you ever been out walking in
the snow?
Tried to get back to where you
were before
You always end up not knowing
where to go
If you've ever been out walking in
the snow
If you'd ever been out walking you
would know.
                    —BRANDI CARLILE

"SHADOW ON THE WALL"

Gone, it's hard for me to say when
I'm wrong
It's hard for me to weep when I'm
strong
But I can never sleep when you're
gone
Oh, but still, if you were going to
crucify me
I wouldn't want nobody to see
'Cause you could kick me hard
when I'm down
Down, down, down

I don't want to be nobody's fool
I've played that part so many
times before
How I long to be a shadow on the
wall
I would make no sound at all
And when the sun goes down
A shadow on the wall cannot be
seen at all
At all

Old friend, it's not that you would
mess with my head

I believe that you believe what
you've said
You think you know me best and
you care
But that's not fair
Because I don't really want to be
saved
It must have been the way I was
raised
To sleep with one eye open I'd say
Hey, hey, hey

I don't want to be nobody's fool
I've played that part so many
times before

How I long to be a shadow on the
wall
I would make no sound at all
And when the sun goes down
The shadow on the wall cannot be
seen at all
At all
                    —BRANDI CARLILE

"CLOSER TO YOU"

It's hard to let the miles pass me
by
Yellow lines that blend together in
my eyes
And when the seasons change
again then I will too
I just want to be closer to you

I'm staring out at endless rows of
green
There are miles of hay like I have
never seen
Just when you think you've had
enough and your dreams come
true
I just want to be closer to you

My mind wanders through all that
I've been hiding from
I tried not to let you down
Now I wonder if I've been doing
something wrong

Help me get my feet back on the
ground

Tomorrow I'll be lying under you
With a heart of gold and arms to
fall into
I know that there might come a
day
where my life is through
But I just want to be closer to you

Someday we might learn to tell
the truth
We might even find the fountains
of our youth
We all needed something real we
all need proof
I just want to be closer to you
I only want to be closer to you
　　　－BRANDI CARLILE

THIS IS ME AND TIM THE FIRST TIME WE PLAYED THE FAMOUS TROUBADOUR. I HAD LUSTED AFTER THIS MYSTICAL STAGE SINCE I FOUND OUT AT 12 THAT IT WAS ELTONS FIRST US STAGE. IT HAS NEVER DISAPPOINTED. NOT THEN FIRST OF 3 AND NOT NOW.

BAGGY JEANS AND CHUCKS, GRUNGE SWAGGER ... SEATTLE KIDS.

HANGING OUT OUTSIDE OUR GEORGETOWN PRACTICE WAREHOUSE WITH FRESH TATTOOS - MATCHING OF COURSE.

BIG DECISIONS IN THE STUDIO
REQUIRE A LOT OF NAIL BITING

ME AT THE DAVE SHOW. GORGE
AMPITHEATRE DEER GARDEN LAWN

BABY PHIL ROUGHING ME UP
AS USUAL

THIS IS ME IN MY "BIRDS NEST" A BED THAT THE TWINS
AND ONE OF KIMS COP BUDDIES HAD BUILT ME IN THE BACK OF OUR
VAN. THIS IS WHERE I WOULD PERCH AND CALL OUT THE SHOTS
OF THE ROAD. HOW FAR WE WOULD BE DRIVING BEFORE STOPPING TO SLEEP,
WHETHER IT WAS STARBUCKS OR TACO BELL, AND SOMETIMES EVEN
KICKING A DRIVER OFF THE WHEEL TO EXCHANGE WITH ANOTHER.
ALL THOSE MILES AND NO ACCIDENTS.

BABIES RECORDING OUR FIRST ALBUM
"BRAND. CARLILE"

CONSTANT SHENANIGANS. WE
ANNOYED EVERYONE AROUND US.

12.

....

THE STORY

had tens of thousands of miles under my belt by the time I met the
fabled T Bone Burnett in a Four Seasons Hotel bar in New York
City. I was eating a burger (I obviously couldn't afford to stay there).
We instantly hit it off. He was towering but not imposing. There was
an intense intelligence in his eye offset by a tendency to self-consciously
flip his white hair away from his eyes. He had some earnest convictions around live recording that really resonated with me. I told him
that I wanted to make my album live with no funny computer stuff
and he had a good chuckle.

He asked me if I wanted to make an album with him. I asked him
if he'd leave L.A. We shook hands and agreed on Ireland . . . we were
drunk.

We wound up in Canada. Compromise isn't all bad.

I was starting to really struggle with my voice. I had struck a deal
with my managers that I would "only do, like, nine shows or something in a row, then I needed a couple days off." I would get up early

during the morning rush-hour traffic to drive to all the radio stations that asked me. You can't say no when you're just starting out. No one wants to pre-record you. It's about paying your dues. You show up on time and you do it live. No shortcuts, no diva shit.

I was also screaming. One night in the Boston Opera House opening for Jamie Cullum, I went for the big a cappella note at the end of "Hallelujah" and nothing came out but air. The audience felt awful for me. I was headed to New York City the next day and I canceled my show and went to the doctor. They found that I was developing hardening polyps from screaming my head off and drinking alcohol during my shows. That's the first time anyone gave me steroids.

You don't know you're abusing steroids when you're younger because no one tells you. You take the pills you're prescribed, and then you further medicate the side effects. Steroids make you unreasonably hungry, so you gain weight and have problems with acid reflux. Then you find yourself on antacids and stomach medications. Worst of all, they lead to sleeplessness, so you find yourself on sleep aids almost inevitably. And that's if you're *not* mostly only sleeping in a frozen coffin out on the great American highway.

I holed up in a New York City hotel room at the top floor of an old building with the twins and our sometimes lead guitar player, Gibb Droll. We idolized him in all ways. I have a big love for that time. We went to sleep to taxicab horns, sirens, and hollering street vendors, and woke up to silence. In total confusion, I went to the window and saw empty streets and cars buried in snow! It was twenty-seven inches. The biggest snowstorm New York had in a hundred years. We had a snowball fight right in the middle of the street and forgot all our collective troubles.

I got right off the road after that, healed my voice, and started preparing to go into a Vancouver recording studio called the Warehouse with T Bone Burnett. Equally as exciting, my longtime hero Matt Chamberlain was going to play the drums. Being from Seattle, I had loved Matt from the work he did with Pearl Jam to Edie Brickell and the New Bohemians to Tori Amos. He was the deep-pocketed groove legend that all the bands coveted.

We all got up to Canada and T Bone Burnett got stuck up there with us somehow. He was afraid to go back over the border and then be told that he couldn't come up and finish the record. I don't remember what it was, something about real estate. The result was that we had T Bone's full attention and ALL of his time. Elvis Costello kept coming to the studio to pick him up and take him to lunch, which was utterly surreal.

T Bone wasn't smoking much weed while we were making our album, but he was VERY eccentric. He tried to explain frequencies, the evils of digital sound waves, and even color to us as it pertained to music. One day, I left the hotel and got in my car to head toward the studio only to realize that a rat had somehow gotten stuck inside my car somewhere. It was making loads of noise and I was completely freaked out. When I got to the studio, I told T Bone what was going on and he spent half the day trying to coax the rat out of my car with a series of long cables attached to a speaker. He was sending experimental frequencies into the vehicle that he believed would confuse or repel the rat, and when one didn't work, he'd just try another one. I laughed until I cried. The rat never left. T Bone really was a blast to be with.

At some point in the session, I felt like he stopped liking my voice. He had grown weary of a particular characteristic in it that he was calling an "affectation." He'd say hurtful shit to me about it like, "A singer making people deaf is the same as a glovemaker cutting people's hands off."

I had come to love and look up to him so much that it was particularly damaging to my self-esteem. I couldn't control this aspect of my voice because it wasn't an affectation to me . . . *yet*. Years later, I would come to understand what he was talking about. But there's something to be said for mentors or pillars in the arts needing to understand that young people are all learning *by* acquiring and eventually shedding affectation. As a producer now myself, it's tempting because potential is a beautiful drug, but you have to let youth take its course.

T Bone and I fell out and lost touch for the better part of a decade. But we eventually reconnected in a big way. I'm always led back to unfinished business in the end. Especially where there's love and dissent. Like I said, he wasn't wrong, and I have a very special place in my heart for T Bone Burnett. He's a good man, a great producer, and a great American icon.

The band and I went overseas for the first time in our lives in 2007. The plan was to start in England to promote *The Story* right after we'd made it. George W. Bush was still the president of the United States. I could not believe I was going to finally get to visit the city where Elton John was born and raised, and the twins were similarly geeking out about the Beatles. We all got the flu immediately after landing at Heathrow and spent two days vomiting in our hotel rooms. But after that it was off to Denmark Street (Britain's Tin Pan Alley) and Abbey Road! While we were doing the Abbey Road street crossing, we saw a Rolls-Royce pull into the studio and watched in total amazement as Sir George Martin stepped out of the backseat. He immediately looked at us, knew exactly what we were doing, and gave us a smile and a wave. Just like that he was gone; we'll never forget it.

We played Birmingham, Leeds, Liverpool, Manchester, London, Dublin, Belfast, Glasgow, and then made our way up to Norway. We were getting really exhausted, cold, and homesick at this point. We started this tour with our heads in the toilet, and as much fun as our first real overseas experience was, it had really taken it out of us.

It was in Norway that I had gotten a phone call from a family member telling me that the twins' lifelong best friend, Jerry, had relapsed in his addiction and decided to take his own life. I had to tell the twins in a tiny dressing room at the back of the bar. It was the first time I saw them cry . . . they would never be the same after that.

Jerry had spent some time as my guitar tech when the twins and I first started touring. He had grown up with the twins and he absolutely worshipped them. I knew he'd had an addiction to speed in the past, but he honestly seemed just like a very enthusiastic, sober do-gooder to me. He was very positive. He carried pictures of his young son, and showed them to everybody he met. We didn't really have pictures on our phones yet.

At some point while we were gone, he hit a rough patch and re-lapsed after many years of sobriety. Jerry struggled with mental illness and in the end decided to check out early . . . he should have never been allowed to own the gun.

In his sober days, Jerry used to love to hike. He'd go out to the peninsula with his sponsor and hike a particular trail. This is where they scattered his ashes. His friend said it's because at some point the trail narrows as it passes a large rock. There's a sharp drop to one side and a monolith to the right. They call it "Jesus Rock" because of the extreme risk you take in passing it. Jerry used to love hanging on to that rock and shuffling on past it, just for the adrenaline rush alone. But one day, he and his friend went on the hike right after Jerry's son was born. When they got to Jesus Rock, Jerry decided to turn around and head back to the trailhead. He said it was because he wanted to be there for his son, and he didn't want to take risks like that anymore.

They scattered Jerry's ashes at Jesus Rock because that was the time in his life that he was the best version of himself. I think he would have liked that.

When we got home, we went back to California. Tim was dating a young musician down there, and Phil was still recovering from his divorce. He and I were together all the time at that point. I flew my little sister down to get her out of the house and take her to Disney-land. It was no secret that she had a massive crush on Phil. But it came as quite a shock that the feeling was mutual.

When Phil started to date my sister, it was very hard for me. I was so confused and didn't know who I was more worried about, my sister who was nineteen, and eleven years younger than crazy tattooed Phil, or my recently divorced, heartbroken friend. To be honest, I was con-cerned it would be the end of our band. I was too protective of my sister and too mixed up about my parenting role to survive a Tiffany-

and-Phil breakup. Thank God they got married and all turned out very well.

One night out on the road in the winter before *The Story*, Tim slipped me a piece of paper without saying anything and I read it. It was a poem:

> *Noon time wind can you blow for me one more time,*
> *And take me back to the start,*
> *Where the midnight moon shined so bright nearly pulled us up to heaven,*
> *By the strings of our heart,*
> *Take me back, Josephine, to that cold and dark December.*

I grabbed a pen and silently wrote a reply:

> *Morning sun, shine on me,*
> *Come light inside my window and rest on my brow.*
> *Kiss my eyes when I sleep and carry me back home,*
> *If my dreams will allow,*
> *Take me back, Josephine*

We didn't know it yet, but we had just named Tiff and Phil's first child.

In retrospect, the fact that I was ever concerned with the age difference between Tiffany and Phil was absurd, considering that I was still with Kim. We'd been together for a while at this point and we loved each other very much . . . but something wasn't settled in my soul. Only in retrospect can I reconcile the way I was drawn to androgynous older women in my youth. At the time I told myself that it was because I was special . . . an old soul. The few friends I had that were my age would tease me, saying shit like "I'd introduce you to this girl I know but I don't think she's lived through enough wars for you." I would fall for police, firefighters, women in the military or in positions of honor and power in their jobs. I would idealize them and then hold their moral failures against them, feeling less and less "safe" every time.

Kim was never sold on monogamy. I found that appalling. I didn't know what I was looking for exactly but it certainly wasn't sexual freedom. I was drawn to her for not just her job but her demeanor. I met police in elementary school. "DARE to keep kids off drugs." They were so friendly and stoic. I would smile and wave when an officer passed by. My interactions with police made me feel safe and my parents squirm! I remember sitting in the backseat and silently judging my mother as she was given a speeding ticket. I didn't know shit.

I learned the truth about police in real time . . . the same way we learn about schoolteachers when we all grow up and go to bars together and they drink you under the table. Our jobs often seem to suggest a paradoxical response at home. It's why I cook, garden, and trim windows.

I remember one of my first dates with Kim after I came of age . . . shooting whiskey and walking out of a gay bar. Kim was fired up! She grabbed a cigarette out of a guy's mouth and threw it on the ground. He was enraged. She smiled like a maniac and I remember pulling her down the sidewalk and walking backward, frantically apologizing for her. I was getting red flags in hits of adrenaline and totally ignoring them. I just continued idealizing her.

It's tricky business falling in love that first couple of times. Never sure which parts of your childhood you're trying to remedy . . . sometimes replicate. I knew I didn't want bar fights and open relationships. I would be disappointed over and over again when my picture-perfect companions would let me down, and I'd find myself backing down life's sidewalks and apologizing for my own failed purity tests.

I missed so many things living in my head like that. The sweet things would go unnoticed because I didn't know how to address them.

Kim talked to me when I was asleep so that I wouldn't argue. Even in the beginning Kim would unfold my gnarled fists while I slept. She would lay my chewed-up fingers out one by one and quietly tell me to take a deep breath. I wasn't ever fully asleep but I never told her. She would mutter something about arthritis and how my hands were "worried." "You might have problems playing guitar when you're older," she'd say. . . . I don't. Thank you, Kim.

Kim said she felt she needed to give me room within the relationship to grow emotionally and to experience authentic feelings. I didn't need to hide them. It drove me crazy that she felt that way because it didn't align with my code. But if I was honest with myself, I never stopped looking. I never stopped scanning the room. I was at an age when I was spending a lot of my time with some really hip older queer people who were telling me that monogamy was at best a heteronormative construct. That I should leave it in the past. Kim was the age I am now. We both had a lot of crushes and she had definitely had her heyday. Kim was (and somehow is) no stranger to sowing oats. Women ADORE her. Hard eye roll.

I was always faithful to her, but sometimes in my travels, my feelings would overtake me, and I would veer dangerously into a sense of "in-loveness." It never lasted. Mostly because the only person I could talk to about it was Kim. She was my best friend. She's wicked funny, and even though she felt jealous every now and then, she fully understood in a way I could only pretend to. We had only been together for four years at this point and it was the longest relationship she'd ever had. She was quite proud of that.

Once upon a time the "in-loveness" *did* last. It lasted for nearly five years. In the beginning I felt really innocent about it. I was protective of it. Repeating the older gals' mantras about queerness already being restricted by society and not imposing hetero restrictions on myself. It was becoming clear that Kim *might* have given me a false sense of security about what I could and couldn't talk about . . . Because this time, it got awkward. The past discussions and late-night gossip sessions about crushes we both used to enjoy were suddenly strained. Something was different this time. It wasn't her fault because she was just as entitled to her real-time reactions and feelings as I was, but my naïveté had finally allowed me to fully submit to something I couldn't handle. It was a mystery to me even as it was happening.

The in-loveness was my muse. And my darkness. I found a woman who passed ALL of my purity tests. Wildly intellectual, sober, talented, heroic, tough, and slightly older than Kim. We talked and sang and traveled all the time. We tortured one another with distance and boundaries. She is the only person I've ever met who can overdose on repression the way I can when shit gets dark. We were perfect for each other. I had crazy dreams and found myself between two worlds again. This love enveloped a significant piece of my youth and I forgot how to feel anything else. I didn't want food and I didn't want peace. During this time, I was addicted to tumult, steroids, and sleep aids. And I didn't think there was a problem with any of those things. I wrote many songs about my great big love that never was. I will never fully understand what hit me; I look back and it seems like a long-spanning dream state.

The era of *The Story* had brought many gifts and some intense growth to my life. I was able to take out my first loan and put my father through rehab for the last time. I made enough money to look after my parents' health for them in a way they hadn't been able to since Dad worked at Boeing. Hilariously, I had finally managed to buy Dad that stupid-ass four-wheeler too.

Perhaps the most significant thing that came of that time happened in Atlanta, Georgia, the week our album came out. I arrived in the dressing room of the Variety Playhouse to find a bouquet of flowers and a gorgeous bottle of wine from none other than Elton John.

Everyone tells you to follow your dreams, but no one tells you what it's going to feel like when your dreams actually come true . . . there's nothing quite like it. It is a shocking, blissful brand of euphoria. Elton liked my voice. He called me on the phone and talked to me for a few minutes. There was nothing for me to say. No way for me to explain to him that I was the Honky Cat in the white suit from the clothing mission. It was the beginning of a friendship that has brought so much healing affirmation and absurdity to my life.

Caroline, Jay's oldest, was born that year. My first baby and the first real bridge to my family. She gave us all a new way to understand what it was to be a Carlile.

I knew immediately that I was a mother the first time I saw her. Even if I had to forget everything else.

"JOSEPHINE"

Take me back Josephine
To that cold and dark December
I am missing someone but I don't
know who
Now I'm standing alone and I'm
trying to remember
Sometimes I wonder how I ever
started loving you

Noontime wind can you blow
For me one more time
And take me on back to the start
Where the midnight moon shines
so bright
Nearly pulled us up to Heaven
By the strings of our heart

Take me back Josephine
To that cold and dark December
I am missing someone but I don't
know who

Now I'm standing alone and I'm
trying to remember
Sometimes I wonder how I ever
started loving you

Morning sun
Shine on me
Come light inside my window
And rest on my brow
Kiss my eyes when I sleep
And carry me back home
If my dreams will allow

Take me back Josephine
To that cold and dark December
I am missing someone but I don't
know who
Now I'm standing alone and I'm
trying to remember
Sometimes I wonder how I ever
started loving you
            —BRANDI CARLILE

"SUGARTOOTH"

He wasn't really known for
breaking the rules
When he arrived in the second
year of my high school
He wasn't so much of a twist of
fate
As a short turn up from a
southern state
He was born with a sweet tooth
he couldn't beat
Always trying to find himself
something sweet
All that he found was the trouble
and me
Or maybe trouble just found him

It was hard to hide that his heart
had scars
He would stay up late talking to
the stars
People tried to blame him for
making bad choices

When he was only listening to the
voices
And searching for some kind of
deeper truth
Between the lines in the bible and
living proof
There's no point now to judge him
in vain
If you haven't been there, you
don't know the pain

He was a liar but not a fraud
Living proof that there was no God
Just the devil stiff as a rod
A slave to the sugartooth

His life became more than he
could take
He found a bad habit he couldn't
break
Nothing could tame him and
nothing could hold him

He only took the pills when the
doctor told him
And looking too hard for that
something sweet
To make his life feel less
incomplete
What in the hell are you going to
do when the world has made its
mind up about you?

He was a liar but not a fraud
Living proof that there was no
God
Just the devil stiff as a rod
A slave to a sugartooth
He wanted to be a better man
Then life kicked him down like an
old tin can
He would give you the shirt on his
back
If not for the sugartooth

They found him lying on his bed
With a gun in his hand and a quiet
head
His broken heart now finally gone

But I know that he had to hurt for
too long
To think he had fought it all on his
own
Just to lose the battle and die
alone
After so many years of feeling lost
He finally made his way back
home

And I heard they put what was
left in a box
And took it to a place called Jesus
Rock
And scattered him all over the
jagged mound
As a symbol to all that peace had
been found
But not for a son who's left behind
With a hand stuck reaching back
in time
To a place in which you can never
unwind
I hope he found something so
sweet

               −BRANDI CARLILE

"LOOKING OUT"

I went out looking for the answers
And never left my town
I'm no good at understanding
But I'm good at standing ground
And when I asked a corner
preacher
I couldn't hear him for my youth
Some people get religion
Some people get the truth.
I never get the truth

I know the darkness pulls on you
But it's just a point of view
When you're outside looking in
You belong to someone
And when you feel like giving in
And the coming of the end
Like your heart could break in two
Someone loves you

I laid a suitcase on my chest

So I could feel somebody's weight
And I laid you to rest
Just to feel the give and take
I got a new interpretation
It's a better point of view

While you were looking for a
landslide
I was looking out for you
I was looking out for you
Someone's looking out for you

I am afraid of crossing lines
I am afraid of flying blind
Afraid of inquiring minds
Afraid of being left behind

I close my eyes, I think of you
I take a step, I think of you
I catch my breath, I think of you
I cannot rest, I think of you

My one and only wrecking ball
And you're crashing through my
walls
When you're outside looking in
You belong to someone
And when you feel like giving in
And the coming of the end
Like your heart could break in two
Someone loves you.
      —BRANDI CARLILE

SIX AM ROLLING OUT OF MY BIRDS NEST
FOR A MOCHA AND MORNING RADIO.

FIRST TOUR BUS. FEELING COZY
AND A LITTLE GROSSED OUT
BY TIMS INABILITY TO GROW
A MOUSTACHE.
BACK TOP PASSENGER LEFT
I'VE NEVER SWITCHED BUNKS.

THIS WAS OUR FIRST FULL TOUR BUS.
IT WAS RANCID AND IT BROKE DOWN
CONSTANTLY - IT WAS PURE BLISS

WRITING SONGS ON THE ROAD.

PHIL AND TIFFANY IN THE BEGINNING

T BONE LOVES THE STUDIO TO FEEL LIKE
A GROCERY STORE REFRIGERATOR (I'D KNOW! I WORKED IN A FEW)
THEY SENT OUT FOR A BLANKET. HE'S AN ICON.

ME AND KIM AT ONE OF HER POLICE FUNCTIONS
SHE HAD BEEN PRESENTED AN AWARD ON THIS
NIGHT. SHE HAS ALWAYS BEEN ON THE RIGHT
SIDE OF THAT JOB

13.

....

GIVING UP GHOSTS AND SATURN RETURNS

I hated the term "Saturn Return." I guess Western astrologers believed that, as Saturn "returns" to the degree in its orbit where it was at the time of one's birth, supposedly a person crosses over some major threshold and enters the next stage of their life. My therapist kept gently mentioning it to me. Anything that had to do with predestiny or mind expansion made my Bible-loving mind pretty nervous. Doomsday prophet Harold Camping was date-setting again. I knew he was a total fraud, but because of the way I grew up, end-times prophecy sent chills down my spine . . . no matter how often I told myself it was complete bullshit.

Nevertheless, by the time I was twenty-eight, I was in two different kinds of love with two incredibly magnetic people, and completely codependent with my parents, not to mention the twins. I was overly invested in my dad's sobriety and my mother's too. I technically didn't own anything, I handed all my money over to Kim, and I was leaning hard on steroids and Xanax to balance each other out. I believed I needed this to get through my tours and the rigors of sleeping on a tour bus.

Sometimes, I wanted the plane to crash . . . or at least just disappear. It would take off and I'd picture it just never landing so that I wouldn't have to go onstage. I was seeing huge swaths of the world through the eyes of an emotionally repressed folk singer and writing some of my best songs ever.

My niece Caroline had taken me by storm, and I was feeling really intense about my lack of familial and emotional stability. I had no real support system because I wasn't being honest with anyone about what I was doing, or the thoughts I was entertaining.

I had distanced myself in my home relationship, but I was seriously considering turning back toward Kim and renewing the nature of our commitment so that I could start the family I desperately wanted. The problem was that there was this invisible wall there that I would soon learn was a result of Kim having a totally predictable and possibly even justifiable affair—albeit *slightly* less honest than my escapade. I don't even know how I felt about it at the time . . . as I mine my memories both hurt and relief come to mind.

I had come back into contact with Rick Rubin in the wrong way at the wrong time. He was now the chairman of my record label and he felt more like my "boss" than he did eight years prior. The first thing he did when he took the job at Columbia was request that we remix and master *The Story*. Man, it pissed me off. He wanted to make our next album with us, and I was still miffed about the year I spent broke and believing I was on his label over at American. I didn't want to make my album with him as a result. For the most part, I told him that. BUT being the total Zen Yoda he is, he basically gave us a budget, his blessing, and permission to try out someone else.

It was a total disaster.

We moved into a small rental in Nashville. Three twin beds in one room. Tim and Phil and me. Huey, Dewey, and Louie.

The "in-loveness" I was experiencing with the woman in my musical life was reaching a peak when she came to see me on that trip. If we didn't see each other, it would become all consuming. Connecting in the real world actually normalized it. But when the distance was there, I was writing about her all the time. We missed each other constantly and we were finding ways to be together more and more while our parallel musical lives crossed as frequently as we were making them. I had idealized plenty of authority figures before . . . but she was *anti-authority*. She was different. She was ten feet tall . . . still disappointing me but in ways that I could get high on. Somehow she was more Brandi than I was even capable of being! In retrospect, I can see that it was classic mirroring. I'm not saying by any stretch of the imagination that she wasn't special, because she was and IS . . . It's just that throughout the years, all the songs about her still apply because everything I loved in this brilliant woman, I wanted in myself too. The relationship had taken on the shape of the muse or a cloak that I could slip on and off.

The young should never deny themselves their feelings. No matter how turbulent they get. Just don't lock them inside, don't keep them secret lest they overpower you from the repression of it. I wanted to talk about it and sing about it . . . so I did. The first song I wrote about this feeling was called "Love Songs." I played it for Kim proudly as she walked in the door one day. She rolled her eyes and said something like "You got it bad." I was in over my head and everyone knew it. I was so much younger than everyone else. I wanted to stay innocent. I didn't want to be denied my feelings. When I sing the song now I sing it to myself. I no longer require completion. "If I ever write a love song, I think I'll write it about you."

When I'm in the grips of my ego I fill my life with restrictions followed by secrets and emotional binging. Declaring myself a vegetarian and driving four towns over to buy a Whopper. Collecting emotional affairs while setting myself phone conversation time limits and deleting emails. Freebasing multivitamins AND also NSAIDs and Xanax. In Nashville I was starting to behave in ways that were conflicted and secretive. I was indulging some strange and self-destructive thoughts. I even did a weird thing where I snuck out on a date with a guy to the Grand Ole Opry. I had made a music video for my song "Turpentine" the previous year, and I'd hit it off with the sweet man who played my brother in the video. We had stayed in touch and I think in some confusing way, I just wanted to hang out with Jay. The guy wound up being a Republican and I laughed at myself and called him the wrong name all evening.

I was absolutely rudderless.

The producer we had chosen to work with in lieu of Rick Rubin didn't believe I was "capable of delivering a live vocal" (his words), which put my ego through a total tornado by the time it was all over. I was having hourly white-knuckle confrontations with him and rage-pacing the rest of the time. I just wanted to play my guitar and sing. It seemed like a reasonable request . . . but I had the hardest time earning that inalienable right as a female artist. I was always too loud, or pitchy . . . too affected, too emotional, or just out of bounds somehow. I was starting to detest making albums.

I went to bed one night in the bedroom with the twins, and my grandfather Vernon came to me in a dream. We were in a laundromat way out in no-man's-land at the end of a dirt road. I heard him before I saw him. He was singing and leaning on a washing machine next to his brother Sonny, who had not died yet but was just about to. Sonny was playing guitar; he was old, but Vern was only about forty. His hair was brown, and I felt confused, remembering him as blond. He was singing:

Anytime you're feeling lonely,
Anytime you're feeling blue,
Anytime you say you want me back again,
That's the time I'll come back home to you.

His voice was lower than I remembered. I walked in and he stopped singing and said, "Here she is, Sonny, you're gonna hear her now," and nodded for me to take over the vocal. As soon as I did, he started grinning, stomping, and elbowing his brother. "Didn't I tell you she could sing?" he said. "Man, she can *really* sing."

No one knew how bad I needed to hear that.

I felt really strongly that it was more than a dream. With one eye open, I grabbed my phone to see what time it was and saw that I had gotten a totally random text message from my mother with a photo of her dad from just before I was born . . . and he had brown hair.

When I woke up the next day, I prayed for the first time in years and thanked God for the access to Vernon and Sonny and for the encouragement. We had the weekend off and I cryptically snuck away from the twins for the day to go and find a church in east Nashville.

I phoned in the rest of the recording session because I knew innately that I had made the wrong decision. It was time for me to find my way back to Rick, who we all now know is notorious for second chances . . . I knew he'd forgive me, and he did. I knew that I was going to be okay because the songs were very good and for the first time in a long time, I believed that *I* was very good.

I dove into an independent Bible study that led me to read the Good Book itself and then thousands of pages on Luther, Calvin, and the Reformation gospels, as well as some of the great pop-culture Christian icons of our time: Brennan Manning, Rob Bell, Rachel Held Evans, Greg Boyd, C. S. Lewis, of course, and many more.

I decided to confront my fear of church and what I came to understand was actually a moderate form of PTSD by sitting through unknown sermons and surrounding myself with strangers. My head would pound, my palms would sweat, and I would even get mild vertigo. It defied all sensibility for me. No amount of "learning" would take it away. The books couldn't touch it. I had to show up.

I knew it was time for my actual baptism.

Brennan Manning was a disgraced, divorced, alcoholic Franciscan priest. I read everything he wrote. *Ragamuffin Gospel* is my favorite. He fell off the wagon and continued to write from a perspective of brokenness. His meditations affected me in a way that no pious teacher ever could have. I imagined him writing page after page while sipping on a Jameson, still believing in himself and in God enough to know that his worthiness was simply irrevocable. He taught me a new way to say the phrase *"The Lord is my shepherd; I shall not want"*—the phrase I'd been carrying around since my grandfather's funeral. He replaces "I shall not want" with the Greek understanding: "I lack nothing."

"The Lord is my shepherd; I lack nothing." This subtle difference is night and day to a self-punishing person.

These songs and heartaches, my misplaced anger and how it led me to seek all this forgiveness on this side of the divide and the other one, were my "second calling," my actual Saturn Return and what ultimately led me to my actual adult baptism.

I WAS FINALLY baptized on Easter Sunday in 2009. I wish I could report the usual feeling of renewal, but I wasn't as present as I would have liked to have been. The botched baptism of my fragile youth still owned that moment in some ways. I light a candle and say a prayer every year on Easter, and every year I feel better, and further away from that day. As the distance between me and that moment grows, it pushes me closer and closer to God.

Maybe baptism, like "coming out," isn't a moment after all.

I considered seminary during this time and I almost enrolled from the passion I had for my faith . . . but ultimately I would find the thing I was really looking for on the other side of the Atlantic Ocean.

I closed the book on the "in-loveness" relationship I was having in my head when I wrote the song "I Will." Saying goodbye to her . . . that imagery and innocence was harder than any of my life's endings up to that point. *Give Up the Ghost* is all about the great finish to my guilelessness and how badly I longed to keep it. It was a one-way split though. I don't really know if she felt it end. It was just for me. At the same time I could feel it slowly ending with Kim. I loved them both so much. I still do, and I credit them with most of the ways I became the woman I am. I needed both of them to learn that I didn't need either one.

I was *actually* head-over-heels in love with my niece Caroline. The song I'd written for her was so personal for me, yet fun and even camp somehow. I thought of Elton and the honky-tonk-swung piano vibes from *Tumbleweed Connection* and *Don't Shoot Me I'm Only the Piano Player*. So I wrote him an email. I didn't expect to hear back. But one day later, I did. I was just waking up in my hotel room and an unknown number came through. Part of me wondered *way* deep down if it might be him. So, obviously I didn't answer! I wasn't dressed properly or awake enough to speak to Elton John on the phone. He left a voicemail:

"Hello, Brandi, it's Elton. Listen, I'm absurdly busy and I don't want to mess you around, so call me back at this number so we can discuss this song of yours." He left a number.

I WAS FREAKING OUT! I jumped out of bed and got dressed, frantically trying to pull together a cup of coffee and some semblance of collectedness. He called again one minute later. And then again and again . . . and again. At this point I was being ridiculous, and I knew I needed to get myself together. I picked up the phone and dialed the number after a good stiff chug on my hotel room coffee.

"'ELLO THERE???" a very loud old British woman shouted into the phone at ninety decibels; she sounded like a witch from a Disney movie.

"H-Hi," I stuttered. "My name is Brandi Carlile. Can I speak to Elton?"

"Oh, sorry, darling. It's Elton speaking. It's just that you never know who's calling nowadays."

Anyone who isn't in love with that man is crazy in my mind. He ended up recording the song "Caroline" with me in Vegas. He sang and played piano. His playing was so skilled and intricate that no piano player I've played with has ever been able to pull it off live. In the studio while we were listening back, every so often he'd elbow me in the ribs and point out that a particular riff was "very Elton" indeed. Love.

He wrote Caroline a note: "Dear Caroline, I loved singing your song."

The next night, I went to see his show and he dedicated "Tiny Dancer" to me from stage. I remember the audible gasp from the twins to my left and my right. They knew.

Give Up the Ghost shaped up to be one of my most honest and shamelessly raw collections of songs. I was and still am so proud of that album. Predictably, I fell out with Rick again at the end of it. My fortitude knew no power differential. My dad had taught me so well to stand up for myself that I would defend my music at all costs. Being wrong didn't deter me one bit. I was fighting for the right to blaze my own trail and standing up to men I loved and respected was honestly par for the course. I have apologized a lot and been apologized to . . . but I've never kept my mouth shut and then wished I hadn't.

SEATTLE WAS IN a total state of shock in July 2009. There was a series of violent crimes against LGBTQ people that ended with the notoriously disturbing and heartbreaking rape of Jen Hopper and the rape and murder of her fiancée, Teresa Butz. Teresa died defending Jen. It was an only-in-your-nightmares, extremely rare, middle-of-the-night home-invasion scenario that you will never be able to get out of your head. I had been with a police officer for almost eight years at this point, and I'd been privy to more of the details than I could emotionally handle. It spun me out. I felt like I knew these women. Being the "out lesbian" celebrity of the moment in Seattle, I was positive they knew me, and I wasn't sleeping.

I talked to my dad about how I was feeling. He told me, rightfully, that I was naturally obsessive and not to get too confused about what my involvement should be. I ignored him and started praying about reaching out to Jenny.

My suspicions were confirmed that they were fans. Jen was a singer and Teresa loved my music. They'd been on the Cayamo Cruise (a singer-songwriter cruise) with me and shook my hand on a beach in the Virgin Islands just a few months prior. After learning this, I asked Jen to dinner. I still don't know why. I felt like I didn't have a purpose— I wasn't sure what, if *any,* role I would be able to play in her healing process and I was totally perplexed and concerned as to why I was even doing it. I put my beloved Taylor guitar that I'd bought with the money from my first record deal in its case—James Taylor himself had signed it for me.

Jen Hopper bravely showed up to meet me in a Mexican restaurant with her best friend in Fremont. She was bandaged on her arms and her throat—which had been cut so badly you almost couldn't believe she'd survived it. I came alone. Our souls connected so naturally that I don't question impulses like that one anymore. We had a margarita and she talked about Teresa all night.

I was meant to hang out with Jen so that she could tell one of Teresa's favorite singers how fucking cool Teresa was and just have a good laugh that she didn't need to feel guilty about. There were no tears. Only a proud would-have-been-wife celebrating her girl. I asked Jen if she'd thought about a healing path yet, and she told me that for her it's music. I gave her my guitar.

Jen has one of the most stunning singing voices in the world. She would eventually start a musical project called Angel Band with a group of family and friends from Teresa's hometown of St. Louis that would help countless people deal with the aftermath of violence in their lives. She also brought up self-defense that night. She was afraid of the dark. She couldn't sleep alone and was trying to think of ways she could feel strong again. She was and is the strongest person I've ever met.

I went home that night and told Kim. She was really moved and motivated. We called a Kung Fu Sifu instructor, who is to this day a dear friend of ours, and with a group of about five women, we started the "Fight the Fear" campaign. We would celebrate Jen and Teresa by teaching at-risk women and girls all over Seattle self-defense for free.

Jenny (as I still call her) spoke at every class we had. She's now one of my closest friends.

All the way over in England, a woman named Catherine Shepherd would read this story in an online newspaper. Catherine had been living and working in London for Sir Paul McCartney for ten years. She started out as his PA but left to travel through Africa and Asia and volunteer in AIDS clinics, orphanages, and a women's mushroom-farming program of all things! Paul called her upon her return and asked her if she'd like her job back. She told him that she saw the world differently than she had before and he said he'd suspected she would. This is how she came to be "Jiminy Cricket." She went back to work as Paul's charity coordinator.

Jenny and Teresa's story had really deeply upset Catherine Shepherd too. She followed it too closely, and when she saw that an American singer was a part of a relief campaign, she reached out to my manager to offer some help. She donated auction items and some memorabilia on behalf of Paul to help us raise money for our classes. She offered to donate money, too, although I declined due to some principles I had around "fundraising," but that's another story. . . .

My longtime manager and friend Mark dreamed up the Looking Out Foundation. I was always fueled by activism, but I was disorganized about it. He was working hard and growing tired of fielding my constant charity foundation questions and my self-righteous convictions around fundraising. Catherine's email intrigued him (thank God) and he suggested I reach out to this woman for some mentoring.

Man, am I glad I did. She gave me advice over email and phone for the better part of a year and it never occurred to me once even that she was a day less than sixty-five years old. I guess I just assumed she was Paul's age . . . ? I still don't know why. She was way too brilliant to be twenty-eight.

A year went by and we met in New York City with our long-term girlfriends by our sides. I had heard she was coming to a show because she happened to be in town for Paul. I wasn't thrilled with meeting the "charity lady" after the show, since all my hip lesbian NYC pals would be there and I wanted to go out. But I agreed and let everyone know I'd catch up with them afterward.

When I walked into that dressing room, I was literally speechless. She was the most beautiful woman I'd ever seen, and the age shock was profoundly funny. Her girlfriend was pretty fucking funny too! I loved them both, but my interest in Catherine only felt platonic. A big part of this was that I was in a religious deep dive, and on top of that, I thought I was only attracted to masculine women.

Cath's girlfriend was a total jock in red lipstick, a PE teacher with an inappropriate sense of humor and a mountain of charisma. I wish they were still friends so we could hang out. They were headed to Memphis. They wanted to see the "city that invented rock 'n' roll." I ditched my friends that night, and Kim and I invited the two of them to Seattle to stay with us for a few days.

The four of us really hit it off. We had barbecues, and Catherine and I played guitar and sang late into the night. It was all really fun and easy . . . I still didn't know I had any feelings for Cath, but when I heard them start their rental car before dawn on the last morning, I jumped out of bed to say goodbye. Poor Cath had her wrist wrapped. She had gotten a really terrible reaction to poison oak. Cath was sleepy, shy, and embarrassed. Her girlfriend was really making fun of her. To be honest, she'd been doing that all weekend. I felt a disproportionate sting of irritation and protectiveness in that moment that I thought about all day. I found myself wishing that Catherine had never left.

The next time I saw her, my feelings were no longer platonic. I knew I'd never see another person ever again.

WE WENT INTO the studio and recorded our album *Bear Creek* pretty quickly after *Give Up the Ghost*. There's a randomness to it that I love—you can tell it was our first taste of freedom from producers. But it was erratic. We had a lot of growing up to do and it was the end of our time on Columbia Records. Getting a record deal is a dream come true for a scrappy kid with big dreams; getting dropped stung. It felt a lot like dropping out of school. But I have such fond memories of my time there and eternal gratefulness for the space they gave me to grow. I mean that. I'd be more than willing to talk shit here if I had something to say.

I was about to turn thirty. Harold Camping died. Jesus didn't come back. The world didn't end. I would soon leave Kim and keep the house. I *actually* ended my emotional affair. I put some healthy distance between me and my parents. And I asked the twins to let me go on my first "solo tour"—that was the scariest thing.

My therapist had warned me that it would be hard to explain an ache for autonomy to identical twins. Innately, the familial connection we had would make it painful to say. They were so upset. Especially Phil. He left the conversation and then came back a couple hours later, but we didn't talk. Just sat by a fire.

I went on my solo tour in the fall.

My bus pulled out of Kentucky, and a text came through from Phil. He'd written a song. It was the song of us. All of us that would soon be. He sang it himself. I sat in the jump seat next to the driver and cried my twenties out as I listened to "Beginning to Feel the Years" for the first time.

"BEGINNING TO FEEL THE YEARS"

You carry me along with you
Keep my spirit strong, you do
Maybe I was meant to be under
your lock and key

The hard times that I've had
Really don't seem all that bad
Yesterday is long ago and far
away

I'm beginning to feel the years,
but I'm going to be okay
As long as you're beside me along
the way
I'm gonna to make it through the
night
And into the morning light

There are things that I said before
I don't mean them anymore
Yesterday is long ago and far
away

And I'm beginning to feel the
years, but I'm going to be okay
As long as you're beside me along
the way
I'm gonna make it through the
night
And into the morning light

With angels by our sides
The spirits there to guide . . .

I'm beginning to feel the years,
but I'm going to be okay
As long as you're beside me along
the way
Going to make it through the
night
And into the morning light
    —BRANDI CARLILE

"I WILL"

It's not the end of the world
It's not even over
But it will be soon
I never learn my lessons
I just change my tune
And no one seems to notice
But you will, you will

It's no big deal
But the last thing I think of when I
close my eyes
And the first thing on my mind
when I rise
It is a day and you're not really in
my life

You can try and you won't find it
where you're looking
You can't hold it 'til it's putty in
your hands
And you can't break a heart that
wasn't even yours to break

You can never be there for me in
the end
And I will do the right thing

I will

You're not fooling me
I'm not the sort of girl who can't
see reason
But it's nothing that a little bit of
time won't heal
I know it don't come easy
But I love you, I do

And coming clean means never
closing curtains
I just change my scene
But you will know what I mean
And I will learn throughout my life
to never lean on what will bend

I can try and I won't find it where
I'm looking

I can't hold it 'til it's putty in my hands
You can't break a heart that wasn't even yours to break
You can never be there for me in the end.
But I will do the right thing

I will

I don't think you ever learned a thing from me
But I know that you want me to learn from you
But you've drawn heavy handed lines around morality

"LOVE SONGS"
I can never write a love song
I can never write a blues song
When I'm in love I am a lover
But I have always had the blues

I am afraid that no one sees me
What will they say when I am gone
It occurs to me I think I miss you
I think I missed you all along

Out of the corner of my eye
I'm not sure if I should think these things of you
Is it the wrong place or the wrong time?
I think it's just my turn to lose

About yourself and I don't share your point of view
It's been time to let you go a thousand times and never know

that it hurts to be the one that you'd regret

I have to say that I am proud to know you
And that I'll never be the same because we met
You might not miss this
But I will.
 —BRANDI CARLILE

Thoughts of you could give me smile lines
I laughed myself to sleep because I knew
We were talking about a fine line
It depends on who you're talking to

If it's any consolation
The blues have always had me too
And if I ever write a love song
I think I'll write it about you
 —BRANDI CARLILE

"CAROLINE"

I woke up long after dawn
20 years had come and gone
I know when it changed for me
The day in June you came to me
I've seen through someone else's
eyes
With nothing on the other side
Every motel, every town
Pieces scattered all around

Promises that I can't beat
Someone's heart that I can't keep
Days so long I couldn't speak
Roads so rocky I can't sleep
But I've seen things so beautiful
All around this broken world
That pale in comparison to you

Caroline, I'm on my way back
home to you
You can't imagine what I'm going
through without you by my side
It's been a long long time
Oh won't you say a prayer for me
I hope you will remember me
You're always on my mind

I have seen the canyon lands
Crooked lines like in your hands
You'd swear the earth was split in
two
I wouldn't lie, I promise you that I
have seen it you will too
You could not believe if not for
photographs I took for you,
Caroline

They've built towers to the sky
It hurts sometimes to watch them
try
They run themselves into the
ground
But I know you will love them and
their city lights and city sounds
There's beauty in the struggle
Anytime I feel it get me down I see
you smiling

Now I have seen things in the sky
stars and lights and birds and I
I've been rocky mountain high and
told them all about you
Because you are still the only
thing that constantly amazes me
I love the road and I have been
blessed but
I love you best

Caroline, I'm on my way back
home to you
You can't imagine what I'm going
through without you by my side
It's been a long long time
Oh won't you say a prayer for me
I hope you will remember me
You're always on my mind
You were always on my mind, My
Caroline
  —BRANDI CARLILE

THE GLITZ AND GLAM OF WASHING MY
HAIR IN A NON-POTABLE WATER BUS SINK
WITH HAND SOAP.

THIS IS THE SHIT AUNTIES WILL DO
THAT MOMS WONT NO WAY I'M
DOING THIS WITH MY KIDS-
CAROLINE GOT THE BEST OF ME
I'M AFRAID

CAROLINE I'M ON MY WAY BACK
HOME TO YOU

SOUL MATES.

THE LYRICS TO CAROLINE SIGNED BY ELTON JOHN.

I KNOW WHEN IT CHANGED FOR ME A DAY IN JUNE
YOU CAME TO ME,
I'VE SEEN THROUGH SOMEONE ELSES EYES,
NOTHING ON THE OTHER SIDE,
EVERY MOTEL EVERY TOWN PIECES SCATTERED ALL AROUN

PROMISES THAT I CAN'T BEAT SOMEONES APART
THAT I CAN'T KEEP DAYS SO LONG I CAN'T SLEEP
ROADS SO ROCKY I CAN'T SLEEP, BUT I'VE SEEN
THINGS SO BEAUTIFUL ALL AROUND THIS BROKEN
WORLD THAT PALE IN COMPARISON TO YOU

CAROLINE IM ON MY WAY BACK HOME
TO YOU,
IMAGINE WHAT I'M GOING THROUGH
WITHOUT YOU BY MY SIDE
ITS BEEN A LONG LONG TIME OH
WON'T YOU SAY A PRAYER FOR ME
I HOPE YOU WILL REMEMBER ME
YOU'RE ALWAYS ON MY MIND

I HAVE SEEN THE CANYON LAND
CROOKED LINES LIKE IN YOUR HANDS
YOU'D SWEAR THE EARTH WAS SPLIT IN TWO
I WOULDN'T LIE I PROMISE YOU THAT
I HAVE SEEN IT YOU WILL TOO
YOU COULD NOT BELIEVE IF NOT FOR
PHOTOGRAPHS I TOOK FOR YOU CAROLINE

After Caroline this
I tried signing this
God
Love EltonJohn

JEREMY COWART - ONE OF MY FAVORITE PHOTOGRAPHERS
CAME TO CAPTURE THE FIRST RECORDING OF GHOST.
LOOKING BACK ON THESE PHOTOS I CAN SEE THAT HE SENSED
THE TENSION AND SIMPLY DECIDED TO DOCUMENT THE GENUINE
ATMOSPHERE... YIKES.

RAIL THIN SELF CONSCIOUS BRANDI OUTSIDE
A NASHVILLE STUDIO FOR THE UN USED RECORDING
SESSIONS THAT WERE OUR FIRST ATTEMPT AT
GIVE UP THE GHOST.

FISHING IN SOME DIRTY URBAN RIVER
STRAIGHT OFF THE BUS WITH MY MORNING
COFFEE. THIS WAS OFTEN HOW I WOULD
GROUND MYSELF AND CONNECT TO A CITY
BEFORE THE SHOW.

14.

....

BEGINNING TO FEEL THE YEARS

My dad's sobriety felt weird. It seemed somehow too easy for him to move on from the past when I so clearly hadn't. After many attempts at AA, he had gone through a kind of aversion therapy. It ends a person's addictive cravings but not necessarily the tendencies. He just flat-out stopped craving alcohol. He hates the smell of it. If he hears two glasses clink together, he gets a quick wave of nausea. He's alive and happy and it's a miracle really . . . but it's complicated.

There's a shamelessness about it that can really hurt a person who is still struggling with the aftershocks. I never could explain it to myself fully, so I started going to Al-Anon to deal with the general lack of resolve around my childhood. To accept that nothing may ever change and not every story ends in epiphanous reconciliation.

The song "That Wasn't Me" was ultimately my deepest healing song. It came with the understanding that my feelings are my own. Reconciliation would have to happen within *my* heart and mind— and I would deal with the lack of resolution alone. This kind of resolve doesn't have the final word, but nothing ever does. I was growing into myself, and my dad's autonomy was pushing me out of my immediate family in an important way. I was starting to understand that I was building a family of my own.

Kim saw something between Cath and me on my thirtieth birthday in New York. Kim and I had become totally platonic and separate people. We simply couldn't get along in a romantic context. I had started looking into what it would take for me to have a baby alone, knowing that I'd have Kim's help as a friend. It didn't seem plausible for us to not live together. We could *always* live together . . . something about us just works. It was certainly unnecessary for either of us to move out, because I was never home anyway. "Parallel lives" is putting it mildly.

Kim loved Cath. After my show in Central Park, Kim and I went to an English pub with Catherine and her friend Christina, plus a group of other singers and local scallywags I loved to hang with. It was good unclean thirtieth-birthday fun. Drinking Jameson, shooting oysters, and trying to teach the Secret Sisters how to yodel. The chemistry between Catherine and me was really intense, and it was noticed by everyone. Nothing was going to happen. Cath lived in London and I was on another path.

I wanted children to screw up immediately . . . and nothing was going to change that.

The next morning, both Kim and Catherine got on flights—to leave me. Cath to London and Kim to Seattle. I returned to my tour with Ray LaMontagne, who I was NOT getting along with at the time. I called Chip Hooper in the middle of the night once a week threatening to leave the tour. I was just furious. With Ray, with Kim, with myself, and I couldn't accept what my life had become. All I wanted was a family and some normalcy, and here I was falling in love again, messing with Kim, passive-aggressively fighting with folk singers, and taking drugs, while the rest of my family was growing up and moving forward.

Ray and I were playing in Boston, and that night was one of the worst thunderstorms the city had ever seen. The crowd was huddled under the tent where we were about to play. They'd delayed the concert by several hours and I stood backstage about as thin as a rail and wrote "Raise Hell," affectionately titled "Ray's Hell," as a personal commitment to give him back the hell I felt he'd been giving me for the rest of the tour. We later reconciled and can now have a very good laugh at our respective tortured phases.

> *You have a mind to keep me quiet and although you can try,*
> *Better men have hit their knees and bigger men have died.*

It took a lot to get me to that point. I have no real enemies. But by the end of the first chorus, I was over it and on to the real problem . . .

> *It came upon a lightning strike with eyes of bright clear blue,*
> *I took the tie from around my neck and gave my heart to you,*
> *I sent my love across the sea and though I didn't cry,*
> *that voice will haunt my every dream until the day I die.*

And if that isn't nauseatingly dramatic enough for you, I woke up on the bus with a hangover the next morning and threw my iPhone into a fountain, determined to never speak to Kim or Catherine, or any other woman ever again.

That tour ended in the hospital like a lot of the long ones had. Walking pneumonia and a debilitating case of cluster migraines with visual disturbances. Of course, always the fatalist, I was convinced I had a brain tumor and started scheduling MRIs and planning my funeral.

When I got home, I was pretty happy to see Kim and, like I always did, I spilled the beans and told her that my "in-loveness" had struck again. I told her that I hadn't talked to Catherine since June, and I hadn't. The relationship I'd had before had taught me to deprive myself. To my amazement and immense relief, Kim told me that she thought it was different this time. She thought that Cath and I were the real thing.

There was mercy in the age difference between me and Kim. We carried each other through really big times in our lives. We fought like crazy and we are best friends to this day. Kim moved out just a couple of months after my thirtieth birthday; she was forty-seven. Before you start canonizing her as a saint, I should tell you that she did take me to the cleaners! But I was happy to see her move on in style. Cath and I decorated her new house. . . . I love lesbians.

Later that summer, Catherine and I locked ourselves into a little cabin on a lake in northern Michigan. It's really hard to "date" internationally. It has nowhere to go but domesticity. There were things to work out, logistics and a culture shock. We needed neutral ground and we wanted to see if we were what we thought we were to each other. Insert U-Haul joke here.

A U.S. marriage ban is very unromantic, and it makes you feel like you have no future when you've fallen in love. It turned out our suspicions were correct: we were absolutely obsessed with each other. I hated for Catherine to leave a room! I still feel exactly the same way. We cooked, went fishing, drove around in a beat-up old Jeep, and listened to music. Cath plays guitar and sings beautifully. We talked about her band back at home and her life working for Paul and wanting to do more with her music. I was enamored beyond reason.

We had one fight: it sounds like I'm making a joke but I'm not. I told her that I didn't like Joni Mitchell after she put on the *Blue* CD in the Jeep. She looked at me deadly serious and said, "I'm not sure I even know what this is if you can't get your head around Joni Mitchell." T Bone had played the song "All I Want" for me in my twenties during the recording of *The Story* and I was not impressed. Now with Cath, I criticized a lyric that I had decided I didn't dig ("I wanna talk to you, I wanna shampoo you") and told her that Joni just didn't sound "tough" to me.

"Do you know what 'Little Green' is about?" she asked.

"No," I said, laughing.

"This isn't funny," Cath said. "Believe me, Joni is tough."

Then she played the song.

Cath didn't talk to me for hours after that. I learned to be careful when I laugh at Cath. She's a moody person because she's an artist and she's got a narrative inside her head that I may only be getting tiny glimpses of at any given time. She's wildly intelligent and deep. She was right; it isn't funny to laugh at Joni Mitchell. It's immature and arrogant. Cath has a way of teaching me about the world through art and music. She picks her battles. Joni Mitchell has changed my life and I now believe that *Blue* is the greatest album ever made, and that "Little Green" is the toughest song in rock-'n'-roll history.

Saying goodbye to Catherine at the Traverse City airport was unbearable. It was also incredibly awkward, which seemed to be the hallmark of our early days together. We kissed goodbye and ended our embrace, only for Cath to get her jacket caught on a stanchion. I backed away, watching her argue with the stanchion, carrying on and saying that she "really had to go" and that she "loved me but it's really not funny anymore" in her thick south London accent before she noticed me on the ground in hysterics twenty feet away, realizing to her horror that she'd been scolding a post.

The following week I flew to England to meet her mother and friends. I'm really affected by jet lag, so the whole trip felt like a fever dream. Catherine's mother and friends are so special. In a world that has a hyperbole problem currently, allow me to tell you what I mean by special. I mean *Stand by Me* special, *My Girl* special, *The Breakfast Club* special . . . the kind of friendships people make sitcoms about. I was as smitten with them as I was disappointed. Smitten because they were brilliant and creative and British and shy and unbearably charismatic all at once. Disappointed because I believed that it meant she would not be moving to the United States of America if hell were freezing over.

Cath and I were in bed early in the morning at the London York & Albany hotel (the first of many nights there). We were drinking mimosas and nursing our hangovers in total style when I got a call from my little sister. She was pregnant. The first baby in our *musical* family was on her way.

Now it was official. Everyone in my family had children except for me. The oldest. And here I am in London drinking alcohol at eight A.M. in bed with my brand-new girlfriend after blowing up my entire life. I wanted to be happy for Tiffany—my nieces and nephews were my life, so the thought of my sister's first baby and the first baby in our band shouldn't have made me feel as hopeless as it did. I was having big doubts about my judgment and life choices.

CATH AND I DATED for several months back and forth across the Atlantic, always desperate to see each other, until we decided it was time for Catherine to tell Paul she was considering emigrating to America. She let him know that she was leaving, and he asked her to lunch to talk about it. He couldn't understand why she was leaving to work with this nobody Brandi Carlile person in the States. When she told him that she was gay and in a relationship with me, he immediately called the waitress over and ordered a bottle of wine. They spent hours laughing and talking about Cath's secret life. She left work in the fall with Paul's blessing and a beautiful Linda McCartney print signed by him that we have hanging in our living room.

We started living together and hired an immigration attorney. Cath was on an ESTA visa, which would only allow her to stay in the States for ninety days at a time, which is more than enough time for lesbians to plan their entire lives together and get a cat (we named her Blue after our first fight). I started thinking about when it would be appropriate for me to propose to Catherine. I bought her a very plain engagement ring because she hates flashy jewelry. The time never seemed to be right though. We kept getting detained at the airport. Border patrol was flagging Catherine's entries into the United States and asking a lot of questions. If we said we were together, they'd put her on a plane and send her back to the UK.

It was soul destroying not being able to just get married and live in the same country together. It didn't even look like marriage equality would happen within my lifetime. Even Barack Obama had famously come out and said he was against gay marriage during the presidential debates.

Before one particularly lengthy detention at the Sea-Tac Airport, I had planned on proposing to Catherine when we got home. My friends had come to the house and gotten everything ready. A bottle of Champagne chilling and a fire in the woodstove. This detention, though, was an unreasonably intrusive one. Our bags and phones were searched, and we were held for more than four hours. We watched families get sent back to the countries they'd come from with tiny children who'd been on overnight flights and traveling for days. I felt ashamed of my country and embarrassed for Catherine. She was so upset on the drive home that she didn't speak to me. She'd begun to doubt America.

I decided just to hold on to the ring.

Catherine had started to dig into and overhaul the Looking Out Foundation and the Fight the Fear Campaign. She was overqualified and whip-smart. She created fundraising avenues that we weren't even aware of: donating a dollar a ticket to the foundation, house concerts and private shows, VIP meet-and-greets, exclusive merch and auctions for interesting personal experiences, like album playbacks for groups of fans. She launched multiple campaigns and recruited volunteers from all over the country—galvanizing and fully integrating our fans, donors, and activists into our foundation. Before too long, Looking Out was officially bigger and more important than our band. The twins were so amazed by Cath's ideas that they started bringing her their own, effectively making the foundation the major focus of our entire family.

A person from my team pointed out that Cath's expertise was so obvious and specialized that she might qualify for a specialized work visa. We reluctantly agreed. I say "reluctantly" because the people we saw turned away at the border had affected us deeply and made us shamefully aware of our privilege. Don't get me wrong: being denied the basic civil right to marry is oppressive and wrong, but we knew too much about displaced people and immigration at this point to not feel the sting of empathy.

The process was quick and decisive. Because of the high-profile work she'd done in the UK, Paul helped us, and so did Elton, Emma Thompson, Roger Daltrey, and many more. Cath rightfully got her O-1B visa, and the stress of separation loosened its hold on us for at least the two years until it would expire.

We got on a plane and came home to the States. My phone was exploding with text messages. Barack Obama had just been the first U.S. president to ever come out in support of marriage equality. He apologized about his earlier opinion on the matter and appealed to those with the power to abolish the marriage ban that LGBTQ citizens should be granted the right to marry. For the first time in my life I believed the laws might change. I was proud of my home again and Catherine was thrilled.

That Obama fella has a way with hope. I wrote him a long letter and he graced my life with a beautiful reply. That's the day I proposed to Cath.

She had gotten in the hot tub to soak off the eleven-hour flight. (Yes, I'm a hot-tub person. I know, I should be eighty and living in Palm Springs.) I grabbed the ring out of the book I was hiding it in and a bottle of Cath's favorite Champagne and went out to join her. I won't tell you exactly how it all happened, but I will tell you that I did this wearing nothing but a hat . . . and that she said *yes*.

We had three weddings. (You're reading that right.) When we called our parents to tell them our exciting news, Catherine's dad was forced to admit to her that he had been battling leukemia for five years and that our wedding date would fall on the day of his chemotherapy trial. It was upsetting to hear he was so sick, but logistically and spiritually, it was no problem. He's a stoic northern Englishman, so he's not keen on attention. We happily decided to take our wedding to him. It was our only religious wedding, and it was very important to me. Cath's dad and stepmom drove us to the city hall in Wareham, Massachusetts, to apply for our marriage license. Gay marriage was recognized as legal in Massachusetts at the time, and it was moving to me beyond explanation to sign that certificate for real. Of course, that reality would end the moment the plane left the tarmac, but there was hope in it. Cath's dad and stepmom drove us there like we were a couple of teenagers being driven to a school dance. Having the Shepherds bear witness to that made me feel weirdly parented . . . it was so functional that I was kind of uncomfortable with it.

My family came out to Boston to be there for us and for Cath's dad. Our respective fathers walked Catherine and me down the aisle together while the twins sang "Beginning to Feel the Years" with a ukulele. We had lobster rolls on the beach at midnight, fishing for striped bass in the high tide. I finally drank the priceless bottle of wine Elton John had sent me all those years ago. We only had paper cups. It was terribly uncivilized and absolute paradise.

We got married again in a barn outside Seattle. We invited 250 guests. Tiffany planned that wedding, and all of our friends helped us. They all know that Cath and I are useless. The Secret Sisters came all the way from Alabama to sing for us, Cath's mom wrote a beautiful speech, and there was karaoke and Champagne and a pizza truck and ice cream. It was and still is the best party I've ever been to.

We got married one final time in London. Cath's parents are divorced, and she tries to keep things as even as she can for them, but I don't think they're bothered about it. It's just one of those childhood dynamics that you can't help but drag along with you for the rest of your life.

Our dear friend Hanalei planned the London wedding. This day was the absolute dream. Our civil-partnership ceremony at Chelsea Town Hall was beautiful but hard for me because I couldn't pray. There was no religion allowed, and we said our vows under a sign that stated that the UK recognized marriage as between a man and a woman. I struggled with the reverse oppression of not being able to bring God into our ceremony because it was a civil partnership. Was there no place in the world for the family we wanted to be? We chose to count our blessings instead. Our friend Holly read "Kathy's Song" in lieu of a prayer . . . but I think God heard us anyway. I have a feeling He likes Simon and Garfunkel.

And from the shelter of my mind,
Through the window of my eyes,
I gaze beyond the rain-drenched streets,
To England where my heart lies.
—PAUL SIMON

We strolled down the steps at Chelsea Town Hall in a legally recognized companionship for the first time on February 15, 2013, followed by a drive to East London in a vintage double-decker bus. We had our reception in an actual crypt (where, fittingly, King Henry VIII once held a three-day wedding banquet). It was entirely candlelit and beautiful. We ate rustic French food and drank our body weight in Champagne before, as all British parties do, it exploded into a shoes-off, raging dance party. Hanalei is still my hero. It was an absolute blast.

The twins and their families were at all three weddings. Baby Josephine, Phil and Tiff's daughter, was our only baby then. She was too little to be a flower girl, but she was pointing the way forward for all of us in those days. The love and support we received from the Hanseroths could only be described as unconditional family love.

When you are told your whole life that it's wrong for two women or two men to marry, when your homeland agrees and when you realize that you believe it, too, deep within your primitive senses, a reckoning is imperative. It is a process but it's mandatory whether you're LGBTQ or not. A person's self-worth is dictated by what inalienable rights are allowed to them. The right to not live your life alone is a big one. If your family can accept you, if they want to celebrate your life and bear witness to your solemn vow, you'll have as many weddings as you need to.

"I BELONG TO YOU"

Last night I had the exact same
dream as you
I killed a bird to save your life and
you gave me your shoes
You said clip my wings and walk
my miles
And I said I would too, then I woke
up
But I wasn't gonna tell you

Today I sang the same damn tune
as you
It was Lady in Red I hate that
song, and I know you do too
You didn't catch me singing along
but I always sing with you
Nice and quietly, 'cause I don't
want to stop you

I know I could be spending a little
too much time with you
But time and too much don't
belong together like we do
If I had all my yesterdays I'd give
them to you too
I belong to you now, I belong to
you

I see the world the exact same
way that you do

We lend our hands, and take our
stands in tandem when we do
When I lied and said I knew the
way, I hid my eyes from you
I still don't know why
I probably didn't want to scare
you

I know I could be spending a little
too much time with you
But time and too much don't
belong together like we do
If I had all my yesterdays I'd give
them to you too
I belong to you now, I belong to
you

I'm gonna die the exact same day
as you.
On the Golden Gate Bridge, I'll
hold your hand and howl at the
moon
We'll scrape the sky with tired
eyes and I will come find you
And I ain't scared
Because I'm never gonna miss you
I belong to you now
I belong to you.
    —BRANDI CARLILE

"KATHY'S SONG"

I hear the drizzle of the rain
Like a memory it falls
Soft and warm continuing
Tapping on my roof and walls

And from the shelter of my mind
Through the window of my eyes
I gaze beyond the rain-drenched
streets
To England where my heart lies

My mind's distracted and diffused
My thoughts are many miles away
They lie with you when you're
asleep

And kiss you when you start your
day

And a song I was writing is left
undone
I don't know why I spend my time
Writing songs I can't believe
With words that tear and strain to
rhyme

And so you see I have come to
doubt
All that I once held as true
I stand alone without beliefs
The only truth I know is you

And as I watch the drops of rain
Weave their weary paths and die

I know that I am like the rain
There but for the grace of you go I
                    —SIMON AND GARFUNKEL

"RAISE HELL"

I've been down with a broken
heart since the day I learned to
speak
The devil gave me a crooked start
when he gave me crooked feet
But Gabriel done came to me and
kissed me in my sleep
And I'll be singing like an angel
until I'm six feet deep
I found myself an omen and I
tattooed on a sign
I set my mind to wandering and
walk a broken line
You have a mind to keep me quiet
and although you can try
Better men have hit their knees
and bigger men have died
I'm gonna raise, raise hell
There's a story no one tells

That you gotta raise, raise hell
Go on now ring that bell
It came upon a lightning strike
with eyes of bright clear blue
I took the tie from around my neck
and gave my heart to you
I sent my love across the sea and
though I didn't cry
That voice will haunt my every
dream until the day I die
I dug a hole inside my heart to put
you in your grave
At this point it was you or me and
mama didn't raise no slave
You took my face in both your
hands and looked me in the eye
And I went down with such a force
that in your grave I lie
                    —BRANDI CARLILE

"THAT WASN'T ME"

Hang on just hang on for a minute
I've got something to say
I'm not asking you to move on or
forget it but these are better days
To be wrong all along and admit it
is not amazing grace
It's to be loved like a song you
remember
Even when you've changed

When you're lost you will toss
every lucky coin you'll ever trust
And you'll hide from your god like
he ever turns his back on us
Then you'll fall all the way to the
bottom and land on your own
knife
And you'll learn who you are even
If it doesn't take your life

Tell me
Did I go on a tangent?
Did I lie through my teeth?
Did I cause you to stumble on your
feet?
Did I bring shame on my family?
Did it show when I was weak?
Whatever you've seen
That wasn't me

Tell me
Did I go on a tangent?
Did I lie through my teeth?
Did I cause you to stumble on your
feet?
Did I bring shame on my family?
Did it show when I was weak?
Whatever you've seen
That wasn't me

But I want you to know that you'll
never be alone

I want to believe

Do I make myself a blessing to
everyone I meet?
When you fall I will get you on
your feet

"LITTLE GREEN"
Born with the moon in Cancer
Choose her a name she'll answer
to
Call her green and the winters
cannot fade her
Call her green for the children
who have made her little, green
Be a gypsy dancer

He went to California
Hearing that everything's warmer
there
So you write him a letter, say, "Her
eyes are blue"
He sends you a poem and she's
lost to you
Little green, he's a nonconformer

Just a little green
Like the color when the spring is
born
There'll be crocuses to bring to
school tomorrow
Just a little green
Like the night's when the Northern
Lights perform

Do I spend time with my family
Does it show when I am weak
When that's what you see
That will be me
That will be me.
    −BRANDI CARLILE

There'll be icicles and birthday
clothes and sometimes
There'll be sorrow

Child with a child pretending
Weary of lies you are sending
home
So you sign all the papers in the
family name
You're sad and you're sorry but
you're not ashamed
Little green, have a happy ending

Just a little green
Like the color when the spring is
born
There'll be crocuses to bring to
school tomorrow
Just a little green
Like the nights when the Northern
Lights perform
There'll be icicles and birthday
clothes
And sometimes there'll be sorrow
    −JONI MITCHELL

CATH AND I SINGING "I BELONG TO YOU" ON STAGE
EVERY TIME I ASK HER TO SING WE HAVE A FIGHT...
BUT SHE ALWAYS THANKS ME FOR MAKING HER DO IT.

OUR DAY TRIP HONEYMOON TO WESTPOINT
FOR FISH AND CHIPS WITH OUR DOG.

CATHERINE AND ME FOR OUR BOSTON WEDDING. TIFFANY DRESSED US
AND DID OUR MAKE UP. YOU SHOULD SEE HOW BAD OUR FINGERNAILS
LOOK FROM THE BEACH.

THIS IS OUR SEATTLE BARN WEDDING. TIFFAN
AGAIN MADE US BOTH PRESENTABLE. CAT
DRANK TOO MUCH TEQUILA AND SANG MADON
ALL NIGHT.

15.
. . . .

FIREWATCHER'S DAUGHTER

Touring with Catherine was amazing. She ended my dependency on sleep aids. No more Ambien, no more Lunesta and Xanax. I went from lorazepam to melatonin, melatonin to chamomile tea and a stern look that says, *It's bedtime.* She was a mother before she was a mother.

If I got sick or lost my voice, she made me cancel the show. No steroids. It all felt very human. I was getting off the bus before three P.M. and eating three meals a day. We had baby Jo with us too. Each night, my sister would do my makeup and Cath would rock Jo to sleep and put her to bed. We had discovered that touring with babies wasn't that hard after all. They like the motion of the road and they love the close quarters. It was never a secret that Cath and I wanted to have kids right away. We were already talking about that up in Michigan.

Tim and his wife, Hanna, were just about to bring our gorgeous nephew, Wilder, into the world . . . now there would be two. The wheels kept turning and the family didn't stop growing. Cath and I were grateful that the Hanseroths took the leap before we did—we learned a lot from them. We were also in a little bit more of a unique position because there was not a realistic way for me to quit working. The band and all of its business-based surroundings were entirely dependent on my ability to get onstage. It was becoming clearer and clearer that I *personally* wasn't going to have a baby this time.

It was a resignation that felt okay in the moment, knowing that I would carry the next time. We did the research and decided to go the IVF route. Our travel schedule was too inconsistent for any of the other methods, and we wanted to give ourselves the best shot we could of having it work the first time.

My old friend David didn't come around much. He hates attention and I shower him with it, so he keeps his distance. He doesn't care for music. Every now and then I'll sing the national anthem at a football game and he'll text me a heart and a wink. I don't really think he knows what I do. When this book comes out, he won't read it. But if there's a leak in my roof, my truck's in a ditch, or something's broken, he'll be there in twenty minutes. He's beautiful. To me, he's still eleven with curly blond hair and a nervous tic: If you dare to look at him and ask him a question, he closes his eyes. He gets really animated and answers you in an assertive voice with a confident chuckle, but he won't open those eyes until he's stopped talking. It's my favorite thing. Cath was drawn to him immediately. Every so often he'd come over for a beer and we'd fuss over him from the moment he walked in until the moment he left—and we never wanted him to leave. To put it simply, we just knew that our kids were a part of him. It's a primitive intuition that for us was undeniable.

We invited him over one day only to reveal, to his horror I'm sure, that we wanted him to father our children. He said a very sweet thing about my childhood and his. Neither of us resented our parents, but he made it clear that he thought it'd be nice to know that we could bring a little person into the world and make them feel truly safe. He said yes and meant it.

Knowing him, I still can't work out how he did it. He had to drive to Seattle and donate several times, see a counselor, and meet with a family lawyer. He is NOTORIOUS for getting shy and flaking out. As an example, he stood me up for his own thirtieth birthday party I'd thrown at my house. I had to give his steak to the dog. But he made every one of those IVF appointments.

We harvested my eggs. Two women living together within a year of marriage, both on IVF hormones and giving each other shots in the abdomen.

Just sit with that for a moment.

The super-ovulation drugs convince you your ovaries are the size of footballs and they make you feel crazy. It was late summer, and I was still irritably working around the land to get it ready for winter, even though they tell you to lie low when you're on those hormones. Obviously, I decided to go ahead and split a half cord of firewood to fill the shed and I threw my lower back into hell. It's never been the same since. Cut to MY back being the focal point of Catherine's pregnancy.

My favorite memory is of my glamorous London wife slaving away in the early summer heat to bury a dead chicken in the yard exactly three days before giving birth. I sat at the fire pit maniacally laughing, thinking about how her life had changed. From Soho Square to pregnant on a chicken farm. Nevertheless, the Carlile egg harvest was a success and we came away with a plethora of viable embryos. The *first* one we implanted in Cath took! We were thrilled beyond belief and I was really hoping it'd be a boy.

I loved that time in our lives . . . but it was complicated. I decided to take a chain saw and cut a massive hole in the side of my house to build an addition. It was an enormous undertaking that lasted Cath's whole pregnancy and beyond. I wish there was some statistic somewhere to show how often people rip their houses apart and take on massive construction projects RIGHT when they're going to have a baby.

We ran out of money in the end and I had to borrow some from my manager. I bought a bunch of saws and taught myself some basic finish carpentry. I sanded, stained, cut, and hand-nailed every trim board. Every time I walk into the nursery now, I'm as amused by my handiwork as I am proud.

The glossy version of my music-business job that a person might see and think automatically makes me rich and glamorous is an illusion. For one thing, I'm stupid and frivolous with money, and for another, it's everyone *around* me that gets rich. My first daughter was about to be born into a closet with a shipping blanket for a wall just like everyone else.

I was working construction on the house and simultaneously recording *The Firewatcher's Daughter* at Bear Creek. I was not fully present during those sessions. I wish someone would have told me I was nesting. I didn't think I had a right to. That was for pregnant women, and I wasn't pregnant. I was feeling really confused about what my role even was. The birthing and breastfeeding classes were excruciating. I'm not big on classes anyway, and I've always thought I'm more famous than I am, so I was positive someone would recognize me. No one did.

The classes were so heteronormative that they were giving me a complex. I knew I was not a dad, but I couldn't get over feeling like I wasn't a mother either. Cath was carrying my child and I was feeling a deep and irreconcilable grief creep into situations where I was being put in a support role usually reserved for "dads."

If you have had children, you will have noticed this. People make fun of dads. I don't like it and I don't really think it's okay. When Mom's pregnant she's a queen. The classes and the support groups all rightfully uphold the woman in this miracle of a position. But the modern practice is to humiliate the "dumbass dad guy" and drag him up to the front of the class so he can put a diaper on a baby doll backwards or demonstrate that he has no idea how to properly wear a BabyBjörn.

This is probably an unhealthy thing. For one, it disempowers a pregnant woman's partner when she needs that person to be the *most* confident, and it also boxes LGBTQ couples into a male-female role paradigm that inevitably just makes them feel more alone. This is what happened to me. I felt useless and humiliated by those classes. It made the confusing grief about not *being* pregnant take on a whole new shape. At least those dads knew how they contributed, and fit into the Christmas-card photo.

I didn't even know what I was anymore.

I was a mother. But I needed someone to tell me that. . . . If only there had been a book.

Same-sex parenting might read clinical, but that's only because it's so new. Gay domesticity has a path, but it isn't well worn yet and we need to humanize these stories because history is happening all around us. Right now.

I wound up bursting into tears in the parking lot outside of one of these classes and telling Catherine that I couldn't be the "dad" for one more day. She felt the same way and felt forced into an ultra-femme world that didn't fit her at all either. She was feeling all the same things I was, but to compound it all, she wasn't sure how to deal with what was happening to her actual body. We pulled out of our parking spot and drove away. Gender identity sneaks up on you around pregnancy no matter how well you've planned it.

Cath found a midwife who specialized in diverse pregnancy situations, and she came to our house and taught us all the classes again in a way that felt like reality to us. She taught us about timed contractions by making me plunge my entire arm into ice and holding it there for the duration of a pretend contraction.

It finally felt right to get excited. We found out our baby was a little girl. We would call her Evangeline: to me, the gospel; to Catherine, the good news . . . they're the same thing.

The band finished the record early and everyone came to help me with my house. Trina Shoemaker, our engineer producer, arrived with a sledgehammer, along with the twins, the whole band, and all the crew. We had a massive work party at my house to prepare for Evangeline. Trina is the one who said:

"Welcome to the end of being alone inside your mind."

Day after day, I would burn construction scraps and think about my faith and my child on the way. I could feel the tide starting to turn politically in the United States, and the debates on TV were ominous, to say the least. I wrote "The Stranger at My Door" staring down a bonfire and trying to make sense of it all. I was building my house on a rock. I wanted Evangeline to know that love isn't a feeling. It's something we do and a promise we keep. I couldn't stop thinking about Syria and the pregnant women leaving their homes for refugee camps. They were heavy themes for June, but I felt like a bird sensing a hurricane. I wish I had been wrong.

The Firewatcher's Daughter ended with "Heroes and Songs." A burial at sea. It was a metamorphosis of that great big in-loveness from my Saturn Return that never was, and the way it left my dreams and became foundational. Endings don't always mean closure. It's when you stop dreaming about something that the book really closes.

Keep the tears that I cried and my youth and my pride
And my sorrow like never before,
I've got thank you's and smiles and affection for miles
And I always will look up to you,
You held open the door for who I'm sent here for
To come in and make my dreams come true.

Evangeline came three days later. Born to two mothers on Father's Day. David came running in during active labor and then raced right back out again. We wouldn't see him for a year after that. It's just who he is.

The midwife told us that we each needed a mantra for every time the world of motherhood felt like it was a template we didn't fit into.

Mine was: "I Am the Mother of Evangeline."

"THE MOTHER"

Welcome to the end of being
alone inside your mind
You're tethered to another and
you're worried all the time

You always knew the melody but
you never heard it rhyme
She's fair and she is quiet lord she
doesn't look like me
She made me love the morning
She's a holiday at sea
The New York streets are as busy
as they always used to be

But I am the mother of Evangeline

The first things that she took from
me were selfishness and sleep
She broke a thousand heirlooms I
was never meant to keep
She filled my life with color,
cancelled plans and trashed my
car

But none of that is ever who we
are
Outside of my windows are the
mountains and the snow
I hold you while you're sleeping
and I wish that I could go
All my rowdy friends are out
accomplishing their dreams

But I am the mother of Evangeline

They've still got their morning
paper and their coffee and their
time
And they still enjoy their evenings
with the skeptics and the wine
But all the wonders I have seen I
will see a second time
From inside of the ages through
your eyes

You were not an accident where
no one thought it through
The world that stood against us
made us mean to fight for you

And when we chose your name
we knew that you'd fight the
power too
You're nothing short of magical
and beautiful to me
I'll never hit the big time without
you
So they can keep their treasure
and their ties to the machine
I am the mother of Evangeline.
    —BRANDI CARLILE

"THE STRANGER AT MY DOOR"

I have seen the firewatcher's
daughter
Watching fires burn from smoke
to black
There's nothing she won't burn
From Styrofoam to urns, to
someone else's ashes in a sack

You can scorch the metal, you can
even melt the glass
You can pass the time here, fire
lives into the past
An all-consuming flame, that
refines and new begins
It'll take your family heirlooms, but
it can take your darkest sins

It's a good ol' bedtime story, give
you nightmares 'til you die
And the ones that love to tell it,
hide the mischief in their eyes
Condemn their sons to Hades
And Gehenna is full of guys, alive
and well

But there ain't no Hell for a
firewatcher's daughter

We exercise the demons of the
things we used to know
The gnashing of the teeth become
the remnants of our homes
We think we're moving on, from
materials we long
To forget we ever sold our souls to
own

There's a chilling absolution that
we're given at our birth
A powerful delusion and a plague
upon the earth
But nothing scares me more
Than the stranger at my door
Who I fail to give shelter, time,
and worth.
        —BRANDI CARLILE

"WILDER (WE'RE CHAINED)"

You came into this world with eyes
as clear as water
You didn't look a thing like your
grandmother's daughter
With a heart so heavy, and
beating like a drum
Neither did you look like your
grandfather's son

Wilder than a brushfire burns
deep inside the bramble
Baby, I think God made your soul
born to ramble
Maybe you'll take to the far away
places
Where life is going to deal you a
hand full of aces
But it doesn't really matter how
great the space is

Life has a fuse and it burns with
quickness
But death ain't the long twisted
branch of sickness
Just as the spark gives birth to a
flame
We'll be bound by our love and in
the family name

We're chained
And when everything else
changes our love will stay the
same
We're chained
And when everything else goes
away our love will still remain
We're chained
        —BRANDI CARLILE

"HEROES AND SONGS"

Some rights and some wrongs
Some heroes and songs
Are much better left unsung
Between fiction and fact illusion
and pact
Where we've been into what
we've become
Although we have changed we
are never estranged
And there's nothing I'd trade from
before

I love you my friend
My dear means to an end
But you're not in my dreams
anymore

Never a lie although this is
goodbye
To the magical mystery tour
Keep the tears that I cried and my
youth and my pride
And my sorrow like never before
I've got thank you's and smiles
and affection for miles

And I always will look up to you
You held open the door for who
I'm sent here for
To come in and make my dreams
come true

Although it was sad and it hurt
'cause it had to
There's nothing I'd change from
before
I love you my friend, my dear
means to an end
But you're not in my dreams
anymore

Although it was sad and it hurt
really bad
There's nothing I'd change from
before
I love you my friend my dear
means to an end
But you're not in my dreams
anymore.
        —BRANDI CARLILE

DAY ONE. WELCOME TO THE
END OF BEING ALONE INSIDE
YOUR MIND.

DAVID AND EVANGELINE

I AM THE MOTHER OF EVANGELINE

EVANGELINE RADIATES DIGNITY AND
STRENGTH. SHE DOESN'T NEED ME, BUT
I KNOW SHE LOVES ME.

CERTIFICATE OF LIVE BIRTH

CERTIFICATE NUMBER: 146-2014-038639   DATE ISSUED: 07/02/2014

GIVEN NAMES: EVANGELINE RUTH**
LAST NAME: CARLILE**

DATE OF BIRTH: JUNE 15,2014**
FACILITY: SWEDISH MEDICAL CENTER - ISSAQUAH
PLACE OF BIRTH: ISSAQUAH, KING COUNTY, WASHINGTON
TIME OF BIRTH: 11:07 P.M.
SEX: FEMALE

MOTHER'S MAIDEN NAME: CATHERINE RUTH SHEPHERD
PLACE OF BIRTH: UNITED KINGDOM
DATE OF BIRTH: 03/20/1980

FATHER'S NAME: BRANDI MARIE CARLILE
PLACE OF BIRTH: WASHINGTON
DATE OF BIRTH: 06/01/1981

FILING DATE: 06/21/2014

FEE NUMBER: 17048901

WHATS IN A WORD? WHATS IN A PIECE OF PAPER?
MORE THAN I THOUGHT. I AM THE MOTHER OF EVANGELINE.

ME HOLDING A VERY OLD SOUL.

EVA AND HER TWIN. BABY DADDY DAVID

EVANGELINE AND AUNT KIM BRO DOWN.

BABIES ON BUSES, LONG DAYS
AND INTERRUPTED NIGHTS.

THE CARULES AND DAVID... UNABLE
TO LOOK AT THE CAMERA AS USUAL

CATH SURPRISING ME ON MY FIRST US
MOTHERS DAY IN NASHVILLE TN

CLASSIC BRANDI AND CATHERINE. 1 WEEK OLD EVA TENT
CAMPING IN EASTERN WASHINGTON.

BARACK OBAMA AND EVANGELINE MEET FOR THE FIRST TIME AND
CRUSH A FIST BUMP. THE OBAMAS BRING OUT THE BEST IN OUR
FAMILY AND PROVIDED SOME DEEP AFFIRMATION WHEN WE NEEDED
IT THE MOST.

DEEP IN CONVERSATION ABOUT LOVE WITH THE LEADER
OF THE FREE WORLD.

16.

. . . .

A PIN DROP, THE LOVE THAT LETS US SHARE OUR NAME

The twins and I had a remarkably efficient way of dreaming up schemes that would result in zero profit. We were even better at designing a loss—claiming victory and artistic excellence. Laughing at capitalism, while our worthy and decent administrators developed ulcers.

The Pin Drop Tour was like that.

The East Coast is the most expensive place in the country to tour for a Seattle band, but it also has the oldest and most beautiful music halls. We had one of our famous ideas: we would tour beautiful old music halls with no PA system, completely sans electronics. We always did an unplugged song in our shows. My voice is obscenely loud and some of these rooms were designed pre-amplification. They were instruments in and of themselves—a feat of engineering specifically designed to honor the human ear. Fast-forward over one hundred years and we're in these places with PA systems, LED lights, fake reverb, and fog machines . . . don't even get me started about the fact that we're filming these shows on our phones.

The idea hit me while I was up in the rafters of the Portsmouth Music Hall in New Hampshire. The venue manager had given us a tour of the place, leading us up a treacherous ladder into the ceiling above the audience. The building designer had carved his initials into the wood next to the date 1878. There were no mics then. He meant for this to be a sacred space of communication between the artist and the audience. The last thing the world needs is more partition.

This would be the site of our first "Pin Drop Concert."

We used Edison bulbs and candlelight for stage lighting and we drove around the Northeast and Midwest playing shows without amplification. It was a complete game-changer. I had to depend on the lyrics. After a few shows, I started to drop songs where I wasn't really *saying* anything important because people noticed . . . and I noticed.

Another thing the acoustic shows laid bare was that Tim had a bad habit of turning away from the crowd when he played a solo on his guitar. He always styled it like it was to interact with Josh (our long-time cellist), or the drummer, but I think it was like David closing his eyes. The problem was he had to learn to face the audience or they wouldn't hear him as soon as he made even a quarter turn. He'd have to thrust his hips forward and the rest of us would take a step back if we wanted a solo to land on the crowd and be heard properly. We were getting rock-star lessons from the artists of the past.

The parenting part of the tour was a comedy of errors. Between the three of us, we had two newborn babies and a two-year-old. Our tour-bus company had to bolt three cribs to the floor of a forty-five-foot Prevost for us. It was so cold, or "way down in the fall," as Dolly would say, in the Northeast, and two of our wives were breastfeeding. Consider this: We'd just embarked on a winter tour where we planned to essentially play silent shows with three babies in tow. We all realized right away that it meant that our families would be stuck on that bus full-time. It was a crazy, terrible family lesson.

Catherine would get to the point where she was about to lose her cool. Music is her life. It always was and always will be. Since moving from London (because she's stubborn and shy) most of her exposure to it was through me, and although we made a great team, it wasn't possible to fly in tandem with Evangeline in the world.

The inside of the bus would get stressful enough for her to take the baby and head inside to the show. She had to stand right next to the door because if that little foghorn of an infant woke up, her blood-curdling scream is all you'd hear for the split second it took Catherine to sprint to the exit and back out into the cold. It was tense. These places were small and had almost no dressing rooms. I tried to make light of it during the show a couple times. "Can someone shut that goddamned kid up?" I'd shout from the stage. The audience would laugh, but not Catherine. It's not fun to be on the road when you're cut out of the music. Water, water, everywhere and not a drop to drink.

We were in Washington, DC, pin-dropping the Barns at Wolf Trap when the Supreme Court officially did away with DOMA. It was a staggering victory for my family and so many like us. The relief was like a warm wave and it washed over our whole family. I fought tears from the moment we played our first note to the last.

I played "Murder in the City" for the first time that night.

Make sure my wife knows that I loved her,
Make sure my daughters know the same,
Always remember there is nothing worth sharing
Like the love that let us share our name.

Cath got her green card on the strength of our legitimate marriage right away. As I type this, the Supreme Court is reviewing a case about whether it should be legal to fire someone if they're gay. . . . As those who would dismantle our rights repeatedly run the protections back on my marriage, it occurs to me that I can't cope with finding out that there's no such thing as precedent. That my family could cease to be protected under the law. I'm not going to sugarcoat it: this is what it means to be an LGBTQ American citizen today.

We got invited to the White House that year. We had a wonderful time with the Obamas. (Didn't we all?) We saw Prince play for two hundred people. If that isn't insane enough for you, Stevie Wonder came out and jammed with him. You can't make this shit up.

We got to tell the Obamas how much they influenced our engagement and made one of those memories that you pass along like a folk song. We always try to keep in touch with them. They were extremely kind and generous to my family. It was the first of several crazy parties we would attend at the White House. The last one was right around the election and I remember looking around at all the people of color, the famous ones and the schoolteachers, the old and young, the haves and have-nots, the queers and freaks, and wondering if the White House would ever look that way again. I hope so, because it was really beautiful.

I was fifteen years into my career and on a flight home from New York when I found out I'd been nominated for my first Grammy. The Grammys were so far from my mind and so out of reach that I didn't even know when they were, how to submit, or when they were announced.

The head of my label texted and said, "Congratulations on your Grammy nom." I didn't even give it a second glance before typing back, "Sorry, this is Brandi." The label had Alabama Shakes on it, I'd never really heard from him before, and I assumed he'd confused me for Brittany Howard.

I jumped out of my seat with a sleeping baby in my arms and started frantically waving to the twins in silence with my one free arm. I wanted to be the one to tell them. I emailed my parents, Jay, Kim, and Elton John. I tended to keep Elton abreast of what was happening in my life like some gay pen-pal father figure. We got all dressed up and dragged the kids down to L.A. for the week—it was a blast! We didn't win, but I met Bonnie Raitt and we had the time of our lives. We were mystified and grateful to have been noticed.

. . .

We were in London for the election in 2016. It was a devastating morning at Heathrow Airport. I was shamelessly crying at the departure gate; random people were walking by and squeezing my shoulder. They could tell I was American. None of them were white.

Cath and I had a fight. We had woken up to the worst news, and with Cath I sometimes felt like I was carrying the United States around on my shoulders. She often used the word "you" to address the whole of the United States. "You don't take care of your citizens" . . . "You have no compassion for asylum seekers." It was a common and honest verbal construct, but I was starting not to want "The United States of America" to mean "you." Anyone else feel like that sometimes? I wish the U.S. didn't spell . . . well . . . us.

The hardest part of waking up on that morning in November was knowing that immigrants, refugees, asylum-seekers, and worst of all, their children would suffer. People told me I was being dramatic. But history will remember this as one of America's most unloving and inhospitable decades. I wasn't being dramatic enough.

The way my child had been born, into (relative) privilege and safety, was a mixture of dumb luck and geography. Why couldn't the rest of us see that? When we got home, I was painting my daughter's new bedroom light purple (dusty lilac) and listening to the terrible news about Aleppo. The guilt was becoming unbearable, but like so many times before, I was learning how to defeat the feeling of helplessness . . . with Catherine. She opened her laptop and searched War Child UK. She'd worked with them for Paul and they had made a real impression on her through their compilation albums. She had an idea she wanted me to pitch to them.

Her plan was to take our most successful album to date at that point, which was *The Story,* and talk all of the administrators into donating their commission as well. Because we owned the songs, it'd be a clean fundraising tool that we could control. Plus, Adele had already covered one of the songs, "Hiding My Heart," but had only released it in the UK! Surely that was a damn good start.

We had simultaneous goosebumps when Catherine's quick search turned up the front page of the War Child site and it *already* said "The Story Campaign" in red bold letters. It was an awareness campaign full of brave refugee children telling their beautiful and harrowing stories.

We knew it was without a doubt a sign. We went to work for War Child immediately.

I HAD TO cancel an entire leg of my tour because I had a hemorrhagic ovarian cyst. It was totally benign and no big deal, but it was irritating the damaged nerves in my lower back from my wood-splitting fiasco and causing weird electric-feeling shocks down my legs onstage. I am a physical performer. I jump around a bit and stomp harder than I'm aware of. I fling my guitar around and whip my head like a coyote with a rabbit. I had to tour during this time with a chiropractor just to barely get through these shows. I would tell myself I was gonna take it easy, but I'd just get out there onstage and flip out instead. I was miserable.

I decided to have surgery to remove the ovarian cyst and a couple other cysts and fibroids while I was at it. So, you guessed it: another summer tour ended in the hospital. . . . I don't see the empty signals, I just flat run out of gas.

I used the recovery time from the surgery to write letters to my heroes instead of songs through late summer and all throughout the fall. I was asking them to be a part of our efforts to support War Child and its new sister organization opening in the United States, Children in Conflict.

The very first person to say yes was Dolly Parton; she covered "The Story." I always said that Elton John and Dolly Parton are the devil and the angel on each of my shoulders . . . I'll let you decide who's who. After that, a lot fell into place. Dolly wanted me to produce and record the track, but I felt out of my depth—this is how I met Dave Cobb.

Dave was booked solid that week, but my bus was quietly passing through Nashville, so with a day's notice, he helped me record Dolly's track in the middle of the night—because his wife is a refugee and he's a good man. The rest of the album, *Cover Stories,* got made with Pearl Jam, Shovels and Rope, Torres, the Secret Sisters, the Avett Brothers, Jim James, Kris Kristofferson, Anderson East, Miranda Lambert, the Indigo Girls, Ruby Amanfu, Margo Price, Old Crow Medicine Show, and yes, ADELE. Barack Obama wrote the foreword. We've raised over $1 million for War Child UK and Children in Conflict. I don't mess around anymore. If I say I'm going to do something, I do it—and I do it on time. I know what it feels like to be dependent on an artist's word now. It took a year to make that album and getting musicians to turn in their homework is like herding cats! (No offense to cats.) But those artists are now my family. They helped me do a really big thing and they made a difference in the lives of thousands of real children.

By now you're noticing my ability to find and create family anywhere. My cultish tendencies run deep! It was starting to bother me that I had family yet to discover and reconcile.

The Carliles decided to find our lost sister, Michelle, that year in May. Mom and I talked about it for a few days before we asked Dad if it was okay with him. He didn't want to betray his promise to Michelle's mom all those years ago to leave her alone, but he eventually agreed that we could try to locate her—IF we spoke to her mother first, just to get an idea about whether Michelle even knew she had siblings. It took about a week for me to find her online and over a month to hear back, but she was thrilled. She only knew that her dad was called JR and had fantasized that he was the guy in the old TV show *Dallas* . . . she didn't even know how close to reality she was. Michelle had always felt like she had siblings and wanted to meet us. She was married with three kids. So, as anyone would, I said, "Come to my house with your whole family and stay with me for four days!" I didn't even see it as a risk. *What's the worst that can happen?*

It was amazing. She was instantly my sister and I felt eerily familiar with her, like we'd known each other our whole lives. She absolutely adores Dad, and it's been really powerful to watch their relationship develop. He didn't raise her, so she only knows him now—it's a clean slate. What a concept . . . I feel lucky to have known him the whole time, for better or worse.

The thing that taught me the most throughout this time was watching both of my parents lose their mothers in the same year. One of them I was very close to—my dad's mom, Grandma Carol.

I was her first known grandchild. I was the first grandchild on both my parents' sides. She could be a hard-ass and was a tad tough on me as a kid. She thought I was obscuring my intelligence. Grandma Carol was a Jesus-loving flaming liberal, and she didn't like me repeating the things my dad had said. She knew I was obsessive and once said, "Girl, I wouldn't cross the street to see Elton John." She was a bit of a cheeky provocateur till the end. She didn't like Evangeline's name and would only call her "Angel."

As soon as I found out who *I* was, Grandma Carol became my best friend and biggest supporter. She toured around the country with me a lot. Sometimes I didn't even know she was there! She didn't want to burden me with her disability—she was in a wheelchair for almost half her life after having a stroke at a very young age and being diagnosed with MS before they had the wonderful maintenance medications they do now. I'd be somewhere in Colorado and look down from the stage and she'd be sitting there in her wheelchair, grinning ear to ear. I'd say, "Grandma, how the hell did you get here?" She hitched rides with fans and friends.

She was a very young single mother to six kids and they're all total unicorns. By the time she died she had an aortic aneurysm, stage-4 cancer, MS, and a disease in her arteries that prevented circulation to her feet. She had the sickest sense of humor. She'd ask my sister to give her pedicures on her "corpse feet" and paint her toenails purple. Sometimes they would fall off and she'd laugh so hard she cried. If I took her on a trip, she'd call it *Weekend at Bernie's* and make me purchase "body bag insurance"—that's what she called it! She didn't want me to pay out the nose just to get her body back from somewhere. She loved the Cayamo Cruise, the singer-songwriter pilgrimage I would take almost every year with Kris Kristofferson, Emmylou Harris, John Prine, Patty Griffin, and pretty much every Americana pioneer you can think of. Grandma would smoke weed out of an apple with the folk stars on Cayamo and stare into the sunset. I still believe she was a little bit gay. She sure loved the fact that I was. She'd call me up before the trip and say, "Sweetheart, it's okay with me if I start this trip on the boat and end it in the freezer. Is that gonna be okay with you?"

It had to be.

She spent Thanksgiving and Christmas with me, Easter too, if I was home. She was never a burden and always a blast. She died at seventy-two. I was at home in Seattle. I was in her room with her kids when she died. I was playing my guitar and singing "Keep On The Sunnyside" when she opened up her eyes and started to cross over. My mom tapped my leg and told me it was time. She'd seen it before. We all put our hands on her and sang "Amazing Grace." Mormons, non-denominational Christians, Atheists, Agnostics, Messianic Jews, Jehovah's Witnesses, and a Jesus-freak lesbian all singing the same song and undeniably watching someone go to heaven.

The day she died I got a phone call on my way home from the hospice. It was the Avett boys. David Letterman was having his last week of shows and he had invited me and the boys to sing "Keep On The Sunnyside," of all songs. There is nothing more real or more practical in this universe than mysticism. Remember that . . . and it's usually sitting right smack in the middle of grief.

My other grandmother, Dolores, was much closer to me when I was young. She was my absolute favorite human. But life was relentlessly unkind to her, and she understandably developed problems that would make her very hard to be close to. Her father committed suicide while he was looking after her when she was eleven. Her husband (Grandpa Vernon) died very young from ALS, and she lost her mother the same year. Just two years later, she lost her last remaining family member when her baby brother, "our beloved uncle Eddy," died of emphysema.

I want to think I would have been able to survive these turns of events, but I don't think so. Grandma Dolores went down roads where the Carliles couldn't follow. We'd had our fill of addictive pain, and the altered states caused me too much agony to ignore. Stronger members of the family could weather it in ways I couldn't, and I always admired that.

When I was young and got sick, Grandma Dolores always took care of me. She was incredibly affectionate, and she believed it was a terrible mistake not to tell someone constantly how wonderful they were. Some of my earliest memories are of her telling me that I was special, that there was no one in the world like me, that I was abnormally talented and clever, and that God had a plan for me. It was why He kept me around after the meningitis.

Grandpa Vernon gets all the credit, but it was Grandma Dolores who started our music. And because of her I thought I was important long before I was.

I call all of the kids in our family "honey" and "baby," and I take them aside constantly to plant the seeds in them that were planted in me: there is nothing in this world or the next one that you can't accomplish if you believe in yourself.

I sound just like her when I answer the phone. When I wake up my children in the morning, her *actual* voice comes out of my mouth.

It's this kind of grief—the mother-losing kind, that I dread the most.

I fear losing a child like everyone else does—but that's crippling and unfathomable. The truth is, though, that we *will* lose our mothers. I saw it happen. I observed my parents' grief and the after-effects of death where the deceased becomes infallible. . . . I think it's a beautiful thing that humans do. It reflects the divine most accurately. It's not that the wrong a person's done in their life goes away, it's just that it doesn't really matter that much. "On earth as it is in heaven." I'll do the same thing with both my parents. I know I will, and I'm looking forward to it. I don't believe in eternal punishment here or beyond.

When the grandmas died, I noticed my aunts and uncles change shape. They became brothers and sisters once again. It was the only thing my folks wanted: their siblings. And they were there. They remembered Mom before Grandma. It's all so profound. "Only children" can and of course often do construct their own support systems. They may even be better off—I couldn't say. It's neither here nor there.

For me, I only know the world through the eyes of the big sister. And my siblings are like my limbs. I know I'll need them when Mom and Dad are gone because I need them now. None of the absurdities of our lives would be funny without them.

This is when and why Catherine and I began to contemplate Elijah.

"KEEP ON THE SUNNYSIDE"

There's a dark and a troubled side
of life
There's a bright and a sunnyside,
too
'though we meet with the
darkness and strife
The sunnyside we also may view

Keep on the sunnyside
Always on the sunnyside
Keep on the sunnyside of life
It will help us everyday
It will brighten all the way
If we'll keep on the sunnyside of
life

Though the storm in its fury break
today
Crushing hopes that we cherish so
dear
Clouds and storm will in time pass
away
And the sun again will shine bright
and clear.

Let us greet with a song of hope
each day
Though the moments be cloudy or
fair
Let us trust in our Savior always
To keep us everyone in His care.
    –THE CARTER FAMILY

WAR CHILD LETTERS

LETTER TO EDDIE VEDDER

Dear Eddie,

My name is Brandi Carlile. I'm a singer songwriter from Seattle and I've been making records for a while and I'm good buddies with Mike!

My wife talked me into writing this letter and I figured it was worth a shot because I have totally idolized you since I was a kid and believe you are one of the brightest lights this city has seen.

About 10 years ago I made a record with T Bone Burnett called The Story and it did modestly quite well for a gay lady rock singer in flared jeans!

I've gotten really involved and fallen in love with an organization called War Child out of the UK. There is nothing I wouldn't do to help these people with what they're doing.

They're seriously doing some of the most dangerous and heartbreaking work in the world with their own two hands. The same people raising money are dodging bombs and sometimes physically helping children whose lives have been torn apart by war. Most of these kids are refugees and orphaned and many are disabled and need a way forward.

War Child focuses primarily right now on Syria and DR Congo but they are ever present all throughout Africa and the Middle East.

We've partnered with War Child on The Story Campaign and decided that in April 2017 on our record's 10th anniversary we will re-release The Story with our friends and heroes covering the songs and donate ALL proceeds to War Child, every last dollar.

Dolly Parton cut the title track for us! We've got Jim James/My Morning Jacket, The Avett Brothers, Kris Kristofferson, Old Crow Medicine Show, and lots more.

I know that we've never met, and I hope someday that we do! But I wanted to take a shot at asking if you and your guys would record a song called "Again Today" for the project? It would bring such a beautiful presence to it and I'd personally be so moved to hear your voice singing a local girl's song!

It'd be a killer rocker!

Having said all this, I know you are a VERY busy man! I bet you'll even find your own way to help War Child knowing what I know about you! I'm proud to know your band and thanks for even reading this! There's no way you can say yes to everything!

What you guys did canceling North Carolina moved me more than I can say. I was SO proud to talk to Mike that day and feel so close to a group of guys on the right side of history.

You are 10 feet tall to me!

Love times infinity,
Brandi C.

PS: I'll have my manager give Kelly Curtis a call tomorrow and fill him in on the details JUST in case you might be interested. Xxoo

LETTER TO ADELE

Dear Adele,

I hope you are enjoying your absolute marathon of a tour season and that it's not kicking your ass too bad! Whew, I can't imagine keeping that pace—but I'm getting old and not unlike you I have a toddler with me 24/7.

I absolutely adore you and like everyone else, I feel like I could get in a bar fight over so much as a backhanded comment about you, haha! I've been truly inspired and impressed over your everyman ability to bring people together over real life and an earthy sense of humor.

At your level of total fame overload, I could truly understand if your team helps you oversee a never-ending barrage of low-level requests by having a response that includes a polite, blanket "no thank you." However, I'd like to just ask something of you that won't require you to do a thing, but it would mean so very much to me personally.

You covered my song "Hiding My Heart" a few years back and your version of it is so gorgeous and free flowing—I absolutely love it.

I'm re-releasing that album The Story on its 10-year anniversary as a charity compilation for War Child UK, and we are donating ALL proceeds to War Child in light of the completely devastating child refugee crisis. Things in my country and in yours changed considerably last week. I personally feel more convicted than ever that the plight of the refugees is the defining crisis of our generation. . . . It's all I care about for the moment as the mother of a child not in need.

As a small artist, I'm not able to make the kind of financial or awareness-based impact that I want to be able to make—so I offered up The Story album and asked my friends and heroes to cover all the tracks on the record. (You would fall in the latter category, although in my head you're both, haha.)

Anyway, Dolly Parton cut "The Story," Kris Kristofferson recorded "Turpentine" with Chris Stapleton, the Avett Brothers cut "Have You Ever," Margo Price covered "Downpour," and many more.

I want to put your version of "Hiding My Heart" on there sooooo badly because I love it and I think you're profoundly powerful and because I know that it'll help the War Child cause immeasurably. There will be no singles, interviews, or spotlight on your involvement other than your quiet inclusion on a project that, unlike other conflict-based efforts, is actually moving the needle and saving little lives.

My wife and I want to thank you for reading and considering this request amongst an ocean of others.

We came and saw you in Seattle and I was laughing hysterically at your banter in between songs, my wife was crying to her horror (she's from London) because she said you reminded her of her school friends. She's homesick and has lived in the States with me for the five years we've been married, and we have a 2-year-old little girl.

Your ability to remind us all of our school friends and bring us to tears with a well-placed joke is a true testament of a person unchanged by flattery. Your stunning voice is a gift and a vehicle because you make people happy on your journey.

Cheers,
XOBC

LETTER TO BARACK OBAMA

Dear Greatest President in the History of America,

I'm putting pen to paper a second time because you've been such a blessing to my family and in my life. I'm with The Guardian and everyone else when I say that yours is one family we will never be ready to see leave the White House—the Lord knows that you left us all better than when you found us.

Recently I've put together this little rag-tag team of artists in an effort to support the cause of children whose lives have been torn apart by violence—so far, it's been truly inspiring!

Someone from my foundation sent me an amazing piece where you're reading a letter from a six-year-old boy asking you to help him find a refugee boy, and it kept me awake for three nights.

I'm too small of an artist to make enough of an impact both financial and in regard to awareness on my own, but in April my album that I made with T Bone Burnett The Story turns 10 years old. I thought maybe I could re-release the album on Sony with my friends and heroes singing all the songs and donate ALL of the proceeds to War Child (an amazing neutral international group that provides a way forward for kids in conflict).

Everyone got on board with the idea and now it's gone crazy in the best possible way.

Dolly Parton cut the title track, Adele cut the closing track, and in between we have Pearl Jam, Avett Brothers, Kris Kristofferson, Margo Price, Brittany Howard from Alabama Shakes, and the list goes on and on.

All the music is coming in sounding amazing.

After I watched the video of you reading the letter, I sought the advice of Pete [Souza] about asking you to write a foreword or a sentence or two for the front page of the album, and he told me that your job is a bit tricky in regard to what you can and can't align with, so I would die of embarrassment if you felt any pressure (haha, strikes me as funny to have said that knowing that you've been the leader of the free world for eight years). I can't imagine the things you are asked to do from morning to night.

If there's a way that you could write a few of your famously inspiring words of compassion for children affected by conflict and our commission by the laws of humanity to act on their behalf, me and my friends on this album would be eternally grateful.

If not—don't think twice! You've already inspired the whole concept in me, and as I've said, you left my family better than where you found us.

No single historical figure has motivated me more than you . . . a simple thank-you seems weird but it's the best I can do.

Thank you.

Love,
Brandi C

"HIDING MY HEART"

This is how the story went
I met someone by accident
That blew me away
That blew me away

It was in the darkest of my days
When you took my sorrow and
you took my pain
And buried them away
You buried them away

I wish I could lay down beside you
When the day is done
And wake up to your face against
the morning sun
But like everything I've ever known
You'll disappear one day
So I'll spend my whole life hiding
my heart away

You dropped me off at the train
station
Put a kiss on top of my head
And watched me wait
And watched you wait
Then you went on home to your
skyscrapers
Neon lights and waiting papers

That you call home
You call it home

I woke up feeling heavy-hearted
I'm going back to where I started
The morning rain
The morning rain
And although I wish that you were
near
But that same old road that
brought me here
Is calling me home,
It's calling me home

And I wish I could lay down beside
you
When the day is done
And wake up to your face against
the morning sun
But like everything I've ever known
You'll disappear one day
So I can spend my whole life
hiding my heart away
And I could spend my whole life
hiding my heart away
    —BRANDI CARLILE

"MURDER IN THE CITY"

If I get murdered in the city
Don't go revenging in my name
A person dead from such is plenty
There's no sense in getting locked
away

And when I leave your arms
The things that I think of
No need to get over-alarmed
I'm coming home

I wondered which of us is better
Which one our parents love the
most
I certainly get in lots of trouble
They seemed to let the other go

A tear fell from my father's eyes
I wondered what my dad would
say
He said I love you, and I'm proud
of you both
In so many different ways

If I get murdered in the city
Go and read the letter in my desk
Don't bother with all my
belongings, no
But pay attention to the list

Make sure my wife knows that I
loved her
Make sure my daughters know the
same
And always remember there's
nothing worth sharing
Like the love that let us share our
name
Always remember there's nothing
worth sharing
Like the love that lets us share our
name
    —AVETT BROTHERS

BUS BAY BABIES MID SUMMER TOUR. THERE WASN'T A VENUE IN THE USA WE DION'T TAG WITH SIDEWALK CHALK

LOAD IN

LIFE ON THE GREAT AMERICAN HIGHWAY

COMPOUND SOUND CHECKS

EASIEST WAY TO GET A TODDLER
THROUGH AN AIRPORT...
YOU'RE WELCOME.

THIS IS THE WAY WE LEFT EVERY
VENUE PARKING LOT

ROAD LIFE CAN BE SO EXHAUSTING THAT
EVEN PIZZA CAN'T TURN YOUR ATTITUDE
AROUND

WE ARE MAKING MEMORIES
EVERY DAY.

PIN DROP. TOUR EXHAUSTION
MAKE UP UNDER MY EYES
NEWBORN BABY EVANGELINE

THE REALITY VS THE FANTASY...
I'D TAKE REAL LIFE EVERY TIME.

PIN DROPPING **LONDON**. THOSE
FLIGHTS RUINED MY LIFE.

PIN DROP. A STEADY KISS AND A
JAMESON WHEN I COME OFF STAGE
IS ALL I EVER ASKED FOR.

SHE'S A SAINT FOLKS... AND SHE
WONT LET YOU FORGET IT!

ME MEETING MY SISTER MICHELLE IN STYLE
FOR THE FIRST TIME

CATH, ME AND BONNIE. LOVE AT
FIRST SIGHT.

I DONT EVEN WANT TO KNOW WHAT
KIND OF SHIT SHE WAS TALKING

EVANGELINE AND GRANDMA TERESA

AGAIN, TELL ME YOU DON'T WANT TO JUST HANG WITH THIS WOMAN! I WISH LIFE HAD BEEN KINDER. I'M GRATEFUL FOR THE PARTS OF HER THAT LIVE IN ME.

ME AND GRANDMA CAROL CAMPING AROUND LILITH FAIR IN 1999. SHE NEVER CONSIDERED ANYTHING OTHER THAN SUPPORT AND ACCEPTANCE FROM DAY ONE.

Dear Grama Dolores it
wood be fun if we cold do
something together. we went
to the lake the other day. It
wasint the same without you.
we cold have Done alot more
with you thar. but it was
ok. Love Brandi. p.s.

writ
back

LETTER TO GRANDMA DOLORES
I WROTE TO HER A LOT. IT
WOULD TAKE ME A LONG TIME
TO GET MY LETTERS FACING THE RIGHT
DIRECTION. A LOT OF RE-STARTS...
STILL DOES.

ME AND GRANDMA CAROL ON ONE
OF OUR CRUISES. SHE NEVER DID
END UP IN A FREEZER. SHE WAS
A LOT OF FUN

17.
....

BY THE WAY

I was beginning to write fewer and fewer songs after Evangeline was born. I was writing a lot more in a literary sense and struggling with whether I could accept that natural inclination. I noticed, though, that when I did write a song it felt much more complete, much more authentic than my younger work because I wasn't experimenting or mimicking as much.

I understand who I am as an artist because I understand that I don't understand who I am as an artist. It can all change at any time. I don't make apologies for that anymore. If I write *one song* in two years and my art takes on the shape of entertainment or finish carpentry for a while instead, that's absolutely okay. I need that one song to mean something. It doesn't have to necessarily be heavy or even profound, it just needs to come from the "muse" and not the "ick," to quote Joni Mitchell. I'm done with song manufacturing. If music needs to find us, it will. I went into the year of writing for *By the Way, I Forgive You* like this, and it felt wonderful.

The first song I heard from the album was "Every Time I Hear That Song." Phil had written it. I was so moved by it. A line in the third verse said:

Now that's twice you broke my heart now
The first was way back when,
And to know you're still unhappy
Only makes it break again.

It put a lump in my throat so bad that I wasn't sure I'd ever be able to sing it. I was there; I knew what he was talking about and it made me proud to be his friend. The way that love never ends. Sure, the feeling ends, but the sheer kindness of it and the honor and the forgiveness part of love never should.

I should address the word "forgiveness." It's got a bad rap. It's become patronizing, whitewashed, upper-middle-class, a suburban kind of word in our culture that is used more often to vilify than to redeem. It's #blessed for the twenty-first century. I hate this because to the divine, it's *radical*. This word sticks in my craw the way the phrase "love the sinner, hate the sin" does. When someone says, "I'll pray for you," I feel like they're saying, "From my platform of purity, I'll pray for your iniquity." When they say, "I forgive you," they're saying, "From my position of righteousness, I will accept you even though you're wrong and inadequate."

I have seen trembling, filthy forgiveness bring light into a dark world like nothing else can—nothing. Not money, not fame, not music, not church, not even "love" as we understand it.

I watched Jenny Hopper forgive Isaiah Kalebu. She would not advocate for the death penalty in his case. She will not advocate for the NRA or a senseless lack of responsible gun laws. And she does not "love" him. Not if you believe love is a feeling.

If Jenny's forgiveness makes you uncomfortable, you understandably haven't changed the way you hear the word "forgiveness," but when you do, you'll see that it actually changes you.

On the other side of this word there lies another legacy. Even worse than its association with condemnation is when this beautiful word is perceived as "to forget" or as a "free pass" in a particularly disturbing situation. When it is seen as an omission or, God forbid, permission. We must detach from the outcome of what happens after we use this word. This is when we discover who the forgiveness is really for. We do it for ourselves. It's for us. Nothing heals otherwise. "Unforgiveness" is a kind of cancer.

After "Every Time I Hear That Song," the forgiveness songs just kept coming:

"I haven't seen my father in some time,
But his face is always staring back at me,
His heavy hands hang at the ends of my arms
And my colors change like the sea."

"Most of all he taught me to forgive,
How to keep a cool head,
How to love the one you're with."

"There's a road left behind me that I'd rather not speak of,
And a hard one ahead of me too,
I love you whatever you do,
But I've got a life to live too."

"I never said I'm sorry, but I meant to.
I never met a coward I don't like."

"I loved you the first time I saw you
And you know I love you still,
I am tired. But I am yours."

"But not for a son he left behind
With his hand stuck reaching back in time,
To a place in which you can never unwind,
I hope he found something so sweet."

"Sometimes I pretend we never met.
Because it's harder to forgive than to forget."

"You are not an accident where no one thought it through,
The world that stood against us made us mean to fight for you,
When we chose your name, we knew you'd fight the power too."

"A morning is coming of silver and light.
There'll be color and language and nobody wanting to fight,
What a glorious sight."

"My mind and spirit are at odds sometimes
And they fight like the north and the south,
I still care enough to bear the weight
Of the heaviness to which my heart is tethered.
She taught me how to be strong and say goodbye
And that love is forever."

A theme was presenting itself.

Before I start sounding too earnest, understand that I wasn't "teaching" forgiveness. I was and still am *learning* it. I'm not evolved. I'm as much a part of the problem as every other person in the world. This isn't wisdom or insight, it's a work in progress and it never did come from me. It came from our parents and grandparents. Our flawed heroes and our favorite TV shows. We were just playing dress-up and trying forgiveness on like a costume. We intend to learn these lessons over and over again the hard way for as long as we're human. If you want the real thing 100 percent pure, the Everclear . . . you should talk to Lazarus.

The twins and I boarded a ferry to Whidbey Island in October 2016 to dig into this forgiveness theme together. When we put the songs together in one place, we knew we had a special album. After a few days, Cath, Tiff, and Hanna came and joined us. It sounds overly idyllic but I remember it as being one of the more peaceful moments of our time together. We had dinner and brought the bottle of wine back to our cabin on the water. We played the new songs for our wives. Hanna did her "office Christmas party" dance for a bit to make us all laugh and then she burst into tears the way she always does about emotional things. They each told us in their own way that they knew this music would change our lives. Something about this album was just different from the beginning.

It was time to go to Nashville.

The ten of us moved into a house in Belle Meade with an old swimming pool and a haunted ancient swing set. I had strep throat so bad that my tonsils looked like a horror film. I sent a picture of them to Jay because he has a weak stomach and upsetting it is my favorite thing to do. I started and ended EVERYTHING important sick. I knew I was somehow manifesting illness and hadn't figured out what to do about it yet.

We had all decided to each have one more child. Tiffany had just given birth to their son Jack, and Tim and Hanna were trying. My need to actually physically have a baby disappeared when I wrote "The Mother." It's almost like it was tied up in my willingness to accept myself as a mom, pregnancy or no pregnancy. And I loved Cath pregnant. She was so incredibly tough and gorgeous. We planned to make this album and then go home and make Elijah.

The first day in the studio was atypical to say the least. I won't bore you with too much studio journaling, but I should set the scene for this album and how it changed us.

Shooter Jennings is my ride or die. He won't say a bad word about anyone no matter what, and it's because he genuinely can find something he loves in EVERYONE . . . even Kid Rock, just to give you some perspective.

Shooter and I are both '80s kids. My favorite movie is *The Never-Ending Story,* and we bonded over the tattoos I have of "the Auryn" on each of my shoulders. In the story, a young boy named Bastian, who has some trauma to overcome and a penchant for unicorns, finds a secret book. Inside of it, there's a place called Fantasia, which is a metaphor for the sanctuary of one's imagination and ability to dream. There is an antagonist called the Nothing, which is its opposite. It seeks to destroy a person's power of manifestation and replace it with conformity. The boy is reading a story about a quest to reverse the Nothing's inevitability. He's in the attic of his school reading this book when suddenly he realizes he's in the story, that he's being written about and spoken to. Shooter and I are total nerds obsessed with this metaphor, so I knew he would be a part of this album. When I brought up Dave Cobb to him and vice versa, they both said the same thing, "He's my brother."

We were off to the races.

We walked in the doors at the historic and visually stunning RCA Studio A. I could see a drum set and microphones already set up. Candles lit, amps and guitars lining the walls, over in the corner was a dim little living room with a record player. The famed Dave Cobb stopped us at the door with glasses of tequila and directed us over to the living room. He wanted to listen to records. It was immediately clear that this recording session was going to be different; we weren't going to spend the afternoon "getting drum sounds."

Sitting on the corner of the couch was a handsome guy in a tweed jacket, cleanly shaven with a head full of curly hair. He introduced himself as Chris Powell, our drummer for the record. I would learn by the next week that this was a costume, not the real Chris Powell. When he walked in like that Dave hit the floor! Chris normally had a ZZ Top beard, a shaved head, and wore only sleeveless T-shirts. No one had seen him any other way. But he didn't think that the twins and I would be able to take him like that, so he cleaned up for our session. He soon got a lesson in our depravity and went back to being himself. We bonded over our love of Nigel Olsson, and we would soon bond over my love for his son, Christopher.

The first thing Dave put on was an album called *White Mansions;* it had influenced him damn near completely and he wanted us to understand where he was coming from. I chose Elton John's *Madman Across the Water* and Joni Mitchell's *Blue* as my go-to albums.

We listened to the Band, the Beatles, Buffy Sainte-Marie, the Roaches, David Bowie, Bonnie Raitt, Carole King, Aretha . . . and it went on like that for most of the day. We made our way over to the instruments with a very slight tequila buzz and started messing around with our song "Most of All." On the final note of our first take, Tim started to really cry for the first time since Jerry died. Phil and I dropped our instruments and ran over to him, wrapping him up in a giant bear hug and joining him in his tears. We had to have looked ridiculous. Everyone must have either thought we were insane or extremely dramatic. There was no way for Dave, Chris, or Shooter to know that we were actually a trio of Seattle-born sociopaths who hadn't cried for more than ten years, since Norway. But we didn't care. No judgment. "No regrets, Coyote."

That was *By the Way, I Forgive You* in a nutshell. Take one is the track on the album.

I'm not saying it was a perfect few weeks. The twins were beside themselves with tension and confusion about the way we were working. It was as if they were blindfolded on horseback and every twist in the trail surprised and alarmed them. It went quick and there was no time to explain—we had given Dave the reins and we had to own that. He wasn't a therapist; he was interested in making a classic album. Period.

It all came to a head toward the end of the sessions when we were listening back. Dave is so sure of himself. He takes on a chilling, even nonchalant attitude toward the end of a session. But the artist is NEVER sure. Approaching the finish line brings on a sense of dread. Tasking a laid-back guy like Dave with deciding when to call it on a song or an album brings on the kind of anxiety you feel when your buddy who is "great with kids" starts throwing your baby up in the air. It fucking stresses you out to no end. But looking back on what I've learned, I'd let Dave throw my baby up in the air again.

The whole time I was in Nashville my mind would wander off and on to a little party that we'd thrown at the Belle Meade house. Cath made chili (she makes it so much that Dave's wife, Ledja Cobb, consistently teases her about it). Chris Powell had brought his son Christopher, or Chris Jr. He was gorgeous. Thick curly hair and uncomfortable in his body, he was wearing a suit blazer like Alex P. Keaton over a white T-shirt. He wanted to talk with the adults and not be with the kids. He was twelve years old.

I'm not saying Chris Jr. is gay . . . and it wouldn't matter if he were.

The kids at school were calling him a fag. He loves gay people and he was being dehumanized on a daily basis for being gay whether he is or not, so he carries the cross regardless. He was honest with the adults in the room. He was so articulate, and the whole time he had the floor, he tugged at that little white T-shirt, pulling it down to his thighs, trying to disappear. I saw the vulnerability in him, twisted and contrasted against his gorgeous future, and I just wanted to tell him: "You don't have to be the kind of man they tell you to be . . . you are going to have a spectacular life . . . you will have the last laugh," but I didn't know him well enough.

I wrote it down.

Dave and his family already had my heart. His wife is a comedic genius of the highest order. His daughter is stoic and sarcastic. They're decidedly Albanian, earthy and dry in the best possible way. Dave and I had really bonded. He loved my voice and he noticed and encouraged every imperfection—so did Shooter. They would egg me on to scream louder and hit higher notes; they wanted to believe me, and I wanted them to be moved and impressed. They were a fantastic audience.

So we were all sitting around in the control room in the eleventh hour, and then . . . Dave said it. The thing you're not supposed to say to an artist. Nostalgia is fool's gold. No one wants to be asked to go backwards.

"Dude! You know what this album is missing?" he blurted out. "A song like 'The Story.' You should write something like 'The Story,' 'cause nothing you've done has been better than that."

I purposely avoided the twins' eye contact knowing EXACTLY what their icy northern glares would look like.

"Yeah, man, I get that," I mediated, "but this isn't *The Story*. That was a long time ago."

Dave, giving zero fucks, said, "Especially vocally—you haven't had a vocal moment as good as 'The Story' since 'The Story.'"

. . . Okay, now *I'm* pissed.

Little did he know that was a vocal moment born of rage. The frustration of having my guitar taken away from me, insecurity from being unable to shed my vocal affectation, and my failure to impress T Bone Burnett—the object of my affection. He was asking me to go back to a dark place.

"Come listen to my favorite song," Dave says.

I begrudgingly followed him out to the living room, and he put on "An American Trilogy."

"Hush, little baby, don't you cry. You know your daddy was bound to die."

Of course, I fucking know "An American Trilogy" like the back of my hand. As Dave knows, once you've backed up Elvis, you'll do-wop your way through every Elvis song you'll ever hear.

Dark places. I was ready to go home.

I got in bed that night with Cath in total silence, *"you've got to dance with the devil on a river to beat the stream"* pinballing through my brain. She asked what was wrong. I explained my feelings and she turned off the light. In the darkness before we went to sleep, she said, "If you're honest with yourself though, *do* you have a vocal moment as good as 'The Story'?"

I knew I didn't. I'd shut that place of recklessness down in me. If you wanted to see it, you had to buy a ticket. Come to a show. I wasn't going to make something that vulnerable *permanent* ever again.

I woke up the next morning with "The Joke" beating at the inside of my chest, trying to get out like a bird. It was a day off. Everyone was gone except my cellist, Josh. I ran into the kitchen and told him we had to go. He threw the ingredients for the sandwich he was making into a ziplock bag and followed me blindly into an Uber. On the way to the studio I called Eddie the engineer and told him I was coming down. I asked him if he'd meet me and let me in. He did.

When we got to RCA Studios around ten in the morning on a Sunday, it was pitch-black. I gave Josh four chords and asked him to go to a corner of the room with just his cello and play them for as long as it took. Two of the chords Dave had given me: D to A minor. I was hearing a verse melody from one of Phil's songs from fifteen years ago that we never wrote.

I thought about Christopher and his T-shirt. I thought about our sneering president and the way he laughed at people who were suffering. I thought about the little girls who wanted a female president. I thought of Aleppo, Jordan, Iraq, and all the beautiful children from the Story Campaign living their lives in refugee camps. I thought about mothers fleeing bombs and violence, carrying their babies on their backs. And I thought about Jesus.

You don't have to like that Jesus is my home base. You can use it to discredit me in the name of ALL the harm Christianity has done. In fact, every single thing I mentioned above has been impacted negatively by Christianity in one way or the other. I am okay with that perspective and I think it's healthy. I, too, have been impacted negatively by it. But something mystical brings me back time and time again to the revolutionary gospel of forgiveness.

I wrote "The Joke" in a half hour. It's not a song as much as the acknowledgment of a promise.

I sent out an all-hands-on-deck message to everyone. They all came in—Dave, the twins, Chris, and Shooter. I couldn't wait to play Dave "The Joke."

"That's it," he said. "That's the best song you've ever written."

The real truth is that we all wrote it. The song wouldn't exist without Dave and the twins.

By the Way, I Forgive You had one more life-changing day in store for me.

. . .

I had a picture of Paul Buckmaster on my wall from the time I was fourteen. I'd cut it out of the vinyl packaging on my favorite Elton album, *Tumbleweed Connection,* along with Bernie and Elton, and Gus Dudgeon, too—my pinup boys.

Paul was the string and orchestral arranger for all of Elton John's early records. His contributions were so profound that I credit him with the marriage of rock 'n' roll with symphony. Many will argue citing Sir George Martin. And I can see that too. But Paul's arrangements were GRAND and traditional, they didn't conform to pop music; pop music had to elevate and conform to the symphony lest it become the subject of one of Paul's legendary temper tantrums. Paul arranged *Space Oddity* for Bowie and *Sticky Fingers* for the Stones. But he fit Elton like an actual glove. His arrangements kept me up at night. I was literally not allowed to play "Sixty Years On" or "First Episode at Hienton" in my bedroom because they upset my little sister.

I met him once when I was sixteen. A guy we knew, Rick Parashar, was recording an orchestral session in Seattle for a British band called Longview, and Paul was going to conduct.

I was invited to this session with my guitar just to look through the glass at Paul. I had been told I couldn't meet him. I watched him flailing about. Laughing, crying, and occasionally storming out the side door. Being a typical guileless and ambitious teenager, I planned to completely violate the order to stay away from Paul. Instead I sat there with my guitar, waiting for my opportunity. Finally, Paul didn't storm out the side door, he stormed out my door, and we found ourselves abruptly face-to-face. I handed him my picture of him and asked him to sign it. He rolled his eyes but obliged and barked something about my guitar playing, and with the bravado only a sixteen-year-old could muster, I took that as an invitation. I didn't even hesitate before launching into "Sixty Years On." Characteristically, Paul cried. He looked me square in the eye and said, "When you grow up, I will arrange your records."

I never forgot it.

Paul Buckmaster arrived at RCA Studios on March 31, 2017, arrangements in hand, to conduct a collection of the best string players in Nashville for the *By the Way, I Forgive You* sessions. The Nashville Symphony, by the way, is breathtaking but that's another story.

RCA wasn't new to him. He'd worked there many times with my friend Ben Folds. Paul had arranged "Whatever You Do" and "Party of One." (You didn't work "with Paul," you used his arrangement or you didn't.) He was absolutely full of life in his tuxedo jacket and NASA T-shirt.

Paul was a gentleman. Half-British, half-Italian (he got the emotional end of the Italian blood). He was an amateur physicist and pronuclear. He had terrible politics, but we just avoided them. He cried about olive oil, he cried over Bach. We sang "Indian Sunset" together, and I was head-over-heels in love with him. Dave was decidedly terrified, both at Paul's volatility and because he absolutely worshipped him. Dave's obsession with Elton John rivals my own and as I'm sure you can see by now—that's saying something.

Paul was mine that day. He conducted with such passion and authority. I didn't cry, but most of the orchestra did. It was extraordinary. I will never forget the end of "Party of One." It was classic Buckmaster, straight out of 1971—pure as the driven snow and *no* layering!!! If you want it thicker, hire more players. The studio was packed with them. It was vibrating in the universal key right through every one of us.

I woke up to a message on my phone from Ben Folds, a couple weeks after the session. "I'm so sorry about Paul," he said. *Oh God*, I thought. *How am I going to tell Catherine that McCartney has died?* Then it hit me. It was coming from Ben, so it had to be Buckmaster. I immediately called Paul and I got his voicemail . . . I wasn't even awake.

"Paul, please tell me you're still here."

He smelled of old paper and Italian cologne. "Party of One" was the last piece of music he touched. I'm so proud to have known him and to have his music and passion with me forever.

That was our last day on *By the Way, I Forgive You.*

"THE JOKE"

You're feeling nervous aren't you
boy?
With your quiet voice
And impeccable style
Don't ever let them steal your joy
And your gentle ways
To keep them from running wild
They can kick dirt in your face
Dress you down and tell you that
your place is in the middle
When they hate the way you shine
I see you tugging on your shirt
Trying to hide inside of it
And hide how much it hurts

Let them laugh while they can
Let them spin,
Let them scatter in the wind
I have been to the movies
I've seen how it ends
And the joke's on them

You get discouraged don't you
girl?
It's your brother's world for a
while longer
You gotta dance with the devil on
a river to beat the stream
Call it living the dream
Call it kicking the ladder
They come to kick dirt in your face
To call you weak and then displace
you after carrying your baby on
your back across the desert
I saw your eyes behind your hair
And you're looking tired but you
don't look scared

Let them laugh while they can
Let them spin
Let them scatter in the wind
I have been to the movies
I've seen how it ends
And the joke's on them.
        —BRANDI CARLILE

"EVERY TIME I HEAR THAT SONG"

A love song was playing
On the radio
It made me kind of sad
Because it made me think of you
And I wonder how you're doing
But I wish I didn't care
Because I gave you all I had
And got the worst of you

By the way
I forgive you
After all
Maybe I should thank you
For giving me what I've found
Because without you around
I've been doing just fine
Except for any time I hear that
song

And didn't it break your heart
When you watched my smile
fading?
Did it ever cross your mind
That one day the tables would be
turned?
They told me the best revenge
Would be a life well lived
And the strongest one that holds
Will be the hardest one to earn

When I woke up in the morning
I was choking on some words
There were things unsaid
between us
There were things you never told
Now that's twice you broke my
heart now
The first was way back when

And to know you're still unhappy
Only makes it break again.

By the way
I forgive you
I never will
Never will forget you

"WHATEVER YOU DO"

If I don't owe you a favor you don't
know me
I don't believe we've ever even
met
If there's a God in heaven you can
show me
Then I guess I should admit I lost
the bet
There are moments I could hold
you forever
And there are moments that
lasted way too long
And there are days when I change
with the weather
To hold you in place would be
wrong

There's a road left behind me that
I'd rather not speak of
And a hard one, ahead of me too
I love you whatever you do
But I got a life to live too

For giving me what I've found
Because without you around
I've been doing just fine
Except for any time I hear that
song
    —BRANDI CARLILE

I never met a morning I could get
through
With nothing on my breath to hold
the night
And I never said I'm sorry but I
meant to
I never met a coward I don't like
There are reasons why a body
stays in motion
But at the moment only demons
come to mind
There are days when I could walk
into the ocean
With no one else but you to leave
behind

There's a road left behind me that
I'd rather not speak of
And a hard one, ahead of me too
I love you whatever you do
But I've got a life to live too
    —BRANDI CARLILE

"PARTY OF ONE"

Waiter send this to the table
The party of one
The only other lonely soul in this
place
And so you're finishing up your
coffee but then where you gonna
run?
Where'd you get that look on your
face?

You should always let the sun go
down on your anger
Let it burn you to sleep
And bring you closer to the
danger, to surrender and retreat
Sing your sad soul to sleep

I loved you the first time I saw you
And you know I love you still
But I am tired
And I am yours

Don't even think about your
freedom or taking that flight
Or going back upon your promise
after fighting for the right
Because your eggshells and your I
statements and your weaponized
words
Are paper tigers now

Your constant overthinking and
your secretive drinking
Are making you more and more
alone

And girl you can slam the door
behind you
It ain't never going to close
Because when you're home you're
already home

I am tired
I am tired
I don't want to go home anymore
I don't want to throw stones
anymore
I don't want to take part in the
war

I loved you the first time I saw you
And you know I love you still
I loved you the first time I saw you
And you know I love you still

I don't want to be right anymore
Lord I don't want to fight anymore
I'm not taking your side anymore

I am tired
I am not my own
And I am leaving
Oh I am tired
And I'm coming home
'Cause I am yours I am yours I am
yours I am yours
I am yours I am yours I am yours I
am yours I am yours
      —BRANDI CARLILE

PETE SNAPPED ONE OF MY FAVORITE PHOTOS EVER.
THIS IS ME AND THE TWINS WAITING TO BE PICKED
UP OUTSIDE A RESTAURANT. THIS IS HOW WE STAY WARM
WHEN ITS COLD.

IN A RARE PHOTO OF SHOOTER SITTING DOWN, HERE WE ARE
CRUSHING A HIGH FIVE BECAUSE WE'VE JUST WITNESSED THE
TWINS HIT THE 3 PART HARMONY ON "FULTON COUNTY JANE"
AND IT SOUNDED SO GOOD WE COULDN'T HELP OURSELVES

ME AND DAVE IN THE HAPPY PLACE.

I'M A PERPETUAL STUDENT IN MY ARTISTRY
I WILL ALWAYS HAVE SO MUCH MORE TO LEARN.

THIS IS A PHOTO PETE SOUZA TOOK OF ME CAPTURING THE ONLY
TAKE IN EXISTENCE OF PARTY OF ONE. IMAGINE IF HE'D STUMBLED!

PHIL EXPLAINING HIS IDEA FOR HOW TO END PARTY OF ONE.
ME LOOKING ANNOYED AND NERVOUS... SHOOTER PACING.

PHIL FIXING BASS PARTS. EVERYONE LAUGHING, TWINS NOT AMUSED
IT CAN BE STRESSFUL BEING PUT UNDER A MICROSCOPE MUSICALLY.

DAVE COBB FELT LIKE HE WAS IN OUR BAND WHEN
WE MADE BY THE WAY. LIKE ONE OF THE TWINS.

THIS IS HOW WE BEGAN EACH DAY IN THE STUDIO. JAMMING AND LISTENING TO RECORDS. SHOOTER IS SOMEWHERE PACING. HE NEVER SITS DOWN.

ME BACKSTAGE WITH CHRIS POWELL JR. A VERY DIFFERENT KID THAN THE ONE I MET BEFORE THE JOKE.
(LITTLE CAPSHAW PHOTO BOMB IN THE BACK)

18.

· · · · · · · · · ·

THE RETURNING OF OUR LIGHT (ELIJAH)

Dad took Jay and me fishing a lot when we were young—less often when we got older but for longer periods of time. It was the ultimate freedom. He let us run around the Cowlitz and other fast-moving rivers unsupervised for hours and hours. We had knives and poles and a serious sense of adventure. Dad has always been ab-surdly good company when we're fishing. I caught the bug early on.

Fishing sometimes defines me. Some days it's all I can think about. I'm so obsessive, but nothing's really ever got ahold of me the way fishing and music have. The only kind of fishing I haven't done is ice and marlin. Me, Dad, Tiff, Jay, and the whole family go to Neah Bay every year in April for the lingcod. Trout starts right after that. I go to Montana to pitch flies, down south for bass, catfish, and game. Florida for king and deep-sea. But my favorite by far is Alaska. I go up in July to fish the reds and kings on the Kenai (kings have been closed the last five years, but I got my king once—forty-three pounds). I fish for halibut in Homer and the list goes on and on. It's my dream to one day own a boat . . . a thirty-foot KingFisher Weekender with twin out-board motors, 200s. As soon as the girls are a bit older, I'll convince Catherine, and I will buy one. My dad will freak out.

All these years have taught me that fishing is really just an attempt to connect to something that you know is there, but that you can't see.

I'm starting this way because this is where my soul went after I recorded *By the Way, I Forgive You.*

I am two women.

One of them is theatrical. She loves attention and detests false humility. She believes the things her grandmothers told her and believes she is an extraordinary singer. That's very important to her. Vocal athletics are her Achilles' heel. A weak voice is debilitating to this person, and the whole house of cards is built on it. She loves fancy shoes, details, being right, and expensive blazers, Champagne and fedoras, and did I mention attention? This person is an entertainer. Perfectly at home on the stage in a darkened auditorium striking a Shakespearean pose and absolutely infatuated with her audience.

The other woman is a gay-handed scallywag. She bites her fingernails no matter how dirty they are, and they are always very dirty. She's got flat hair. She wears only faded, baggy jeans for yard work. Loves finish carpentry and horses. Spends hours into days on a tractor or a four-wheeler and grows tomatoes. She wears glasses; cooks breakfast, lunch, and dinner; has a weakness for very expensive candles, bedding, and soap; and she builds a fire every day. She's bad with money and doesn't care. More than all this, she fishes . . . Catherine prefers her.

Both of these women showed up for *By the Way, I Forgive You,* but the scallywag dominated on this one.

For this reason, I felt I needed a break to reevaluate and contemplate bringing her more into my music—and onto the road. *"Are there chances in life for little dirt cowboys? Should I make my way out of my home in the woods?"* I knew because of the honesty on the album that the earthier part of me was trying to find more of a place in my life and music. It was time to step away for a bit. Time to put "Captain Fantastic" on ice.

I spent most of that summer in the woods with a machete and a hedge trimmer. I made miles of beautiful trails. Some for the four-wheelers, some for Cath to hike. The twins would join me, and we'd work until we were covered in sweat. We never can relax. Evangeline was often with me collecting sticks, rocks, and snails. We'd come home filthy and dehydrated, ripping down the driveway on a four-wheeler.

In the woods, I thought so much about what was coming up, as it was about to be a time in my career that I absolutely dread: Artwork. The cover. The photos. Videos, "content pieces" that the label needs to promote any album. It has always felt like acting to me. But I know that it's also good for me because I always get a new "look," a fresh perspective on my makeup, a new hairstyle, and usually a whole new wardrobe too! The twins then adjust their appearance based on all that, and we look that way until we make another album. This one felt different though. I couldn't get past knowing that the "other" version of me was the one who wrote this album, and I didn't want to cover her up with glam . . . even for fun.

Pete Souza is a very dear friend of mine. He was Obama's White House photographer for all eight years, and I think he's an absolute genius. He's also an empath, a real truth facilitator. I think he saw past the part of Barack Obama that the president maybe wanted us to see and instead photographed a real man—a father and a husband, a basketball player and a goofball. Pete helped the world fall in love with Obama in a way that it hadn't with any other president. (Equally, his humanization fueled the hatred in the hearts that were so inclined, but that's another story.) Pete did the same thing for Ronald Reagan. It was all Pete. I had an idea.

I asked Pete to come to my house and live with me for a week. He would photograph me getting up in the morning, disoriented and cantankerous, making my coffee, feeding the animals, arguing with my wife, wielding a machete, installing various household accoutrements, and even fishing. He wound up fitting right in. He would read bedtime stories to my daughter, eat at my table, and run random cow herds off my lawn. For a city guy living in DC, he was great at chasing cows on an ATV. He blended in. I wanted to forget about his presence and find out what I really looked like.

I love old family band photos. I love the way the Allman Brothers look in their album artwork. Like they were literally just passing around a joint and a baby or two when someone snapped the photo. Cutoff jean shorts, bruised knees, and dad hats. That's what the twins and I really look like. One day we all went down to the river for a picnic and got into the water with the kids so that Pete could take a photo. He risked his camera on several occasions following me into rivers, and it was worth it. . . . We look like a real family. It was starting to happen. I was becoming one woman.

We had one final shoot to get the cover of our album. We went back to Whidbey Island where we wrote our songs for the album and walked along the beach at Fort Casey. Pete snapped one of my favorite photos ever of the twins and me skipping down a ridge. Tim is jumping in the air. There's a lot of joy in it, and it's soul-capturing for the three of us. Everything you want to know about us can be found in this photo. But it wasn't the cover.

Scott Avett and Joni Mitchell, two of my favorite painters, actually both paint themselves a lot. It's not vain; it's a superpower to know what you look like—not on the surface, but what you *really* look like. It's even more of a superpower to know and *accept* it. Now, here's the truly unattainable nirvana . . . what if you could actually know—even *love* it? Most people are unaware of the story their eyes tell or the way their lines show us how often they've laughed. I don't want to be worried about my face or my body. I want to love it. With Pete, I wanted to know what I look like and not just accept it but completely embrace it.

I thought that Scott might know what I looked like, so I asked him to paint me. He said that he would, but not from a photo. Which means he got it: he knew I would choose said photo, which would mean that I was still controlling my image (made worse by the fact that I have a harmless gay-girl crush on Scott Avett).

I flew to North Carolina and sat for Scott so that I could find out what I look like to an artist who is a painter. I didn't want to see the painting until it was on the cover of *By the Way, I Forgive You,* and I didn't.

Many people tried to talk me out of this. It's not the way it's done. I had to fight to be myself—it wasn't the first time and it probably won't be the last. The songs, the photos, the cover, and the videos were all one attempt to be audaciously honest. It was me wanting people to really see us for the first time. Not the way our egos want people to see us, but the way we really are. I was so proud of that painting, I hung it right up in my living room, where it will stay always. I recommend hanging a photo of yourself being honest in your living room. Why shouldn't you?

After I saw that vision through, I decided to do a one-eighty and adorn myself with sparkles and sequins. I maxed out my credit cards on jackets I couldn't afford in the hopes that if I aimed high, I'd get there. Anyone who hasn't read this book wouldn't understand the dance between the rugged side of me and the one who loves to shine, but I was reaching back in time to the Honky Cat, embracing my spirit of eccentricity . . . it was expensive, but it still wasn't hip.

Chip Hooper died that year. He had a rare brain cancer and left us too early. I have had some of the most amazing men in my life. Incredible women, too, and I think I speak on that a whole lot. You may disagree with me when I say that we are living in a time when good men, who are feminists and fabulous fathers, are understandably lost in the noise because the righteous shift in human consciousness demands it . . . and so do I. But Chip was one of the best and the hardest to lose. There's a Chip Hooper memorial at the Gorge, where I first entered his psyche, and I'll never not think of him when I'm there. He was a brilliant photographer; his favorite songwriter was Shawn Colvin.

Live music has become increasingly difficult for women. It wasn't always so. Years ago, I was on a conference call with Chip, Duffy, and a couple other guys. We were talking about my tour at the time and when the call ended, I couldn't get my phone to hang up.

"Okay, she gone?" I heard one of the guys say.

"Yep," replied my *then* manager.

"Okay, so about Lilith, shouldn't she just do the three California dates? This routing is crazy."

Now, pause.

To say that Lilith Fair changed my life is a significant understatement. I went to *all* of them and, even though I was flat broke, I bought every CD. The thought of Lilith coming back sent chills down my spine!

"Um, guys. First of all, I'm still here. And second of all, I can't help but notice that you've secretly waited until the ONE woman on the call jumped off to discuss whether I should play FUCKING LILITH FAIR!! Fuck the routing, I'm there!"

Chip roared with laughter. "That's what we knew you'd say! We're just trying to get our damn ducks in a row."

A couple of years ago, Chip talked me off a ledge when I had been removed from a tour that I was beyond excited about. I would be opening for a male-fronted rock-'n'-roll band I love. A couple promoters had complained about having a female-fronted opener on the shows because they believed they'd sell fewer tickets and less beer. I was getting pretty upset about this stuff, so Duffy and I started to dream up a plan.

What if they're all wrong? What if we could get thousands of women to leave the United States and spend thousands of dollars just to see women headline a festival? What if Lilith Fair was always right and we really can move tickets? Surely, this would send a message to promoters back home? This was the idea behind our all-women's festival, "Girls Just Wanna Weekend." We did it in Mexico and it was an instant success! It did send a message back home, but *I* learned a lot too. It's not all the festival bookers and promoters' fault like I had previously believed. When it had suddenly become *my* job to book women on a festival, I found very few women to choose from.

That's when I started to uncover how systemic the gender disparity in music is. And it's ALL kinds of women. The lack of representation for LGBTQ people and women of color is abysmal.

It's not a small problem. It's not even a first-world problem. Music and art *are* who we are! That's how ALL of us discover ourselves! Go back over these pages and picture my life without these songs and these people.

Now imagine your family *loves* country music. It's not the '70s, '80s, and '90s, when we had Tanya Tucker and the Judds, Trisha, Patty, Dolly, Reba, Martina, Loretta, Brenda, Pam, Lori, Jessi, Deana, Rosanne, Patsy, Shania, Tammy, Faith, Alison, Lee Ann, LeAnn, Mary Chapin, Sara, Linda, and Bobbie. I could fill two pages with just country. Even the guys were singing about real life then. Country music was still poetry:

> You know a dream is like a river, ever changing as it flows
> And a dreamer's just a vessel that must follow where it goes
> Trying to learn from what's behind you
> And never knowing what's in store,
> Makes each day a constant battle
> Just to stay between the shores.

"The River" was a smash hit song in the '90s. It was saying something important to us. But in this analogy you and your family love country music NOW. Turn on the radio and listen to what is being said to your daughter right this minute: That she's an ass in a pair of blue jeans. That she belongs in the passenger seat of a pickup truck with a koozie. That she's only into "backroad" guys. Show me even a right-wing mother or father who wants their daughter to believe this about herself and I'll show you a liar.

I had adequate mirroring. The soundtrack of my life existed. I could hear women everywhere, yet here we are in 2020, where we are hearing one woman an hour on country radio. What's worse is that now women are not even getting signed. They're not even getting a job at the label that *could* sign enough women to tell the story of the other half of the human race.

I don't know where I would be without women and queer people creating art during my childhood . . . but if you want to find out, look no further than the country kids born at the end of the 2000s.

CATH GOT PREGNANT with Elijah in June 2017. We did IUI this time. We knew that IVF was an option, and we still had embryos, but Cath had really struggled with the hormones and wanted to try to avoid them if at all possible. We hadn't seen David in a couple of years, but he had set us up with plenty of what we needed (gross) to approach parenting in many different ways.

We decided to try IUI four times, and after that we would revisit the existing-Brandi-embryos conversation. Once again though, we were extremely lucky, and it worked the first time.

I always loved the pregnancy-test moment. The first time we did one we did it too early. They tell you to wait weeks after IVF, but we started testing after two days. The blue line was so incredibly faint that Cath was sure it was a negative. I watched it get bolder and bolder as we continued to test in the coming weeks. I kept telling her she was pregnant, but her mind wouldn't let her believe me. Finally, I went to CVS and got one of those tests that says PREGNANT in bold letters. That did it.

This time though, we did wait. We understood how pregnancy tests work and we were ready. As Cath walked out of the bathroom holding the stick with a big smile on her face, we heard the familiar sound of gravel crunching under car wheels. (I love an unannounced guest. It reminds me of good things about my childhood and living in the moment.) It was David. Coming by for the first time in *two years* to visit Evangeline at the very moment we had learned he was about to become a father for the second time. He burst out laughing when he walked in the door and we told him Catherine was still holding the pregnancy test.

I signed over fifteen thousand copies of *By the Way, I Forgive You* while we waited for the baby to be born. I still love physical music, and I had put so much heart into the artwork that I promised fans that

I'd sign every copy they preordered. I made good on that because I'm a nervous hustler and it got us a number-one album. Number five on Billboard—I was so proud of that—but it was just the beginning.

I'd made a promise to myself on New Year's Eve that I was going to make the biggest impact on music that I'd ever made, and I was going to do it by really being myself. I was committing to working harder than I ever had in my life for one year. I talked it over with my wife and she wanted to help me, even knowing that we would have a newborn. We would say yes to EVERYTHING; I didn't care if I got paid. I was on a plane three times a week. I spoke and represented, I did benefits and galas. I tributed everyone from Aretha to Chris Cornell. I was tapping into some of the work ethic that sustained me and Sovereign in my youth.

Elijah Shepherd Carlile was born a month after the album's release. It was an ambitious time. She was breech and then late and we had to induce Cath on March 18, 2018, which was the exact same day that Tim and his wife, Hanna, rushed to the hospital and had Waverly Hanseroth prematurely. It's fitting and not surprising that I would have a baby on the same day as a twin. The way things were going, this kind of synchronicity was becoming as common as corn.

Elijah was such an easy baby. She came out with a full head of black hair and went silent every time she heard my voice (FYI, that didn't last). I had an ease with her that I didn't have with Eva, and Cath was less protective, so I really got some special time. I sang to her constantly, and her sister was in love with her beyond measure. I had to travel more than I'm proud of, but Cath and I had made a plan and a pact. We wanted to break through. We wanted something for our girls. Eli hit the road with her crazy family at just under thirty days old. It was hard to wait that long. Our doctor told us that if we went out sooner and Eli wound up with a fever, she'd have to get a spinal tap because of an increased risk of meningitis. . . . That sealed the deal for me.

It was mid-April and we were playing in New York when I started to struggle with my voice and realized I needed to make some life changes. I had been invited to *The Howard Stern Show*. I had a policy for years leading up to this morning that I couldn't sing before two P.M. if I was on the East Coast—even later if I hadn't adjusted to the time zone. But I was excited to meet Howard. I hadn't really been beating up on my voice too bad, so I agreed to give it a try if we brought out a voice coach that I'd met a few times and really liked.

His name is RAab Stevenson. Once again, Dave Matthews had brought someone important into my life when he introduced us at the Gorge right after *The Firewatcher's Daughter* came out. For a while there, Dave and I were horrible about our voices. Drinking all day and then spraying topical anti-inflammatory into each other's throats just before going out onstage and singing.

I was opening for Dave that day but hadn't seen him in a while. I ran backstage to find a very peaceful and healthy-looking Dave. He gently turned down my offer of a glass of Jameson: "I've got three shows; I'll throw down with you on Sunday. Remind me to introduce you to RAab today."

It took me a year to call RAab.

RAab made me get out of bed at seven A.M. the day of Howard Stern ON THE EAST FUCKING COAST, which was so counter-intuitive because I feel like sleep is the best thing for my voice. We got on a treadmill to trick my body into thinking it'd been awake longer than it had. Right before I sang "The Joke" that morning, I did a shot of Jameson with Howard. It was like nine in the morning, but I can shoot whiskey pretty much whenever and love it. RAab was scream-ing through the soundproof glass, "Nooooo!" and clutching his chest. I loved his drama. I thought I had nailed "The Joke" and I felt really proud of it, but RAab could hear two subtle things: One was that I was getting sick. The other worried him enough to put me straight into a car and take me to the doctor to get my vocal cords scoped. Sure enough, I had a cyst on my vocal cord. It wasn't the cyst that mattered so much as the visibly enlarged capillary inside of it and the fact that it looked quite prone to hemorrhage.

This revelation freaked me out so bad that I vowed to stop drinking before I sang from now on and to train and exercise my voice regularly. I needed to make some lifestyle changes. My voice wouldn't have lasted another year the way I was treating it with alcohol, late-night food, never enough water, no rest, and constant colds. I was so stressed out that I got very sick.

I had to play the first of three nights at the Beacon Theatre starting on the night after they discovered the cyst. I was sicker than I've ever been onstage all three nights. I would have to get up, take steroids, and go to the doctor to have my sinus cavities cleared and my throat scoped. I played every show with a fever.

A steroid med pack tapers down. The first day you take six, you take five the next day, then four, three, two, one, until they're gone. It's important not to confuse a med pack of prednisone with the kind of steroids athletes take. It's a totally different drug, and singers don't take them to cheat. You don't get any superpower or strength from them. You take them when you're sick and you need to keep going—before you understand fully that looking after yourself isn't "letting everyone down." Steroids feel awful. It's better to just cancel. I didn't.

It was an old pattern, and my ambition and love for *By the Way, I Forgive You* was taking me down a familiar road. I needed to turn around.

I got the scare of my life on the morning before the second night at the Beacon. Since I needed steroids to get through the shows and to cure my tonsillitis, I had been prescribed sleep aids again. Xanax. It'd been a few years since I'd taken them, or anything like them, and I wasn't happy about it, but I had three nights at the Beacon and Austin City Limits to get through. For this reason, I agreed to use them until I got home. My family wasn't with me because Eli was too young, and I didn't tell Catherine. Being in hotel rooms alone is the worst thing for me. I get dark, homesick, and apocalyptic.

I set my alarm for 4:30 A.M. to take my first round of steroids and go back to sleep. I had gone to sleep earlier that night with no sleep aids because I hadn't taken any steroids yet. I reached for the steroids and poured six of them into my hand and unscrewed the cap on my water bottle. I sat there frozen and staring at my hand for a long time. I couldn't move. It was like I've heard people describe sleep paralysis, except that I was basically awake. It was like moving my hand to my mouth was a puzzle that I would have had to solve before I did it, and I just *couldn't* move a single muscle. I suddenly realized with a shot of adrenaline and shame that I was staring down at six Xanax that I was about to pop into my mouth and go back to sleep . . . I don't know if I would have ever woken up. I had a newborn baby and instead of the impact I had wanted to leave on the world for my kids, I would have died as a perceived drug addict or possible suicide. No amount of defense by Catherine or the twins would have been enough to remove the stain left by a simple accident. Just a tired mom alone in a hotel room afraid to let anyone down and wanting the show to go on. I will always think about that before I pass judgment on a person who's had a drug overdose. I left the Xanax in NYC for good.

By the time I got to Austin, I was so sick I couldn't swallow. Evangeline flew down with my sister to be with me and she had it too. One of her eyes was almost swollen shut from the virus. We were gorgeous.

RAab was with me, and somehow with all his tricks and teas, he'd get me singing perfectly by showtime. No one from the Beacon knew I was sick, and when I watch my ACL performance, I can't tell either . . . although over the course of the year I became a much better singer. I stopped drinking alcohol onstage, or even on tour, completely. I started training with RAab regularly and decided to totally change my life and focus on my health. I wasn't quite ready for it yet, but this was when I started entertaining the idea of getting hypnotized to get to the bottom of why I would get so sick during really pivotal moments in my life.

About four months after the album came out, I was being interviewed by one of my favorite conversationalists, Scott Goldman. I was talking about how "Party of One" wouldn't exist without "The Last Time I Saw Richard" from Joni Mitchell's *Blue*. I was quoting Joni and how she has often alluded to the idea that she has left the beginnings of concepts and art out in the ether for people to find and finish. She has famously stated something like: "If you find me in my work, I haven't done my job. If you find yourself, then I'm an artist." He pointed out that Joni's seventy-fifth birthday was coming up and that there would be a tribute concert. I gasped and the two of us wondered aloud if the notoriously reclusive and recovering Joni would be in attendance. Then I went to work on trying my damnedest to get invited.

I wrote letters to everyone I could think of. I literally begged. In the end I made it into the lineup. I would sing for Joni on her birthday. I sang "A Case of You" with my beloved Kris Kristofferson. He spoke it and I sang on the choruses. He struggles with memory loss, but I asked him that night: "What do you remember about Joni?" He replied, "Only everything . . . and that she was ALWAYS perfect."

That night was surreal. I met Joni but I acted a fool and she'd never remember me. I was incredibly nervous. It struck me that a tribute of this magnitude could have been held in the Staples Center and sold out immediately.

Joni came onstage at the end. The curtain was lowered for the encore. She was recovering from an aneurysm that left her unconscious and all alone for several days in 2015. All she wanted was to stand alone on that stage so that when the curtain came up, there she'd be on her own two feet. James Taylor, Chaka Khan, Graham Nash, Kris Kristofferson, and many more of us stood on the stage behind that lowered curtain and prayed while she tried to stand. She gave it all she had at the time, but the curtain had been down for too long, and in the end, she had to sit in a chair when the curtain went up. I hated seeing that. Joni radiates dignity. She is as regal as a human can get. We all sang "Big Yellow Taxi" staring at her in total admiration and disbelief that she was onstage with us at all—sitting *or* standing, it made no difference to us, but it did to her. She was determined to walk again. "For a third time," as she would explain it to me later. *"Once out of infancy, once out of the polio, and one final time now."*

After being a part of her birthday celebration, I had an epiphany.

No one would hear Joni perform her beloved *Blue* album live again. She's a self-professed painter and if she did sing again, she would probably innovate; it would most likely be recent work. So what if I did it? What if I kept the original keys and sang it almost verbatim in service to its legacy? To Joni's legacy? *Could* I even do it?

I WAS IN upstate New York when I learned that the twins and I had been nominated for song, album, and artist of the year at the Americana Awards! I had always loved the thought of being considered "Americana," and we celebrated by running down the street in the rain to get back on the bus and tell our wives and kids! It was a very happy day.

We immediately called up Dave Cobb and he'd already heard. It's not hokey to say that it is an honor to be nominated. When it finally does happen, it's simply life-affirming. Being upheld by your friends and peers for an accomplishment you are proud of feels good because it's supposed to feel good.

The families headed to Nashville that September for the awards and got all dressed up! The catch is that we were in the impossible situation of being in all the same categories with the spectacularly talented Jason Isbell. It'd be a bit like him being up against me in the "Seattle Lesbian Awards," and I mean that with COMPLETE admiration and respect—to Jason and Seattle lesbians. The two of us are paralleled as kindred spirits in a way I can't describe. If there's such a thing as past lives, he's some kind of distant brother from one of mine. I suspect that he's deeply special to many people whom he's not quite as intensely aware of. I've pulled him aside quietly on several occasions to gain insight on things pertaining to addiction and fear. He exudes a kind of calm everyman wisdom that is so needed in our community.

The feeling you get when you're up for an award is so physical. You don't get to make a moral decision about how you should feel, your adrenal system does it for you. Your heart pumps blood to your brain like you're in a high-speed chase. And the award goes to . . . eternity . . . "Someone else," then an immediate drop in heart rate. A mixture of relief and extreme disappointment. A pet peeve of mine is the "award denier," the "I don't care about these self-aggrandizing dog-and-pony-shows" types.

Kindly fuck off, please. Heart emoji.

You do and you should care. I'm not saying that competition can't be art- and soul-destroying, but don't act like you don't care. Either way . . . I guess I care. The cat's out of the bag! I'm not cool.

I had never won an award in my life at that point. Not when I was the Honky Cat, or in any of the pageants from my childhood. Not even at karaoke! But here I was, sweating in my seat at the Ryman and up for three of them.

The song "We Are the Champions" by Queen has never not made me cry. Teams, winning, losing, being picked or rejected. These themes are traumatic for some LGBTQ folks. *We* get to own that song—and Freddie, for that matter. It's okay to want to be champions for a little while. Our path is long and fraught with submission. Triumph is a beautiful theme for 2020 queers. Freddie, Elton, Dolly, Bette . . . these are names I shan't forget.

I was contemplating this when a handsome, white, extremely talented young fella won the Best New Artist Award and promptly denounced the genre—"Americana ain't no part of nothin'," I remember him saying as he scolded the room full of misfits. "I consider myself a country singer," he said . . . right before he walked off the stage with his award instead of leaving it there for Courtney Marie Andrews or anyone else whose heart had pounded while his name was being called. Do you know what that sounded like to the people of color or the LGBTQ folks in attendance?

Here's what I heard from where I sat: "I don't belong here with you. I'm normal. I belong in the bigger room." It was uncomfortable and upsetting for me to hear. We have a long way to go when it comes to addressing some of the concerns that I can see he had about the industry in retrospect . . . but damn. It really set the scene for the evening and made things more tense than they should have been.

k.d. lang was there to accept her Trailblazer Award. Buddy Guy and Irma Thomas were all dressed up to accept their Lifetime Achievement awards. A pioneering all-female and predominantly gay record label, Olivia Records, was being honored for its three decades of contribution to Americana. These are not people often recognized by mainstream music of any kind. They deserved it. They weren't a part of "nothin'"; we were a part of "something" for once. These are the legends of the misfits. Read the room.

The famous Ryman Auditorium was full of hardworking people who have been overlooked by the mainstream establishment and want to make life better for those of us on the fringe. Some because of their music but some of us (me) because of circumstance and the fact that we're different. Clearly, I was a tad offended.

I held Cath's hand as each award went to Jason Isbell, just as they had at the Grammys the year before, and the final one went to the godfather of Americana, my hero, John Prine.

Hard to argue with any of that . . . but it still took the wind out of me.

I felt an energetic shift. It wasn't just from me. It was in the room. Everyone knew those guys deserved those accolades and more. It's so hard to describe mixed feelings like these, so I didn't try. Not even to myself. I went backstage and loved on Jason and Mr. Prine, because I do. When I got in that car, I promised the twins and the girls that we were gonna win the Grammy for the Best Americana Album if it was the last goddamned thing I did.

Don't worry. I apologized to God for scapegoating the guy that won Best New Artist. I was just tired of being reminded that I may never fully belong.

I needed a villain, and he looked a hell of a lot more worthy of it at the time than Jason and handsome Johnny.

As we got into the fall, we just worked harder.

We were writing songs for an upcoming Tanya Tucker album that I was losing sleep about. I was stressed-out for two really important reasons: One was that, as I'm sure you remember me mentioning, she was one of my great childhood heroes. The other was that she kept canceling the album as her bus rambled at a snail's pace through the United States toward California.

Shooter had invited me to co-produce the album with him after seeing me freak out at the mention that he was doing it. "Please, please, please, can I fly down, Shooter? Can I swing by? Can she still sing? Is she cool?"

"Do it with me!" Shooter said. "We'll record it together."

Shooter connected Tanya and me via text message that night. It was one of those group threads, but Tanya didn't understand; her reply to my emoji-ridden and obnoxiously enthusiastic text was: "Who the hell is this Brandy bitch?"

. . . If you're honest with yourself, that's exactly what you'd want Tanya Tucker to say.

We had also just made our first album in the home studio we'd been building for six months. The Secret Sisters had decided, to our delight, to make their fourth album with me and the twins producing. We had made album number three for them at Bear Creek, but we'd been fans since day one. Laura and Lydia Rogers are two sisters from Florence, Alabama. They're Church of Christ girls and they won't say "hell," but they sang at my wedding and they've let my gay ass follow them around for over ten years, singing three-part harmonies and writing songs. They're inseparable in every way, but especially vocally.

Their third album, *You Don't Own Me Anymore,* was a total coming-of-age album in response to being dropped by their label and sued by their manager in their twenties. They had to file for bankruptcy and barely made it through that decade. They literally had nothing to their names. After three albums on a major, they were cleaning houses and couldn't get a credit card. I was outraged. I assembled a team and started consulting on their career. We did a Kickstarter campaign to make the album. The fans brought them back to life and the album was nominated for a Grammy.

Fast-forward and they're both married, and all grown-up. The songs they brought to me this time were way different from before. Instead of the puritanical Louvin Brothers church-hymnal vocal style I had been used to, these voices felt . . . different. Older, sensual, soulful, but strangely "at odds."

This is when I discovered what it means to be a producer. I began to unravel the tangled source of the tension *so that I could record it.*

Laura showed up pregnant. It used to be that she didn't want kids. She loves dogs. She had spent some time as a nanny and loved kids but had a pretty solid "nah" resolve when it came to the possibility of having her own. Lydia DID want kids. She's younger but she got married first. She had been struggling to get pregnant or stay pregnant . . . I don't know because she never had to say. She had written it.

I recalled London on that early morning when I found out about Josephine. It's complicated. There's so much love there for your sister . . . but there's something otherworldly and beyond your control when you've got your mind made up that you are a mother before you get to be one in the world.

Laura is hilarious. She makes me roll on the floor laughing. She's so gross and self-deprecating, I keep a journal of things that she says. From the outside looking in, I could see that she was worried about her little sister. Worried that she wasn't getting pregnant and wanting her to have the family she so desperately wanted.

She felt guilty and wasn't really letting herself fall in love with her baby because Lydia didn't have one. So she complained and joked a lot about her discomfort, described in detail her bodily functions as kind of a comedy routine to try to make the whole "pregnancy ordeal" seem overrated. (To be fair, poor Laura did have a hell of a time.) But all that irreverence made things harder for Lydia. She was frustrated that Laura would complain about something precious that she was trying so hard for and wanted so badly. She's sensitive and more serious than her sister, but she's also very funny, so she tried to remain good-spirited about it all.

It all comes out in the words and the voice. Lydia is actually a soul singer in need of permission.

Lydia wrote:

> *Sugar water to the brim they told me it'd be spring.*
> *Early September and my first glimpse of tiny wings,*
> *Summer's coming to an end, magnolias are in bloom,*
> *Birmingham this time of year was giving me hope, too.*
> *But I'm a late bloomer this is surely true,*
> *It doesn't matter when you bloom,*
> *It matters that you do.*
> *Keeping track and counting down again I'm overdue,*
> *Watching everyone around get there before I do,*
> *Looking in the mirror at this body that betrays,*
> *But looking out the window late bloomers on parade,*
> *It doesn't matter when you bloom,*
> *It matters that you do.*

Laura wrote:

> *You're a part of me and the one I love,*
> *The sweetest years won't tarry,*
> *You will reach for me when my arms are full*
> *And I will lay down the things I carry.*
> *I will hold you dear.*
> *While my shadows long and my eyes are clear*
> *I know these days will pass away so I will hold you dear.*

These weren't kids anymore. And these weren't harmony songs. They were confessions, and for the first time in their lives, the Rogers sisters were separate women. In the past, they didn't tell you who wrote which songs but suddenly you could tell, and I was caught up in the sheer truth of it all. So I asked them not to sing together on this album. They had only ever sung into one mic, but not this time. Their love for each other could sustain the artistic separation.

One of the sessions took place on the stage of the Fitzgerald Theater in Saint Paul, Minnesota. We had three shows there and the girls opened up for us. We wanted to capture all that big, beautiful reverb, so we packed up our gear and took it with us. It was December in Minnesota and it felt dark at noon. I thought "Hold You Dear" was the right song to get in that space. Right before Laura sang it, I told her quietly that, all joking aside, it was okay to be excited and have affection for the baby growing inside of her. I told her that Lydia was happy for her and that she'd find what she was looking for in time. By the time Laura got to the verse about the baby, she was crying so hard she couldn't sing. She kind of got it the third time around, but we kept the tears because it was brave and because . . . when do you get to hear a mother falling in love with her baby for the first time on an album? Never.

The album ended during a power outage. We said goodbye by candlelight in the chaotic upcoming Christmas season. No matter what happens with that album, it's the truth and it needed to be made. It's not the Everly Brothers sound that fans are used to, but it had to come out that way because the Rogers girls once again were being carried through hardship on the catharsis of music.

Lydia was pregnant within a month of getting through that album. She got up onstage and whispered it into my ear. And now they each have a gorgeous baby boy.

I was ready for Tanya Tucker now . . . what could possibly go wrong?

By the time Christmas rolled around, I had lived several lifetimes inside of *By the Way, I Forgive You*. It felt like the curtain was closing.

It was in the end of this era that Sovereign left me. His work on me was finished and he passed away quietly after spending his whole twenty-year life by my side and holding me together. God sent me what seemed like broken horses twice. Both times I believed I was car-ing for them. That they were so inherently flawed that they could only belong to me. When Sovereign left I looked back at the climb and realized how none of it would have happened without him. . . . I would have always had music, but horses force you by survival to overcome your fears. Sometimes because you have no choice. You're too deep in the woods—too far from home and there's no turning back. Sometimes with the kindness in their eyes they fool you into thinking they're somehow dependent on you . . . that *you* are their person. This is a gift and a lie. They are so much more mystical than that. A horse can kill you. Especially a broken one. Every moment you spend with him is a moment he's simply deciding to let you live.

I HAD TWO broken horses . . . and they were the most unbroken creatures I've met here on earth.

"LATE BLOOMER"

Sugar water to the brim, they told me it'd be spring
Early September and my first glimpse of tiny wings
Summer's coming to an end, magnolias are in bloom
Birmingham this time of year is giving me hope, too
Giving me hope, too

I'm a late bloomer
I'm a late bloomer
This is surely true
It doesn't matter when you bloom
It matters that you do

Keeping track and counting down again, I'm overdue
Watching everyone around get there before I do
Looking in the mirror at this body that betrays
But looking out the window, late bloomers on parade

I'm a late bloomer
I'm a late bloomer
This is surely true
It doesn't matter when you bloom
It matters that you do
                    —THE SECRET SISTERS

"HOLD YOU DEAR"

To the lover of my youth, the solace for my age
My protection from what harms
You will reach for me on our darkest days
And I will come home to your arms

And I will hold you dear
While my shadow's long and my eyes are clear
I know these days will pass away
So, I will hold you dear

Oh, blessed mother and the father I adore
There is time upon your faces
I will cherish you til you leave me for your eternal holy places

And I will hold you dear
While my shadow's long and my eyes are clear

I know these days will pass away
So, I will hold you dear

You're a part of me and the one I love
The sweetest years won't tarry
You will reach for me when my arms are full
And I will lay down the things I carry

And I will hold you dear
While my shadow's long and my eyes are clear
I know these days will pass away
So, I will hold you dear
                    —THE SECRET SISTERS

THE THREE OF US LOVE MAKING TRAILS AND
MAINTAINING THEM

PETE RIDING ON THE BACK OF CATHERINES QUAD
RISKING LIFE AND CAMERA TO CAPTURE MY JOY
AS PHIL TRIES TO PASS ME

THIS IS A REAL FAMILY PHOTO

ME AND THE SECRET SISTERS
MY ANGELS ♡

ME AND THE TWINS WANTED TO REVEAL OURSELVES
IN THESE PHOTOS — WE ARE OVER TRYING TO LOOK
COOL.

THE BEAUTIFUL MOMENT PETE CAPTURED ON THE
RIDGE AT WHIDBEY

I HAD TWIN GOATS AND I NAMED THEM TIM AND PHIL
BUT TIM DIED ON MY WEDDING DAY. I LOVED PLAYING
DOZERS WITH PHIL. WE WOULD PUSH EACH OTHER FOR HOURS.

ME INSTALLING CATHS SWINGING CHAIR. GETTING IMPATIENT
AND BREAKING OUT THE SLEDGE HAMMER IS AN EVERY
DAY THING FOR ME. THIS WORKED BY THE WAY.

FLY FISHING IN THE CEDAR RIVER. CAN YOU IMAGINE
WHAT PETES CAMERA COSTS?

EVANGELINE RUNNING THE SHOW

MAKING BRIDGES IN THE WOODS FOR
THE KIDS-GOONIES STYLE.

MORNING MELODIES AND COFFEE IN PJS

ONLY CATH CAN LOOK THIS COLLECTED
MOMENTS AFTER GIVING BIRTH...
LOOK AT ELIJAHS HAIR!

ME AND BABY ELI - DAY ONE

THIS IS THE LAST PHOTO TAKEN OF ME AND MY OLD PAL SOVEREIGN. HE DIED SUDDENLY SHORTLY AFTER IT WAS TAKEN. I HAD 20 AMAZING YEARS WITH HIM AND HE ALTERED THE COURSE OF MY LIFE TOWARDS THIS BEAUTIFUL REALITY.

THIS IS WHAT MY PARTICULAR BRAND OF MOTHERHOOD LOOKS LIKE. SIX KIDS ON A 45 FT BUS.

FISHING

MY BELOVED SCOTT AVETT PAINTED THE COVER OF BY THE WAY I FORGIVE YOU.

19.

· · · · · · · · · ·

BRING MY FLOWERS NOW WHILE I'M LIVIN'

It was pitch-black and five A.M. when my ringing phone woke me up in the middle of my sleep.

I had gone to bed that night knowing that at some point the next morning we'd hear about the Grammys and whether we got that Best Americana Album nomination I had been so hoping for. I would also be boarding a plane at eight A.M. to head to Vegas to meet Tanya Tucker for the first time. My plan was to try and convince her that she should recommit to making the record with Shooter and me—we were supposed to start in less than a week.

I don't know about you, but when your phone rings like that in the middle of the night, someone's dead—that's the first thing I think. I picked it up and the screen said "Asha calling"—my publicist and friend. I STILL didn't get it! What in the hell was she doing up this late?

Then it HIT me! I got it. I got the Americana nomination. She must have found out earlier because she was in Nashville.

"Hello?!" I gasped into the phone. "Did I get it?"

Now, Asha is literally a Zen master, but her voice was shaking. "Brandi. You got Song, Record, and Album of the Year in the MAIN categories. . . . I saw it on *Good Morning America* . . . they just kept saying your name . . . they just kept saying your name."

I tried to make sense of what I'd just heard. Catherine's phone started blowing up. I was getting text messages so fast it was like an elaborate prank. Over the next few minutes, I would learn that our album had gotten SIX Grammy nominations. My phone never stopped ringing that day . . . I had no idea how many people I had given my number to over the years. Everyone had heard.

Not David though! Still had to tell him. . . . Spoiler alert: he didn't care.

Elton called me. "Can you hear me screaming from England????!!!!"

I heard from the lovely Harry Styles, who revealed that he was a fan.

Asha said I couldn't go to Vegas. I had to stay put and talk to press. Good thing, 'cause both my kids woke up vomiting. That's what I love about the juxtaposition of my jobs. You'd think that it would be a total downer to spend a day like that getting life-affirming news and simultaneously being thrown up on and stuck in front of *Dora the Explorer* all day, but it was PERFECT. Courier after courier showed up that day with at least seven or eight different bottles of fancy Champagne. I could see the confusion as they handed me the bottles of Dom and Cristal with "Congratulations on the Grammy Noms!" messages. They'd look at my little cabin and my green little fever babies and be thoroughly confused. It's one of my all-time favorite days.

The twins came over that night and we drank all that Champagne. Tiffany made us a key lime pie, and the kids made us a banner on butcher paper. Another banner flashed across the evening news while we watched TV: "Kendrick Lamar, Drake, and Brandi Carlile lead with the most Grammy nominations." I was the most nominated woman at the 2019 Grammys.

I got a call the next day and was told I would be performing on the show. No distracting bells and whistles, no collaborations, just me and my special rock-'n'-roll band against a beautifully lit stage with the song lyrics appearing behind me. What a tremendous and organic honor. The only catch was I had to shorten the song to fit the time constraints. I was relieved! My idea was to end "The Joke" after the second chorus and not do the big note. The choruses were so huge that I didn't think we needed it. . . . The truth was that I was afraid I wouldn't hit the note.

The same thing had happened with "The Story." For years, I never really could hit that note and then eventually my voice just somehow expanded and suddenly I was able to always reach it. I wasn't there yet on the end of "The Joke." The big "theeeeem" moment would come out right only about one out of twenty times. Dave Cobb had always loved "The Story." I told him in passing that I had a different ending planned for "The Joke" on the Grammys and he freaked out!

"No, no, no! Please don't do that! This is the exact moment we've been waiting for, don't duck out of this. That moment is the whole point!"

Without really knowing it, once again Dave Cobb had just pushed me beyond my belief in myself. I put the note back in and I started practicing it with RAab and by myself, obsessing over the vowel and the volume. It was exactly like when I was a teenager. I never want to stop needing to get better or pushing myself beyond where I think my limits are. The trick is having someone who believes in you. It never once occurred to Dave that I wouldn't nail it.

Meanwhile, Tanya Tucker agreed to point her bus back toward California and at least *meet* in the studio with me and Shooter. I reached out to my old friend Rick Rubin for some advice, because I was seeing this opportunity as something similar to what he had done with Johnny Cash on *American Recordings*. He showed a generation of rock-'n'-roll kids where their punk-rock country music had come from, and I felt that there was a generation of especially young women who were just longing to know who their punk-rock country matriarchs are. Rick confirmed that it was indeed a hard sell convincing

Cash to cover Nine Inch Nails and the rest, but that if we focused on the lyrics, and helping them resonate with her, she would soon connect to the vision. The reception Cash received had really encouraged him to carry on. I was hoping that would happen with Tanya as well. The hardest thing sometimes is convincing your heroes that they're worthy.

She wasn't sure about the songs. She wasn't sure about anything really. It'd been seventeen years since she made an album. She's a recovered drug addict with a lot of hard stories. She lost both her parents in the early aughts and would explain to me that her success in music brought so much joy to her parents, especially her father, that when they died, she just didn't see the point anymore. "When they got their wings, I knew that there was more love behind me in this life than there is ahead of me," she said one day while I sat at the piano.

I wanted to show Tanya that it wasn't true. I wished she could have seen me at nine years old, forced into a skirt with a perm, and the only thing that was making me feel like myself was that I was singing "Delta Dawn" or "San Antonio Stroll." Tanya made me feel tough when I needed her. She brings all of us so much joy with her music and her personality. I wanted her to see how loved she is and that there's more love ahead of her than she thinks. But once again I was shocked to see the double standard that folks are willing to impose on women in this realm. We know about Cash, Hank, Merle, Waylon, and George—we know all these men were delightfully self-destructive drug addicts, some even convicted criminals who left their wives and kids on multiple occasions. Total hell-raisers, yet we literally sing their songs in church! Our undying love and reverence for these men (mine included) rivals any religious deity I can think of, yet Tanya Tucker is considered "finished" in the world of country music. She's held permanently accountable for her addictions and her past shenanigans. She's in her sixties now and bears a cross of regret that you just find yourself wanting to carry for her for a while. That was my plan.

When I met T that day at Sunset Sound in L.A., we hit it off right away. She kept calling Shooter "Little Waylon." She had pink hair and wore an American flag T-shirt. "I love the pink hair, Tanya," I said while she twisted her cigarette out into the sole of her boot. "Oh you know, baby, I gotta be struttin' my stuff or I ain't Tanya Tucker. But I don't wear my miniskirts anymore since my balls started showin'." You can't make this shit up.

We started with "High Ridin' Heroes" because it's a song she felt confident about, but we changed the pronoun so that emotionally she was speaking in first person. She slipped that song on like a skin.

> *Time was when she was queen*
> *Now the rodeo's just this old girl's dream,*
> *The highs are few and far between*
> *The lows get the rest,*
> *These old hard times ain't nothin' new,*
> *Once you've done the best you can do*
> *You just tip your hat to the wild and blue*
> *And ya ride off to the west.*

After that, she was in. We all knew we had something special. It was working.

The songs that the twins and I had written for her were all about her life. The landscapes from places she's lived and loved: Texas, Vegas, the Arizona skyline, always on the run. Her time with Glen Campbell, her addictions, her relationship with her father and children, being poor—these are themes that we refined during our time in the studio with her. She'd tell a story and we'd run off with an eraser to fix a line or two based on something she'd said.

Toward the end of the album, she told me a story about a poem she'd left on Loretta Lynn's answering machine. It went:

> *Bring my flowers now while I'm livin',*
> *I won't need your love when I'm gone,*
> *Don't spend time, tears, or money on my old, breathless body,*
> *If your heart is in them flowers, bring them now.*

I was riveted. Biting my fingernails, frantically waiting for her to finish.

"Bring them ON!" I blurted out.

Tanya looked confused. "Nah, baby. It was *now,*" she grunted.

"Tanya, that's a song! It might even be THE song. If your heart is in them flowers, bring 'em *on,*" I said.

She said that it wasn't a song because she's not a writer. We went to the piano right then, and I just listened to her. She told me about her brother and sister and how she wishes they'd forgive each other. She talked about her horse that died, "Jessie Ray," the great love of her life. She talked about how fast her kids grew up, her mama, how she regrets not playing guitar and not being clean by the time her father died. I wrote the verses and the melody to "Bring My Flowers Now" while she talked to me, but it's all her. It's her real story. She's a writer.

We laid that track down live and I'm still haunted by it.

When I started talking about the album in the industry and in the country community, I heard countless times that no one would be willing to give Tanya a second chance. I don't know if they ever will . . . She's not even in the Country Music Hall of Fame, but I will fight for her no matter what happens. She's human, she's brilliant, she's country, but most important she's my family.

My festival, Girls Just Wanna Weekend, happened in Mexico right after we recorded Tanya's album and before the 2019 Grammys. It was the first year and I was very proud of it. It was sold out, and I brought my whole family: Mom, Dad, Jay, Tiff, Michelle, and ALL of our kids and friends, past and present. Amber Lee came and even sang! It really reminded me of Lilith Fair. Everyone there knew it was something special. It had so little to do with me and so much to do with the collective consciousness and the turning of the tide. The Indigo Girls were there, too, which made it feel even more full circle. I knew that no one who had been at the festival that first year would ever be able to miss it.

When we got home, there was two feet of snow on the ground and all of our roofs were damaged. We spent the three days in between

Mexico and the Grammys working outside in the snow and . . . you guessed it, I got sick!

I went into that week with another cold. I had RAab but it was time for me to call the language specialist/hypnotherapist woman I'd been putting off calling and see if there was something deep inside my mind that I could unlock. I don't consciously remember much about that first session, but somehow it worked. I didn't take steroids, and I worked nonstop with RAab and drank lots of water. The kids were the best medicine, and by the night of Clive Davis's pre-party, things were already starting to shift.

I loved everything about that week, all the parties and the fancy clothes and the new people. I met Quincy Jones at the Clive Davis party—it was really overwhelming and outrageous. Clive himself was pretty dreamy and positively encyclopedic. I've never met a person with a vault of memory like that. Greatest of all though, Joni was there. She watched me sing "The Joke" and after I got offstage, I walked up to her so that I could meet her *properly*. She was alone at her table and I sat down. "Hi, Joni," I said. "My name's Brandi, I sang to you at your birthday."

"I remember," she said, her eyes twinkling with mischief. She grabbed my striped sequin sleeve. "What are you supposed to be? A referee?" We both burst out laughing and I kissed her cheek and left her to her admirers.

The Grammy Awards are very intense. It's a powerful thing, an undertaking that big. If you're lucky enough to perform, and your performance design has any weight to it, you know from the time you walk through the door that you are on the precipice of a make-or-break moment. You try not to dwell on it, and put it out of your mind because the pressure is too much. I knew damn well that I wasn't going to win one of those big main-category awards. I didn't even write anything down for them. All I could think about was that Americana Grammy I promised the twins we'd win, and of course the performance. I had stubbornly decided somewhere in between the

Ryman and the Staples Center that the word "Americana" was very important to me and I wanted to call it home this year.

They had scheduled our rehearsal at the precise moment that the Americana Grammys were being given out in the other room. We had been explicitly told that we would have to choose: Americana or the TV performance.

I understood their reasons. It's a big deal. The cameras and lighting need adjusting; they have to test all the gear and the broadcast equipment, they also need to see you run the song so they know you can stay within the requirements and time constraints. If we didn't rehearse, we'd lose the performance. But if we weren't there when the awards were given out for our genre, I would miss my only chance ever to accept an award. Worst of all, the people who voted for me would think I didn't appreciate it. So, I chose Americana. Shooter stayed onstage at his piano to hold it down for us, and the twins and I sprinted down the hall just in time to hear the host begin to shift to the Roots genre.

My mom and Jay were even in the audience. It meant so much to me that they were there. I was terrified that we wouldn't win and that I'd let everyone down. I knew if I did not win an Americana/Roots Grammy that I wouldn't win one at all. And I was pretty positive that at least two of the Grammys were deservedly going to John Prine.

When you've never won at anything you can really only fathom losing.

The suspense was almost unbearable. It's not what you think. If you're not in the music business, you probably don't know that most Grammys are given out in a brightly lit, half-empty room during the day. The big, glitzy event takes place much later. I imagine it'd be really intimidating to accept an award in that dark, pressurized, televised scenario but to me . . . even at noon in a half-empty theater, my heartbeat was positioned squarely between my ears when the envelope was being opened.

"And the Grammy for the Best American Roots Performance goes to . . . 'THE JOKE'!"

I couldn't believe what I heard. Cath was jumping up and down, Duffy and Mark were crying. I hugged the twins and we all ran up onstage giggling. I blanked and forgot to thank anyone and just ran offstage. Just as the dread started to sink in about the people I forgot to thank, I heard it again: "And the Grammy for Best Americana Album goes to Brandi Carlile for *By the Way, I Forgive You!*"

That was it. We had done it. Dave Cobb came running up! I had written a little speech about how it felt to be seen in this way and to be included by my Americana misfit peers. I had no sooner tearfully read it before they announced that we had won a THIRD Grammy. It was positively euphoric.

I think that because of the way I grew up poor and failing in school, because I was the only gay person in such a small town, because I was often nervous, humiliated, and turned away from *even church,* I had an unresolved hurt deep within me that I wasn't paying too much attention to. I'm incredibly aware of my privilege . . . to a fault. I often convince myself that I don't have a right to address my upbringing and the way that the hard parts of my childhood made me feel—which was panicked, exposed, and excluded. The work I've done with War Child, incarcerated people, and even the friendship I have with Jenny Hopper has given me tremendous perspective. But as I've learned to empathize and cope with the injustice and pain in the world, I have learned to ignore my own because it feels less and less important. I have often felt ashamed of my own internal struggle. This has fed an insatiable case of impostor syndrome that I don't know if I'll ever fully kick. But I do know now that pain is relative and never naming it contributes to the way I feel in almost any scenario where attention may be drawn to me that could result in my embarrassment or rejection.

The people and events that had come along and healed me never went unnoticed. My dad pointed out recently that after my botched baptism, I started to gather people—congregants, squads, cheerleaders. I knew in some way that if I was ever going to see this or any dream come true, I needed people. I now realized where this instinct had come from. It was an early childhood tactic that I had been given by being the first child born on both sides of my family. I was adored by my grandparents, parents, and aunts and uncles. Showered with affection. That religious rejection was enough to send me back to one of my earliest and most primitive instincts: to simply surround myself with love and acceptance. It saved my life many times.

I was standing onstage accepting these Grammys and they meant more to me than they probably should have. I had made it more than it was, but it felt good. *We are the champions.* I wanted to thank everyone I knew. I was inarticulate and gracious and forgetful and human. I freaked out and said that Dave Cobb wrote "The Joke." I forgot to thank RAab and my friend Tracy, and I didn't give the twins enough time to speak in general. Worst of all, I forgot to thank John Prine, who made the album of a lifetime and was one of the people I loved and admired most in the world. It was still awesome. I wished I could've thanked everyone from my past that I should have forgiven, because there was a lot of catharsis in that moment for me. I didn't need to be on TV. The whole thing was exhilarating.

We sprinted down the hall and into the Staples Center for the rehearsal we were late for, not knowing if we had actually lost our performance! But we arrived to an applauding production crew and hugs from the director. Poor Shooter had sat at his piano and missed the whole thing. He didn't care though . . . he's so fucking cool. Even the rehearsal was monumental . . . but I missed the note.

I still hadn't gotten my teeth into the big "them" at the end of the song. I set it aside so that I could continue celebrating, but I had started to secretly fantasize a catastrophic failure. In my mind I could see myself holding the long note, *"The joke's oooooon . . ."* and then the silence before the drum fill . . . but when the cymbal comes down my voice cracks and falls apart like a defunct firework. The expected spectacular bombshell fountain revealing itself as a sputtering sparkler.

I was going to be okay. RAab was there. I didn't tell him what I was feeling, because it was complicated. I also knew deep down that I was going to smash it. When this kind of pressure is on a performer, he or she absolutely needs to be able to visualize total victory and bliss, but there's also a necessary apprehension, sometimes even dread. The tension this creates is a perfect cocktail. It's rare, but when you get it right, something really magical happens. I kept telling myself, *This is what you know how to do. You just gotta sing "The Joke." You're not a kid anymore. You're ready for this.*

I could hear the host as I walked onstage and plugged in my guitar. There was a video wall in front of me so that I could tune and line-check. I loved the ordinariness of it all: managing my own gear, the twins to my right and left, Chris, Shooter, and Josh right behind me. No click track, no in-ear monitors, just rock-club wedges . . . at the Grammys. Such a rarity in this futuristic era for performance. The cables and the hardware of a live show are comforting. The tools of my trade reminded me JUST in time that I knew exactly how to do what I was just about to do. I tuned up my old Gibson just like I would have down the street at the Troubadour . . . and I waited to hear my name.

When I began the song, the audience was sitting down. They were mostly wondering who I was, and to my surprise and discomfort, *really* listening. It was silent. When I cleared that first monster of a chorus, I saw someone stand up all alone in the middle center and I locked eyes with her for support as I stepped into the second verse. It was Janelle Monáe. It was such a kind thing she did . . . I've tried to tell her what that felt like, what it meant to me, but she may never really understand. She stood that way by herself for what seemed like almost a minute and it kicked me into high gear. Suddenly I was performing for her. One by one, people started standing up around her until it was a wave of people . . . stars, heroes, friends, Dave and Ledja Cobb, and my wife. I lost all semblance of fear about the last note. Before I knew it, the silence was upon me . . . and then the drum fill. I said *fuck it,* and just screamed the last note. Left it all out there.

"The joke's on . . . theeeeem!"

We didn't go to any parties that night. We went out for sushi. Me, Cath, Mom, Jay, the twins, Tiff, Hanna, our team, and a small group of friends. The thing I loved was watching the team that had stuck by me for so long celebrate that win. Elliot, Mark, Duffy, and Will sat around a table with me and we toasted Chip because we knew he was there. When you win a Grammy, your whole team wins a Grammy.

I went to a quiet dinner with Joni Mitchell the day after the Grammys, along with a couple of her hilarious friends. Joni and her fiery best friend, Marcy, had become acquainted with Cath, and they all overlooked my fan-girl issues and agreed to let me attend the meal. I got all dressed up and expected a cancellation call all day long, but it never came. Cath and I took an Uber to the quiet little Italian restaurant Joni had chosen and sat in the car waiting for her. We saw a small dark car park around the corner and watched as Joni got out with a cane. She stood up, handed her cane to her friend and straightened her cloak.

It was then that I knew Joni Mitchell is everything you hope she will be. Fighting to get on her feet behind a closed curtain was a distant memory. She walked right into that restaurant on her own two legs and sat down. "Pinot Grigio for the table," she said proudly to the waiter.

The hours ticked by and I eventually asked her permission to play the *Blue* album in its entirety at Disney Hall in L.A. I'd had too much wine and Cath couldn't believe I had done it. Joni put her hand on my arm and told me that she'd be honored. What she said next would come to change me as an artist forever.

"You know I'm a painter now, right?"

"Of course," I said, "one of the greatest."

She smiled her impervious-to-flattery smile. "It doesn't bother me to not sing anymore, but there is music in my house and a lot of great instruments too . . . sometimes that does bother me."

I wasn't quite following, but I was obviously mesmerized.

Marcy jumped in: "Maybe we could get some fun folks together."

And then Joni said it: "Maybe we could have a *jam*."

I was struggling not to shake when Joni looked me right through and said, *"Are you in?"*

I can tell you that with the week's events leading to this moment, I'd never felt quite so "in" in my whole life.

The next day, I woke up to a message from Ellen DeGeneres asking me to come on her show. I canceled my flight home and flew my mother back to L.A. the same day to sing "The Joke" on her show by myself. It was a whirlwind and a dream.

After I performed, Ellen invited Catherine and me over to her house that evening. I ended my journey sitting around a fire with Ellen DeGeneres, my wife, and a bottle of wine, talking about life all night long. She knows the role she's played in my life and so many others'. I didn't even need to tell her.

At this point it's probably not hard to understand how humbled, changed, and healed I've been by this time in my life, but I still can't quite make sense of it. I don't think I should try.

I left L.A. and immediately took my wife and kids on a vacation to Mexico. We ate great food and stayed on a beautiful beach in a tiny, one-room hut, where we all slept in the same bed. I only want to be with them. . . . But I never relaxed. If there was ever going to be a "moment" for me, surely this was it? It felt much more like a midlife beginning than a resting point.

"BRING MY FLOWERS NOW"

Bring my flowers now, while I'm livin'
I won't need your love when I'm gone
Don't spend time, tears, or money on my old breathless body
If your heart is in them flowers, bring 'em on

All the miles cast a long shadow
I'd take a couple back if I could
I'd've learned to play guitar
Told my daddy more I loved him
But I believe, for the most part, I done good
There's always sunrise and rainbows and babies
And the little things I cherish on my way
Even though one day, they'll bury me and Jessie Ray
I just know we're gonna ride again someday

Bring my flowers now, while I'm livin'
I won't need your love when I'm gone
Don't spend time, tears, or money on my old breathless body

Well, if your heart is in them flowers, bring 'em on

The days are long but the years are lightning
They're bright and they will never strike again
I wish I'd been a better friend, a better daughter to my mother
There's no goin' back when your back's against the wind
So if you got love, then you're sittin' on a gold mine
And you can't take it with you when you go
So don't wait to help your sister
Forgive your brother and your neighbor
We all think we got the time until we don't

Bring my flowers now, while I'm livin'
I won't need your love when I'm gone
Don't spend time, tears, or money on my old breathless body
If your heart is in them flowers, bring 'em on
　　　—BRANDI CARLILE AND TANYA
　　　　TUCKER

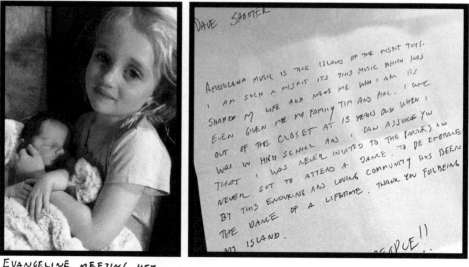

EVANGELINE MEETING HER
BIGGEST FAN

Dave Shooter

AMERICANA MUSIC IS THE ISLAND OF THE MISFIT TOYS.
I AM SUCH A MISFIT. ITS THIS MUSIC WHICH HAS
SHAPED MY LIFE AND MADE ME WHO I AM. ITS
EVEN GIVEN ME MY FAMILY TIM AND PHIL. I CAME
OUT OF THE CLOSET AT 15 YEARS OLD WHEN I
WAS IN HIGH SCHOOL AND I CAN ASSURE YOU
THAT I WAS NEVER INVITED TO THE PARTIES AND
NEVER GOT TO ATTEND A DANCE. TO BE EMBRACE
BY THIS ENDURING AND LOVING COMMUNITY HAS BEEN
THE DANCE OF A LIFETIME. THANK YOU FOR BEING
MY ISLAND.

PEOPLE!!

YOU'VE MADE IT WHEN YOU SELL OUT MSG.

ME, SHOOTER, CHRIS POWELL JR.
AND THE TWINS RIGHT AFTER
WINNING THREE GRAMMYS

FUCK IT... THEEEEEM

ME AND THE BOYS FEELING VERY PROUD

SOME KISSES ARE THEIR OWN REWARD

TANYA MOTHER TUCKER YALL

20.

. . . .

SONGS ARE LIKE TATTOOS

Things were different after the Grammys. More people recognized me, and my shows got bigger. I told myself I was gonna slow down, but I didn't. I was holding on for dear life. There's no telling when the ride's gonna stop and you'll have to go get back in line. It's the way it's supposed to be. Ebbs and flows; sometimes you're first and sometimes you're last. You meet the exact same people on the way up that you do on the way down, so be prepared for anyone to be your future boss. All these things are true.

The more adversity and resistance I encountered with Tanya Tucker and her tattered reputation, the more determined and protective I became. I was ready to put anything I had earned on the line for that woman and her album—and I did.

Amanda Shires (who is married to Jason Isbell) approached me backstage at a gig one night with a drink in her hand. "I wanna start a band with you called the Highwomen."

I thought I'd misheard her . . . "The Highwaymen?" I said.

"No, the Highwomen."

Which incidentally sounds exactly the same in a Texas accent.

I couldn't get the idea out of my head. I'd wanted to help assemble an all-female country/Americana supergroup for a while to address the disparity pertaining to women in the roots genre. The High-women was the PERFECT name. And Amanda Shires was the perfect bandmate to start with too: creative, spontaneous, brave, and outspoken. Like for most of the exciting concepts I'd been a part of up to that point, Dave Cobb had a hand in the plan and had sent Amanda to me for direction and support. I stalked her about it for quite a while before our tour buses wound up parked next to each other in a remote location. We both had sick kids and wound up in a "Tylenol share" situation.

Amanda flew out to my house in the winter and we spent a few days writing songs and talking about women we wanted to play music with. There were so many who inspired us. Maren Morris, Margo Price, Kacey Musgraves, Tanya Blount-Trotter, Cary Ann Hearst, Sheryl Crow, Maggie Rogers, Yola, Lori McKenna, Natalie Hemby, Gillian Welch, Andra Day, Janelle Monáe, on and on, and we talked to all of them. We got so much love and support for the idea that we knew at the end of the day, no matter who joined our band, we were all Highwomen.

The Newport Folk Festival was scheduled to happen in July. Newport is known for its historic superjams that go down right after the final act. . . . Newport is known for its "moments."

The moment Bob Dylan plugged in was at the 1965 Newport Folk Fest. The day Cash introduced Kris Kristofferson to the world was in 1970. In 1962, the freedom singers with Joan Baez led the congregants of the festival marching through the streets of Newport in protest during the civil rights movement, singing "We Shall Overcome." Newport's moments set the tone for so much of pop-culture history that it was astounding to think that the festival had never had an all-female headlining set. They accidentally had their share of all-male ones, I'm sure, and no one would have even noticed that. But

Newport's extremely passionate curator and booker, Jay Sweet, had given me a really important job the previous year after an honest conversation about women and live music. He asked me to put together a main-stage, all-female headlining show.

I'm not going to get too far down the road of describing that kind of pressure to you, but out of reverence alone, I will say that Judy Collins was given a *side stage* in 1967, and she booked some of the most iconic songwriters the world has ever known! She also managed to somehow introduce Joni Mitchel to Leonard Cohen mere minutes before Joni made her Newport debut that day.

I meditated on these Newport "moments" in the final days of summer until it landed on me one day like a piano dropped out of a second-story window.

What has Newport never had? DOLLY. Dolly Parton at Newport would be the moment of a lifetime. Who better to illustrate the feminine and its tenacity through the ages than Dolly? I started writing her letters in September, and I got a very kind and thoughtful "please don't ask me this again until closer to the time." I sent my second letter at Thanksgiving and my third at Christmas. I got the phone call from the Butterfly herself in early spring.

"Alright, I'm coming! Here's my song choices. Teach them to your band and get 'em right! '9 to 5,' 'Just Because I'm a Woman,' 'She's an Eagle,' 'Jolene,' and you and I will be singing 'I Will Always Love You,' which will be beautiful." All of the above in a measured, stern voice, followed by a giggle. "I'll see ya there if the creek don't rise!"

And with that, the first ever Newport Folk Festival's tribute to women was set to make history. "She's an Eagle with Brandi Carlile and Friends" was born.

All these projects were on a fast track and they were a FULL-time job. Newport was set to be the Highwomen's debut show on the Friday, and I had my all-female stage on Saturday night. As I dove head-on into Highwomen, Tanya Tucker, the Secret Sisters, and getting my Newport shows and Dolly's songs together, it became clear to Cath and the twins that I was definitely not planning to slow down.

To be honest, neither was Catherine, but her heart was in something else . . . she was worried. She was watching a fragile part of my artistry get buried in all the things I was going to *accomplish* in my "moment" and she never stopped thinking about Joni and her question to me: *"Are you in?"*

She was afraid that I would fall out of love with the most innocent part of my music. She sent me all Joni's old interviews and quotes . . . *I heard someone from the music business saying they are no longer looking for talent; they want people with a certain look and a willingness to cooperate. I thought, That's interesting, because I believe a total unwillingness to cooperate is what is necessary to be an artist—not for perverse reasons, but to protect your vision. The considerations of a corporation, especially now, have nothing to do with art or music. That's why I spend my time now painting.*

Joni's songs and quotes became a touchstone for me when I overpowered myself. A tether to my calmer, more unique and fragile self.

Catherine brought it up every day for weeks on end. I had decided to finally book the terrifying *Blue* show, and I was assembling the band. I needed to do something brave. I went to L.A. to scout the venue and get my bearings, when I ran into the Irish folk god that is Andrew Hozier in the lobby of my hotel. We ordered a drink and started to talk about Joni. I told Andrew about my invitation and asked him if he thought it was real. He told me that he'd sure as hell better be invited if it was. So, I started daydreaming.

The flight home the next day was delayed on the tarmac, so I decided to just buck up and reach out to Marcy, Joni's friend. I told her about the conversation I'd had with Hozier and asked if I was indeed invited to put together a little jam for Joni. Marcy gave me the green light and we started planning together. I called up Hozier and we set a date for May.

Our first Joni jam was kind of an otherworldly prank. . . . I guess we didn't know what to expect, but no one was prepared for what the evening would reveal. Joni always has the mischief in her eyes. We showed up—me, the twins, Hozier, and Catherine—with a giant orchid and a bottle of Champagne. Joni walked out to greet us and feed her koi fish. She looked strong and stunning in bright lipstick and a designer hat. Her friend "Chef Steph" had prepared Mexican food, and we sat around drinking Joni's favorite Pinot Grigio and asking her questions, all of which she politely answered like it was story time with a preschool class. She has the presence of a white cat. She could sort of take you or leave you . . . she's regal and sly. She must know, in a sense, that to be with her is its own reward. Compliments and pleasantries would stand out like a sore thumb.

We moved into Joni's living room, which is adorned with paintings and wooden instruments. She's proud of her house and it's one of a kind, custom in every way. She's hand-painted the beams and cabinets. To use the restroom, you have to push on a hidden wall panel that's actually a secret door she's painted cats on. There are orchids on every surface. A single Grammy seems to be the only sign of a proud rock star until you lean in and read that it was awarded to her only for the album artwork . . . that's when it finally makes sense. You would walk in and immediately know whose house it is . . . even without the self-portraits.

I sat down and asked permission to play one of her sacred Martins. She nodded and smiled. I mean . . . can you imagine JUST that? Just touching the guitar. Forget about where I'm sitting or the fact that she had just explained the lyrics to "This Flight."

I struggled so much with the concept of which song to play for Joni. . . . What will she think is a good song? Does it have to be complicated? Profound? Not too obviously derivative of her songs? I settled on "Cannonball" to exploit the twins' harmony and lean on them. It was an exhilarating three and a half minutes, but I felt proud of our song and relieved when Andrew started his. He played an old Irish folk song and it was absolutely breathtaking. Joni was sitting across from us in her chair smiling and sparkling when it suddenly became clear why . . .

Apropos of nothing, in walked Chaka Khan! Joni laughed as our jaws hit the floor, and that's when Herbie Hancock joined the party. The place exploded in laughter and shock as the songs got a whole lot groovier and the wine flowed. We tossed songs back and forth and tried not to implode while Herbie made the piano sound like a thousand people were playing it. At one point, Chaka took my wine while I was mid-conversation. "Bitch, you ain't drinking that thing," she said as she poured it into her own glass. Herbie Hancock was playing some jazzy diminished chord and the living room was alive with music and murmur when from out of nowhere came a quiet but confident singing voice that no one had heard in years . . . *"Summer-tiiiiiiiiiime, and the living is easy . . ."*

It was Joni Mitchell.

She had decided to open her mouth and sing for the first time since her aneurysm had left her silent on that very floor and unable to stand all those years prior. Joni Mitchell always has a plan. It was just time.

Joni sang all night that night.

From then until now, the Joni jams have never stopped. We've lost count of our special nights. No phones. Joni always says, "Park your pistols at the door." Our friend Reuben James has become one of Joni's favorite pianists. He flies all the way from London every time. He plays all her favorite songs to sing, while I try my best to harmonize, sitting on the floor next to Joni. She smiles and tilts the lyrics my way with a twinkle in her eye but teases me with the timing and chooses intentionally misleading notes that I'm simply too white to follow.

It's been low-key, humble, and lighthearted in every way. We've done at least one a month as Joni sings more and more: loud and clear with that famous vibrato and no sign of cigarettes or even an ego. She's the last living diamond.

The legends who pass through Joni's jams insist that they will never be the same.

NEWPORT HAPPENED IN July like a dream or a wedding . . . or a dream of a wedding. It was so idyllic that you'd swear it was already a part of folk history. The world was just ready for it. Women's voices absolutely dominated the sacred fort that year. The Highwomen's set was vulnerable and sweaty but a steady freight train. It was a relentless celebration that I'll never forget. Our dressing room was a bunkhouse with a painting of Joni on the wall.

On the day of She's an Eagle, I had myself believing 100 percent that Dolly would not show up. I was positive that it was all too good to be true. This is so irrational to anyone who knows Dolly, because she *always* shows up, and on time. To be honest, even if she hadn't, the show would have been so special. We had Sheryl Crow, Maren Morris, the Highwomen, Amy Ray, and Lucy Dacus singing the Indigo Girls' classic "Go." We had Judy Collins singing "Both Sides Now"; we had Linda Perry doing "What's Up?"; Sheryl Crow, Maggie Rogers, and Yola singing "Strong Enough to Be My Man" . . . There were more amazing women on that stage than I can list here. Linda Perry helped me with the Dolly set and the Highwomen learned all Dolly's background vocals.

Newport was completely in the dark. No one at the festival knew that Dolly Parton was coming . . . Maybe. When they brought Dolly onto the festival site, she was draped in a black canvas bag. She made her way through the muddy coastal grass with no part of her visible but impossibly high heels and long brightly colored fingernails. I was in her trailer when she took it off. "HI, honey!" she said. "How you doin'?!"

"I bit off more than I can chew!" I blurted out, fighting back nervous tears.

I'll never forget what happened next. She took my face in her hands and closed her eyes. "Alright, then . . . let's pray," she said.

When Dolly Parton prayed over me, I believed in God again. Every part of my soul came crashing to the earth like it was riding on lightning. I became connected to it again. I remembered that I was just a tiny part of that day and that little moment in time. Most important, that I was in fact responsible for none of it. Good, bad, or indifferent. The prayer is just between me and Dolly. But it was life-affirming and I like to think Dolly prays for all of us like that.

That day is indelible for women in music history. You can see it now everywhere, and I loved every terrifying second of it.

These endorphin rushes were leading to days of sleeping and big spiritual lulls that were becoming increasingly more addictive. I was about to take it too far.

AS THE *BLUE* show was approaching, I was hoping more and more that I'd be struck mute and unable to perform. The songs were HARD. *Blue* is seen as one of Joni's least complicated albums, and singing it still feels something like learning to breathe underwater. Her tendencies are so otherworldly and unnatural to a performer. She's an artist.

We had put the show up on sale and it sold out immediately. The guest list was instantly maxed and there were going to be lots of interesting famous Hollywood types in attendance. Everyone from Marilyn Manson to Kevin Bacon . . . Bonnie Raitt was coming, and to my utter disbelief so was Bernie Taupin. The idea that folks could see someone take a shot at *Blue* was obviously very popular . . . but so was the film *Faces of Death,* and it's for the same reason.

Of course, that was just in my head. There was so much support and affection for the show.

The moment that took the wind out of me, though, was when I got confirmation that Joni was coming.

Elton John had kept in touch with me all year and I really enjoyed hearing that loud and joyful voice burst through the phone. I now answered every time an unknown number would come through. I could be mid-song at sound check at Red Rocks and I'd be flailing around trying to silence the room: "SHHHHHH!!!!! It's 'Unknown,' it could be Elton John!!"

It had been more than twenty-five years since I read *Elton John* by Philip Norman, and I had preordered my copy of *Me* and was anxiously awaiting its arrival. Elton's first book in his own voice is a big deal. You gotta consider the fact that he simply does not "write"; he composes and communicates. But to read HIS personal thoughts on himself sent many an Elton John fan into a total frenzy.

For me, this frenzy peaked when I got an email explaining that Elton had chosen me to interview him in person about the book and that I would be getting my copy early. I had to simply read the book and come up with an interview full of questions and observations. A call from Elton followed shortly after: "What's your shoe size, darling? I'm on a mission."

Moment of silence for twelve-year-old Brandi . . . the Honky Cat.

Cath and I would be having lunch with Elton and David in Vancouver the following week at their vacation home and interviewing him the same day. What kind of questions would I ask? Would I go off-script? What would YOU ask your heroes? I LOVED that book. I had already started writing the one you're reading now, and I was so inspired by its candidness. It's a fearless, touching, and self-deprecating piece of work. The interview was easy.

Elton makes you feel like an old friend . . . some awkward little sister he can tease about fashion, and try to shock with delightfully inappropriate humor made all the more hilarious by his straight man (so to speak), the eye-rolling and seemingly mortified David Furnish, who clearly adores Elton and his sense of humor.

David is vividly intelligent. When they begin their comedy routine, you get the subtle sense that it's fine you're there . . . but that there's no one Elton likes to make laugh more than David. He ramps it up bit by bit while his husband, hand to forehead, exasperatedly asks everyone to "please not look at him or he'll keep doing it." It's real love.

We stayed for dinner that night too. Elton said something about the *Blue* show. He was the first person I invited obviously, but he had plans. He was tickled by the probability of my impending failure. "Is it all original keys, then?" he asked, looking over his glasses in evil delight. I nodded. "Yep! All OG keys and NO teleprompter. PLUS . . . *she's* coming."

Elton's eyes widened. "You crazy bitch," he said slowly. "Use the fucking teleprompter." He followed that up with a story about the pressure of singing different words to "Candle in the Wind" at his beloved Princess Diana's funeral. I was letting it all sink in.

"Fuck it," he said, as he picked up his iPad and started plunking his fingers violently at his calendar screen. "I had plans but I'm canceling them. I can't miss it. I'm coming too."

I should have been excited, and I was! But something was really bothering me. It had just gone from being a very big deal to WAY too much pressure, and I began to struggle psychologically. Something about this final straw was making the *Blue* show too much for me. It didn't feel like the present, it felt like the past crashing into my new station in life like a tsunami and I had just wandered out too far on the beach, fascinated by the receding water. I had lifted more than I could carry. I started to manifest sore throats and sickness before I knew what I was doing, and I reached out for help.

I never have known how to leave my childhood self at home. I don't have the heart to put her in the past. I want to protect her and keep her here in her wonderful future *and my* present, but she gets freaked out too easily for this job. I have a family to support now, and at some point I need to start believing that I belong here.

I have been "getting sick" to drop out of hard things since I was a baby. Sick to keep from being scared, to keep from finishing school, to end scary tours, to prioritize my mental health, and I would even get sick to get out of something spectacular, something I wanted more than anything in the world. Sickness and my "specialness" go hand in hand. That's an early pattern that's been there since my near death and rebirth.

I was writing this very book during this time, and let me tell you that it was NOT helping me circumvent any drama. My whole life was flashing before my eyes on a daily basis.

I trained for the show like it was a marathon. I didn't drink alcohol. I worked my voice out with RAab on the daily. Emotionally, the twins were NO help. Neither was Cath. No one was. They were all just excited. The closest thing anyone said to the profound was Evangeline, as usual.

"What's wrong, Mom? Why am I supposed to leave you alone?"

"Nothing, bud. Momma's just very nervous about my *Blue* show."

"But why? You really want to do it, don't you?"

It really is supposed to be that simple.

The woman I called for help a second time specializes in language and hypnosis. She told me to stop writing this book. She told me to imagine a glass vase filled with blue marbles and to put all my sickness and fear into a single green marble. Then she told me to push that green marble all the way down into the middle of that vase and asked me if I could still see it. I couldn't.

It was the day before *Blue*. I was lying in bed on the phone with her and I had tears streaming down my face. I just knew my throat was closing and that I would wake up the next day unable to sing. I imagined all the phone calls I would make apologizing, the emails and flowers I would send in my stead . . . but there were so many blue marbles *and only one tiny green one*. It didn't have the power to even be seen in all that blue. Surely, I could overcome it. I knew I could, but only if I had a talk with eleven-year-old Brandi.

It went something like this:

"Just because Elton John is going to see you sing doesn't mean you can bring our childhood to this show, you crazy little lesbian. I know you wanna come and I want you there, but please stay in your fucking seat and let me do my job. . . . We'll freak out later."

I woke up feeling like a million bucks. I'm not saying I wasn't nervous, 'cause I was. I was very quiet. Everyone around me was treating me like an origami bird, and I took advantage of the space. Bella Freud had made me a gorgeous custom royal-blue suit. I was in blue head to toe, even my socks.

We set up a dressing room for Joni. Orchids and Pinot Grigio. She showed up in a floor-length dress and looked every bit the legend. She glided down a long hallway and silenced every person she passed with the confidence she exuded that night. Danny Clinch was there to photograph the moment. Elton and David turned up in Gucci. Carey was even there! From the Mermaid Café! Carey, get out your cane! We were all buzzing with the promise of a crazy night and sticking glittery blue stars on our faces. None of it was lost on me as I ran around waiting on everyone in my blue socks. I was pouring their wine and taking photos like it was someone else that was about to do what I was just about to do.

I made one last stop by Joni's room before I made my way to the stage.

"Please don't tell me where you're sitting," I said.

"Don't be silly," she replied dryly.

"One more thing . . . 'when I think of your kisses, my mind sees stars'? Is that the lyric?" I asked.

" 'My mind seesaws' . . . it seesaws," she said with a wink, and she walked away, leaving me in her room alone.

I sauntered onto the stage determined to just be there and feel every second of this miracle. I had a head full of blue marbles and a brand-new suit; nothing was going to shake me.

"*I am on a lonely road and I am travelling, travelling, travelling . . .*" that's about how far I got before I saw the whiteness of Joni's teeth in the darkened auditorium. Sitting right next to and holding hands with Elton John.

When my life flashes before my eyes, I'll see all of that.

I loved it. It was one of the greatest nights of my life.

The next night, we went to Joni's. Bonnie Raitt came too. We ate hot dogs and laughed about the night before. Joni carefully handed out a few compliments and told me in her way that I had honored her. Just after dinner, Elton turned up and brought me a diamond ring in the shape of one of the little glittery stars from the night before. It's the only ring I own besides my wedding ring—and I prefer it!

I sang Grandpa Vernon's songs while Elton played piano. We all sang along to "Tiny Dancer," and Elton and David did their comedy routine.

The single most profound musical moment of my whole life came in an instant as the night crash-landed in a beautiful heap . . . picture this:

I'm sitting on the floor, leaning back against Joni's knees, her hand on my shoulder. I'm holding Cath's hand. The twins and wives, our whole little family is piled onto Joni's couch with David and Marcy. Bonnie is sitting across from me, draped across her guitar, riveted because Elton has just sat down looking a bit serious behind the piano and asked if he could please play a song for Joni. He told her that he was so proud of her recovery and lamented that "things like this don't happen anymore." He was right. They don't. No one kept it together as he played the iconic intro to "Your Song." Some people cried, but not me and not Joni. We couldn't wipe the smiles off our faces.

I DON'T KNOW who I am as an artist after this album and after Joni, but I know I'm not Joni Mitchell. *"I'm a country station, I'm a little bit corny"* doesn't ring true to me anymore either, though. I'll never stop trying to write a song that impresses her.

Good fucking luck.

The best part of all this is that I remain my ordinary self in this dream. It's lucid and I'm observing all of it. I haven't changed. Writing these memories down has shown me that. The upside of impostor syndrome is that you're always aware of how surreal these gifts are. I never expect it, so I'm actually incapable of taking it for granted.

Maybe we all just want to be immortal. To leave imprints and art and moments and words. To forgive and be forgiven. I hope I can.

You don't have to be famous to be a hero. Anyone can do that.

I will never *be* my heroes, but I'll always have them.

"YOUR SONG"

It's a little bit funny, this feeling
inside
I'm not one of those who can
easily hide
I don't have much money, but boy,
if I did
I'd buy a big house where we both
could live

If I was a sculptor, but then again,
no
Or a man who makes potions in a
travelin' show
Oh, I know it's not much, but it's
the best I can do
My gift is my song and this one's
for you

And you can tell everybody this is
your song
It may be quite simple but now
that it's done
I hope you don't mind
I hope you don't mind
That I put down in words
How wonderful life is while you're
in the world

I sat on the roof and kicked off the
moss
Well, a few of the verses, well,
they've got me quite cross
But the sun's been quite kind
while I wrote this song
It's for people like you that keep it
turned on

So excuse me forgetting, but
these things I do
You see, I've forgotten if they're
green or they're blue
Anyway, the thing is, what I really
mean
Yours are the sweetest eyes I've
ever seen

And you can tell everybody this is
your song
It may be quite simple but now
that it's done
I hope you don't mind
I hope you don't mind
That I put down in words
How wonderful life is while you're
in the world
     —ELTON JOHN AND BERNIE
        TAUPIN

"BLUE"

Songs are like tattoos
You know I've been to sea before
Crown and anchor me
Or let me sail away
Hey Blue
And there is a song for you
Ink on a pin
Underneath the skin
An empty space to fill in
Well there're so many sinking
Now you've got to keep thinking
You can make it thru these waves
Acid, booze, and ass
Needles, guns, and grass

Lots of laughs
Lots of laughs
Everybody's saying that hell's the
hippest way to go well
I don't think so, but I'm
Gonna take a look around it
though Blue
I love you
Blue
Here is a shell for you
Inside you'll hear a sigh
A foggy lullaby
There is your song from me
     —JONI MITCHELL

EAR TO EAR NEXT TO THE
BEST WE'VE EVER HAD.
THE CAPTAIN AND THE KID.

FACE TO FACE WITH THE CAPTAIN.
THE BAND IS ON STAGE WAITING FOR
ME TO TAKE THE FINAL BOW... BUT
I'M NOT IN A HURRY.

"WHEN I THINK OF YOUR KISSES MY MIND SEESAWS"
JUST BEFORE GETTING DRESSED. ONE FOR GOOD LUCK.

LISTENING TO JONI. ALWAYS REMEMBERING. LIFE IS CRAZY BEAUTIFUL
ALWAYS GRATEFUL.

BONNIE RAITT MAKING ME TAKE A COMPLIMENT.
MY ADMIRATION FOR HER RUNS SO DEEP THAT I
CAN HARDLY LOOK HER IN THE EYE...
CLEARLY SHE WASN'T HAVING IT.

WHEN JONI WRITES
"APPROVED" WHAT ELSE IS
THERE TO SAY? WHATS
LEFT?

21.

· · · · · · · · · ·

STARDUST AND THE CONTINUUM

Sometimes in these latter days I wish it had all ended there. In Joni's living room with my family and my heroes. Like that's the moment a meteor hits the earth and milliseconds later we're stardust. Sometimes I think I'm living through the most powerful and spiritual awakening in human history. I don't know yet . . . By the time you are reading these words you will know much more than I do now.

When I started this journey, I was on such an emotional high. Running a victory lap to top all victory laps. I won five Grammys; Tanya won Country Album of the Year; the Highwomen came out swinging; I sold out the Gorge and Madison Square Garden . . . shit was getting crazier and crazier. I wasn't slowing down.

I was in Florida when I first heard about Covid-19. I played a show one night and the next night I came out onstage and half the auditorium was empty.

My adopted city of Nashville had just been hit with a horrible tornado and the plan was to stop on the way home and help all our friends raise money for the community to rebuild their homes and businesses. By the time the plane touched down the information was everywhere.

I arrived backstage and saw my friends Jason, Sheryl, Asha, Hemby, Yola, and on and on. We were all so scared. We started talking about whether we should hug or not. We decided almost unanimously to just do it, worried that it might be the last time any of us would embrace one another for a while. I was leaned up against a bathroom-stall door anxiously discussing Australia with Yola. We were embarking on a tour there together in just a couple short weeks when I got a text saying that Pearl Jam had just canceled their world tour. That's when I knew.

Imagine you're watching a movie about a group of friends and fuck-up musicians, like in, say, *Almost Famous*. Then in some strange twist in plot they're all suddenly ripped apart after all they've been through and given new marching orders. No more planes, or shows, no buses, dressing rooms, stages or studios, or any type of collaboration in real life. No more audience, no applause or laughter. No more work. No more dream. Effective immediately and until further notice.

That's not the way it happened, because it would have been too painful to realize it all at once like that . . . but that's how it turned out.

Quite a few people caught the virus that night. We had come to that club from all over the world.

When we lost John Prine to Covid, it seemed too much to bear. It was too high a price to pay. That we couldn't be together and be with Fiona made our grief all the more real. Many of us would have released it onstage, where we could have celebrated him and told stories and jokes . . . all the things he taught us to do. But we couldn't. I just tried to stay up past my kids so that I could cry and sing into my phone. We will celebrate him again soon. He's still with us because so much of what makes us songwriters came from him.

It all settled into reality slowly for me. There was mercy in that. Then after the mercy there was hope and clarity.

ONE OF THE things I realized right away was that the veil of fame and celebrity would be righteously lifted. As a person too new to any kind of mainstream exposure to have seen any of the real-life effects of it, I suddenly and completely recognized the problem.

What many of us really are is a subculture. Sure, there exists the lifestyle of the glorious elite and their fabulous wealth, the lines they don't have to wait in and the bills they don't have to pay . . . but that really describes so few of my peers that I was able to understand how effective and destructive the fantasy of stardom can be. It's easy to sell too! When an artist is getting their picture taken, they are almost always wearing things they will immediately have to give back the second the lens cap is on. Some stylist will be holding the horrendous outfit you showed up in out to you for its retrieval like it's radioactive. You get into the backseat of a car that some label is paying for and then charging you back in some other hidden way. The artist is branded by the dream and its marketability . . . but what happens if that machine breaks down?

Suddenly you're out of work, back in your ill-fitting jeans, and no one's worried about you because they believe your address is Beverly Hills 90210. *But it's not.* Most of us are pretty normal, flawed people digging our own drainage ditches and remembering to keep jumper cables in the car in case we leave the lights on. It's not even about money, 'cause even when we have it, we don't know for how long or what to do with it. God forbid you're a woman and you wind up like a football player in forced retirement at thirty-five but with a sliver of the income. Musicians are rarely as "buttoned-up" or as glamorous as our industry would like you to believe.

Touring was the only way for an artist to earn a living, and that was already very expensive and burdened by corporate co-opting.

It went away in an instant.

The moment the shows ended, many of us flocked to the internet and started streaming our performances for free. Everyone was worried about the real-life emotional impact that isolation would have on us and society as a whole. We had been with "the people" for years. Not behind a desk but laughing and singing with them. When the world locked down, the artists I love recognized the collective despair . . . they began to serve the people. We knew we were gonna have to figure something out financially at some point, but music first— everything else later. So many of my friends realized they were alone without their audience at that point. I realized it. Clothes got real casual, people started seeing our living rooms and the dog hair on our couches, every multibazillion-dollar music industry–affiliated entity started trying to get the artists to engage for free . . . but it wasn't necessary this time. It's simpler to do it ourselves. They haven't found a way to get between the artist and the people yet in the age of a global pandemic.

It's a silver lining. I'm not even sure I like the word "fan" anymore, but something is reemerging in the relationship between an artist and a fan . . . for some reason I want to point that out . . . I can't know how it ends.

I will learn to be comfortable with the continuum.

Everyone will remember where they were when George Floyd was killed. I was in the garden taking a break and scrolling on Instagram. It was so repulsive and so many of us had so much passion bottled up from the quarantine that I knew America was about to receive a reckoning. From Emmett Till to MLK to Rodney King to Elijah McClain to Breonna Taylor to George Floyd . . . and So. Many. More. A spiritual awakening and a shift were beginning to take place in the absence of our mobility . . . our never-ending stamina for consumption. In the hours following news of his murder and the subsequent protests I remembered something important that I learned a few years ago.

In 2016, I was on a plane that was touching down in Seattle when I got a call from our governor and his wife. People were protesting in airports all over the country. Trump had just implemented his famed "Muslim ban" and was blocking entry and sending back mostly non-white people and families from an extensive list of countries that predominantly practiced Islam. It was an emergency. The governor was redirecting protesters to the city center for a peaceful rally where he would speak, and he was inquiring whether I'd like to sing. I was with the twins and our sound guy Alex; also I had guitars! So I immediately said we'd be there. I decided to play "The Times They Are A-Changin'" by Bob Dylan. By the time we got downtown, thousands of people were there. We dragged our suitcases and guitars through the airtight crowd and made our way to the stage. I still don't know how we did it. It was a hastily built platform with a barely operational tiny PA, and I was having my doubts, but I spotted the governor and his wife crammed into the wings and made my way up next to him. He whispered something to one of the organizers and pointed me out. The woman made eye contact with me and slowly nodded. She was wearing a hijab, along with almost all the other women on the stage. I don't remember seeing any men or white people other than the governor and his wife and the twins. When he spoke it was almost inaudible. I was worried because, due to the lack of space, my head was basically against the small plastic speaker atop a flimsy stand. It became clear that this particular plastic speaker (one of only two) wasn't even on.

If you're not cringing at this point in the story, just picture me squeezed onto a mostly melanated, largely marginalized community's stage . . . in my cowboy hat holding an acoustic guitar . . . next to my white twin brothers and waiting to play a Bob Dylan song.

To do this I would have to step in front of a line of ALL Islamic immigrant activists and address a rightfully angry crowd of largely the same people. What does Dylan have to do with any of that? Fuck if I know.

At this point more than an hour had gone by. The sideways glances I was getting from the speakers on the stage waiting to speak were starting to sink in. I will never really understand why no one told me to fuck off. Things were getting tense. The PA had a broken speaker and so much of the value in what these women were saying was lost in the hissing and popping the remaining one would emit. All the powerful moments came from someone giving up and just starting a chant.

I sing. I didn't know how else to help. I was waking up to the fact that the only thing I felt I had to offer wasn't a solution at all. . . . And that's when I remembered that we had brought our sound guy.

We put down our guitar cases and went to work untangling wires and plugging in/unplugging microphones to identify shorts in faulty cables while Alex worked on the dinner-plate-sized mixer to EQ for people speaking and leading the movement. It felt better than singing because the glory came from quite literally amplifying the human beings who were actually affected by this atrocity.

It's the new way. We all will learn this lesson one way or the other. I pray for your sake that you don't learn it on a stage, but that's where I learn most things.

We didn't "save the day" or "fix the protest" but we didn't cover Dylan either. We fixed the broken speaker and made things a little clearer and we went home having learned a really important lesson.

People in this country who are in positions of privilege must learn to find ways of fighting for the just treatment of others not by centering and platforming themselves but by holding up the ones who are suffering. It's not about shame or repentance, it's about understanding that Dr. King still gets the bullhorn while many of us must organize, galvanize voters, peacefully protest, teach our children, plead with our parents, pray, resist, and *amplify*.

I'm not ashamed that I went to the city to sing and found myself on my knees untangling the cables. I'm proud of that. Mostly I'm just grateful I got to listen. Are there cables in your life that you might be able to untangle for someone? Are you waiting to sing but still learning to listen? Me too.

The protests are still happening. Everywhere. I pray they don't stop. I want this to be THE moment. I want to see it in my lifetime and for my kids to grow up knowing the innate worth that can still define all of us. I wish I could tell you how it ends . . .

But I have to get comfortable with the continuum.

In the days following the great transition, I've built a garden and revived a broken-down greenhouse here on the property. I built the garden out of stacked stone because it retains heat at nighttime, and we have a short cold growing season here in the Northwest. For the first few months the local nursery owner would let me come in before she opened and pick out my starts and seeds.

I live with the twins and all our kids. Josh is married to Cath's sister now and she's pregnant with a little girl. We are beyond lucky to have one another. Soon to be seven kids and a handful of dogs. My ex Kim lives here too (so lesbian). We ride four-wheelers to each other's homes and share a tractor. We have cocktails in the woods around happy hour every couple of days just to talk about what's in the news and get some of the fear off our chests. We bought a few cameras and integrated our longtime sound engineer into our pod so that we can film a little variety show in my barn to keep paying the salaries of our crew and keep some income flowing into our group.

Jay lives in eastern Washington in a tiny town where he used to hunt with Dad when he was a little boy. Mom and Dad had to move out there with him because things are getting a little bit tough on our side of the mountains for people like my parents. It's not just the lifestyle but the pace of things and the intensity that seems to conjure their demons. This all used to be rural farmland and untouched redwoods. It was the country out here . . . now it's just the country for people who can afford it.

We all get together when we can and play our music and drink Mom's radioactive filthy margaritas. Jay and his kids started a bluegrass band, and Jay has finally found his way into being an artist. One where he doesn't have to learn his lessons on a stage, but he speaks the language fluently. He's started writing songs looking hard at forty, and they are unbelievable. It's like he never missed a decade. His kids are fearless. My girls worship them.

The election hasn't happened yet. You're in the future, so you know. *I'm not yet comfortable with this part of the continuum.*

I WILL MAKE my next album in the fall, which is upon me.

The first time I sat down at a piano I wrote these words:

"You've got a beautiful mind, and the soul of a coyote. Hunger driving you mad, throwing good after bad."

To sit alone with my mind is dangerous company sometimes. Being judgmental is hard work!

I know I'm not alone in that. So many of us feel that way. That the wanting and searching is sometimes so never-ending that we often seize our spiritual gifts of empathy, or art, or communication and employ them in ways that don't serve the soul. Yours or mine.

I need more walks with Evangeline and Jesus. Less Twitter . . . maybe another broken horse will find me?

In the adrenal void, the bottomless crater left by my ability to perform live music, I found an opportunity for me to do something new and big with my life. I went online and took a boat captain's test and I bought that damn fishing boat. The KingFisher 3025 aluminum boat of my fishing dreams that I thought was another decade or so away. My wife nearly ended me for making a big purchase the instant our natural ability to earn an income evaporated. . . . So I financed it and assured her that if things didn't correct themselves in a year, they can come and get the son of a bitch and at least we will have had some fun!

Since we've had the boat, Catherine and our little girls and I spend a lot of time camping up on the Canadian border in the northern part of the San Juan Islands. We catch greenlings and crabs, spot prawns, and we all sleep in the same V-berth bed. We've gotten used to it. I've never been more intimately connected to my family and now I'll always need it to be this way.

Sometimes we cram the whole compound onto the boat and head out to Whidbey Island where we wrote *By the Way, I Forgive You*. Tim gets seasick, the kids get their ice cream, and we get to feel the energy of a tour bus. It's the non-potable water, the swaying, the annoyance mixed with affection, it's the junk food and the weird tiny toilet. . . . But mostly it's the close quarters. The not-aloneness that we always needed the most.

We want the music and the people back. We know it will happen, but we don't know when. One thing I do know though is that WHEN we get back onstage again, whether it's Red Rocks or the Crocodile Café, we will know exactly who we really are for the first time and you will know who you are as well. Stardust without the meteor.

Surely this is the beginning of the next level of consciousness.

I will learn to accept the continuum,

Until we meet again.

Xobc

CATH TOOK THIS PHOTO OF ME AND THE GIRLS
IN THE SAN JUANS. THIS WAS IN MAY.
TRAFFIC OF ANY KIND WAS SIMPLY NON-EXISTENT
FOR THIS REASON WE COULD SEE FOR MILES AND MILES.

FISHING FOR LING COD WITH
THE GIRLS

ME AND MY PERFECTLY NAMED BOAT

ACKNOWLEDGMENTS

I t's strange to write a memoir-ish book when one is approaching forty years old. I've never been one to let the truth get in the way of a good story! But this time it's different. Most everyone mentioned within these pages is alive and they will have opinions . . . feelings and more. Young memoirs need to be as honest as possible for the author to survive them. It's an all-consuming responsibility to tell the truth and hold very little back. I have to face my characters every day and I am willing to walk that wire and find this balance.

I dropped out of school pretty young and I wasn't exactly an honor student while I was there. I've had to overcome some massive literacy issues and moderate dyslexia to accomplish this goal. I think I will finally stop having nightmares of being back in that classroom in my thirties and still failing. With these words I have healed deep wounds and feelings of inadequacy within myself. If you get this far . . . if you're still reading this: Write your life. No matter how young or old. Even if you feel like you're not interesting enough. Do it. Believe me you are. Your life is in fact twisted and beautiful and you'll find that as you peel back the layers, the unexpected side effect is that it feels wonderful to be known.

Even if it's just by you.

I used to believe that writing a book would be a near-impossible feat. You do it once in your life and it takes up the whole damn thing. This would be true if not for the following people who helped me do it.

Catherine Carlile, my shepherd, who never once laughed at my chicken scratch and became my constantly opened thesaurus. You've taught me to see every person as a child through the eyes of a child. You are grace. I don't think I ever even knew the woman in this story until you did.

"Fishing is the pursuit of what is elusive but attainable. A perpetual series of occasions for hope."—John Buchan

Next we write YOUR story, Trinset.

Lauren Munselle, my assistant and friend, who probably finally met me through this book while systematically teaching me how to use an actual computer and verbally editing with me for hours into days. Thank you for not giving up on me.

My dad, JR, for pointing me in the abstract direction of Jesus and for his insistence that I become articulate and honest above every other virtue. You are the ever-present standard.

Evangeline, my indigo child, for naming this story.

You in all your seriousness and soulfulness have piqued my curiosity, earned my respect and my semi-aggressive and uncontrollable affection. When you speak, I will listen.

Elijah for bringing our family into the laughter, drama, and joy we all needed. Why can't I tell you "no"? Thank God for you! Now we know how to have fun.

Glennon Doyle, for deep-diving into the life of someone she barely knew and being willing to shine her ever-present light. You and Abby are the forever kind of friends . . . even in a global pandemic I can feel that. We will fish.

My editor, Gillian Blake, for truly seeing me and amplifying my awkward voice above all things proper. I will continue to call you with thoughts and ideas long after this book has collected its dust on the shelf.

My agent David for understanding me through the twisted root of our shared queer experience.

My beloved Elton for his guidance and humor. With respect to the only advice I've gotten from you and not taken: although I never did end up naming the book "Rug Muncher," I do appreciate you screaming it down the phone to me on several occasions.

Joni. I'll never know where to start. In your quiet wisdom you made me loud enough to drown out all other voices and pointed me toward the artist inside me. It's never just music. You are a lonely painter, and I now know that I am a lonely writer.

The twins. The right and the left. The guardians of the story.

All of the songwriters who freely gave me permission to print their life-altering words.

My loved ones . . . especially my Carlile family; Mom, Tiff, and Jay, who live this life latched to my soul and who gave me their blessing, allowing me to use their names to tell my side of this story.

Thank you forever.

Xobc

PERMISSIONS

CHAPTER 2

"Stand By Me" by Ben E. King, written by Ben E. King, Jerry Leiber, and Mike Stoller

   ©1961 Sony/ATV Music Publishing LLC.

   All rights administered by Sony/ATV Music Publishing LLC, 424 Church Street, Suite 1200, Nashville, TN 37219.

   All rights reserved. Used by permission.

CHAPTER 3

"I Don't Hurt Anymore" by Hank Snow, written by Jack Rollins and Don Robertson

   Words and Music by JACK ROLLINS and DON ROBERTSON

   Copyright © 1953 (Renewed) CHAPPELL & CO., INC.

   All Rights Reserved.

   Used By Permission of ALFRED MUSIC.

CHAPTER 4

"Fancy"by Reba McEntire
Words and Music by Bobbie Gentry
Copyright © 1969 Northridge Music Company
Copyright Renewed
All Rights in the United States and Canada Controlled and Adminis-
tered by Spirit Two Music, Inc.
All Rights Reserved. Used by Permission.
Reprinted by permission of Hal Leonard LLC.

"Ride On Out" By Brandi Carlile
Written by Brandi Marie Carlile
© Songs Of Universal, Inc. on behalf of Itself and Music of Southern
Oracle (BMI)
All Rights Reserved
Used by Permission of Universal Music Publishing.

"Jose Cuervo" by Shelly West, written by Cindy Jordan
Words and Music by Cindy Jordan
© Universal Music Corp. (ASCAP) All rights reserved. Used by Per-
mission of Universal Music Publishing.
Copyright © 1981 EMI/EASY LISTENING MUSIC CORP. and
UNIVERSAL-MCA MUSIC PUBLISHING
Exclusive Print Rights on behalf of EMI/EASY LISTENING MUSIC
CORP.
Controlled and Administered by ALFRED MUSIC
All Rights Reserved
Used By Permission of ALFRED MUSIC

"Tennessee Flat Top Box" by Johnny Cash
Words and Music by JOHNNY R. CASH
Copyright © 1961 (Renewed) CHAPPELL & CO., INC.
All Rights Reserved
Used By Permission of ALFRED MUSIC

"Coat of Many Colors" by Dolly Parton
© 1971 Velvet Apple Music. All rights administered by Sony/ATV
Music Publishing LLC, 424 Church Street, Suite 1200, Nashville,
Tennessee 37219. All rights reserved. Used by permission.

CHAPTER 5

"Honky Cat" by Elton John and Bernie Taupin
Written by Elton John and Bernard Taupin
Performed by Elton John
© Universal Songs Of PolyGram Int., Inc. on behalf of Universal/
Dick James Music Ltd. (BMI).
All rights reserved.
Used by permission.

"Skyline Pigeon" by Elton John and Bernie Taupin
Written by Elton John and Bernard Taupin
Performed by Elton John
© Universal Songs Of PolyGram Int., Inc. on behalf of Universal/
Dick James Music Ltd. (BMI).
All rights reserved.
Used by permission.

CHAPTER 6

"Philadelphia" by Neil Young
Words and Music by Neil Young
Copyright © 1993 by Silver Fiddle Music
All Rights Reserved. Reprinted by Permissionof Hal Leonard LLC.

"I Don't Want To Talk About It" written by Danny Whitten, performed
by the Indigo Girls
"I Don't Want To Talk About It" by Danny Whitten, Used with Permission Crazy Horse Music 1972

"Happy" by Brandi Carlile
Written by Brandi Marie Carlile, Phillip John Hanseroth, Timothy Jay
Hanseroth © Universal Music Corp. on behalf of itself and Southern
Oracle Music, LLC (ASCAP) All Rights Reserved. Used by Permission
of Universal Music Publishing.

CHAPTER 7

"That Year" by Brandi Carlile
Written by Brandi Marie Carlile, Phillip John Hanseroth, Timothy Jay
Hanseroth © Universal Music Corp. on behalf of itself and Southern
Oracle Music, LLC (ASCAP) All Rights Reserved. Used by Permission
of Universal Music Publishing.

"Fare Thee Well" by Indigo Girls
Written by Emily Ann Saliers and Amy Elizabeth Ray
Performed by Indigo Girls
© Songs Of Universal, Inc. on behalf of Godhap Music. All rights reserved. Used by Permission.

CHAPTER 8

"Hallelujah" by Leonard Cohen
Collected in STRANGER MUSIC: Selected Poems and Songs. Copyright © 1993 by Leonard Cohen and Leonard Cohen Stranger Music, Inc., used by permission of The Wylie Agency LLC.

"Eye of the Needle" by Brandi Carlile
Written by Brandi Marie Carlile, Phillip John Hanseroth, Timothy Jay Hanseroth © Universal Music Corp. on behalf of itself and Southern Oracle Music, LLC (ASCAP) All Rights Reserved. Used by Permission of Universal Music Publishing.

"In My Own Eyes" by Brandi Carlile
Written by Brandi Marie Carlile, Phillip John Hanseroth, Timothy Jay Hanseroth © Universal Music Corp. on behalf of itself and Southern Oracle Music, LLC (ASCAP) All Rights Reserved. Used by Permission of Universal Music Publishing.

CHAPTER 9

"Turpentine" by Brandi Carlile
Written by Brandi Marie Carlile, Phillip John Hanseroth, Timothy Jay Hanseroth © Universal Music Corp. on behalf of itself and Southern Oracle Music, LLC (ASCAP) All Rights Reserved. Used by Permission of Universal Music Publishing.

"My Song" by Brandi Carlile
Written by Brandi Marie Carlile, Phillip John Hanseroth, Timothy Jay Hanseroth © Universal Music Corp. on behalf of itself and Southern Oracle Music, LLC (ASCAP) All Rights Reserved. Used by Permission of Universal Music Publishing.

"Wasted" by Brandi Carlile
Written by Brandi Marie Carlile, Phillip John Hanseroth, Timothy Jay Hanseroth © Universal Music Corp. on behalf of itself and Southern

Oracle Music, LLC (ASCAP) All Rights Reserved. Used by Permission of Universal Music Publishing.

"Heart's Content" by Brandi Carlile
Written by Brandi Marie Carlile, Phillip John Hanseroth, Timothy Jay Hanseroth © Universal Music Corp. on behalf of itself and Southern Oracle Music, LLC (ASCAP) All Rights Reserved. Used by Permission of Universal Music Publishing.

CHAPTER 10
"The Story" by Brandi Carlile
Written by Brandi Marie Carlile, Phillip John Hanseroth, Timothy Jay Hanseroth © Universal Music Corp. on behalf of itself and Southern Oracle Music, LLC (ASCAP) All Rights Reserved. Used by Permission of Universal Music Publishing.

"Follow" by Brandi Carlile
Written by Brandi Marie Carlile, Phillip John Hanseroth, Timothy Jay Hanseroth © Universal Music Corp. on behalf of itself and Southern Oracle Music, LLC (ASCAP) All Rights Reserved. Used by Permission of Universal Music Publishing.

"Fall Apart Again" by Brandi Carlile
Written by Brandi Marie Carlile, Phillip John Hanseroth, Timothy Jay Hanseroth © Universal Music Corp. on behalf of itself and Southern Oracle Music, LLC (ASCAP) All Rights Reserved. Used by Permission of Universal Music Publishing.

"Psycho Bitch" by Phil and Tim Hanseroth
Written by Phillip John Hanseroth and Timothy Jay Hanseroth © Songs Of Universal, Inc. on behalf of Itself and Music of Southern Oracle (BMI) All Rights Reserved. Used by Permission of Universal Music Publishing.

CHAPTER 11
"Have You Ever" by Brandi Carlile
Written by Brandi Marie Carlile, Phillip John Hanseroth, Timothy Jay Hanseroth © Universal Music Corp. on behalf of itself and Southern Oracle Music, LLC (ASCAP) All Rights Reserved. Used by Permission of Universal Music Publishing.

"Shadow on the Wall" by Brandi Carlile
Written by Brandi Marie Carlile, Phillip John Hanseroth, Timothy Jay
Hanseroth © Universal Music Corp. on behalf of itself and Southern
Oracle Music, LLC (ASCAP) All Rights Reserved. Used by Permission
of Universal Music Publishing.

"Closer to You" by Brandi Carlile
Written by Brandi Marie Carlile, Phillip John Hanseroth, Timothy Jay
Hanseroth © Universal Music Corp. on behalf of itself and Southern
Oracle Music, LLC (ASCAP) All Rights Reserved. Used by Permission
of Universal Music Publishing.

CHAPTER 12

"Josephine" by Brandi Carlile
Written by Brandi Marie Carlile, Phillip John Hanseroth, Timothy Jay
Hanseroth © Universal Music Corp. on behalf of itself and Southern
Oracle Music, LLC (ASCAP) All Rights Reserved. Used by Permission
of Universal Music Publishing.

"Sugartooth" by Brandi Carlile
Written by Brandi Marie Carlile, Phillip John Hanseroth, Timothy Jay
Hanseroth © Universal Music Corp. on behalf of itself and Southern
Oracle Music, LLC (ASCAP) All Rights Reserved. Used by Permission
of Universal Music Publishing.

"Looking Out" by Brandi Carlile
Written by Brandi Marie Carlile, Phillip John Hanseroth, Timothy Jay
Hanseroth © Universal Music Corp. on behalf of itself and Southern
Oracle Music, LLC (ASCAP) All Rights Reserved. Used by Permission
of Universal Music Publishing.

CHAPTER 13

"Beginning to Feel the Years" by Brandi Carlile
Written by Brandi Marie Carlile, Phillip John Hanseroth, Timothy Jay
Hanseroth © Universal Music Corp. on behalf of itself and Southern
Oracle Music, LLC (ASCAP) All Rights Reserved. Used by Permission
of Universal Music Publishing.

"Anytime" by Happy Lawson
  Words and Music by HAPPY LAWSON
  Copyright © 1921 (Renewed) UNICHAPPELL MUSIC, INC.
  All Rights Reserved.
  Used By Permission of ALFRED MUSIC.

"I Will" by Brandi Carlile
  Written by Brandi Marie Carlile, Phillip John Hanseroth, Timothy Jay
  Hanseroth © Universal Music Corp. on behalf of itself and Southern
  Oracle Music, LLC (ASCAP) All Rights Reserved. Used by Permission
  of Universal Music Publishing.

"Love Songs" by Brandi Carlile
  Written by Brandi Marie Carlile, Phillip John Hanseroth, Timothy Jay
  Hanseroth © Universal Music Corp. on behalf of itself and Southern
  Oracle Music, LLC (ASCAP) All Rights Reserved. Used by Permission
  of Universal Music Publishing.

"Caroline" by Brandi Carlile
  Written by Brandi Marie Carlile, Phillip John Hanseroth, Timothy Jay
  Hanseroth © Universal Music Corp. on behalf of itself and Southern
  Oracle Music, LLC (ASCAP) All Rights Reserved. Used by Permission
  of Universal Music Publishing.

CHAPTER 14
"I Belong to You" by Brandi Carlile
  Written by Brandi Marie Carlile, Phillip John Hanseroth, Timothy Jay
  Hanseroth © Universal Music Corp. on behalf of itself and Southern
  Oracle Music, LLC (ASCAP) All Rights Reserved. Used by Permission
  of Universal Music Publishing.

"Kathy's Song" by Paul Simon
  Written by Paul Simon
  Performed by Simon & Garfunkel
  © Paul Simon Music administered by Songs Of Universal, Inc. (BMI).

CHAPTER 15

"Heroes and Songs" by Brandi Carlile
Written by Brandi Marie Carlile, Phillip John Hanseroth, Timothy Jay Hanseroth © Universal Music Corp. on behalf of itself and Southern Oracle Music, LLC (ASCAP) All Rights Reserved. Used by Permission of Universal Music Publishing.

CHAPTER 16

"Keep On The Sunnyside" by The Carter Family
Written by Alvin Carter.
Copyright © 1928 by Peer International Corporation Copyright Renewed.
Used by Permission. All Rights Reserved.

"Hiding My Heart" by Brandi Carlile
Written by Brandi Marie Carlile, Phillip John Hanseroth, Timothy Jay Hanseroth © Universal Music Corp. on behalf of itself and Southern Oracle Music, LLC (ASCAP) All Rights Reserved. Used by Permission of Universal Music Publishing.

"Murder In the City" by The Avett Brothers
Words and Music by Scott Avett and Timothy Avett
Copyright © 2006 First Big Snow Publishing, Ramseur Family Fold Music and Nemoivmusic
All Rights Administered by BMG Rights Management (US) LLC
All Rights Reserved Used by Permission
Reprinted by permission of Hal Leonard LLC.

CHAPTER 17

"The Joke" by Brandi Carlile
Written by Brandi Marie Carlile, Phillip John Hanseroth, Timothy Jay Hanseroth, (Dave Cobb) © Universal Music Corp. on behalf of itself and Southern Oracle Music, LLC (ASCAP) All Rights Reserved. Used by Permission of Universal Music Publishing.

"An American Trilogy" by Elvis Presley
Written by Mickey Newbury
© 1971 Sony/ATV Music Publishing LLC. All rights administered by Sony/ATV Music Publishing LLC, 424 Church Street, Suite 1200, Nashville, Tennessee 37219. All rights reserved. Used by permission.

"Every Time I Hear that Song" by Brandi Carlile
    Written by Brandi Marie Carlile, Phillip John Hanseroth, Timothy Jay
    Hanseroth © Universal Music Corp. on behalf of itself and Southern
    Oracle Music, LLC (ASCAP) All Rights Reserved. Used by Permission
    of Universal Music Publishing.

"Whatever You Do" by Brandi Carlile
    Written by Brandi Marie Carlile, Phillip John Hanseroth, Timothy Jay
    Hanseroth © Universal Music Corp. on behalf of itself and Southern
    Oracle Music, LLC (ASCAP) All Rights Reserved. Used by Permission
    of Universal Music Publishing.

"Party of One" by Brandi Carlile
    Written by Brandi Marie Carlile, Phillip John Hanseroth, Timothy Jay
    Hanseroth © Universal Music Corp. on behalf of itself and Southern
    Oracle Music, LLC (ASCAP) All Rights Reserved. Used by Permission
    of Universal Music Publishing.

CHAPTER 18

"Late Bloomer" by The Secret Sisters
    Written by Laura Rogers/Lydia Rogers
    Published by Reservoir 416 (BMI) obo itself, Songs of One Riot (BMI),
    Fake Bird Eggs Music (BMI) and Lydia Lane Couldn't Catch A Train
    (BMI)

"River" by Garth Brooks
    Written By Victoria Lynn Shaw and Garth Brooks
    © UNIVERSAL MUSIC—MGB SONGS (ASCAP)
    © BMG SONGS, INC., MAJOR BOB MUSIC CO., INC. and MID-
    SUMMER MUSIC, INC. (ASCAP)
    All Rights Reserved
    Used by Permission of Universal Music Publishing and Alfred Music

"Hold You Dear" by The Secret Sisters
    Written by Laura Rogers/Lydia Rogers
    Published by Reservoir 416 (BMI) obo itself, Songs of One Riot (BMI),
    Fake Bird Eggs Music (BMI) and Lydia Lane Couldn't Catch A Train
    (BMI)

CHAPTER 19

"Bring My Flowers Now" by Brandi Carlile and Tanya Tucker
Written by Brandi Marie Carlile, Phillip John Hanseroth, Timothy Jay
Hanseroth and Tanya Tucker
Performed by Tanya Tucker
© Universal Music Corp. on behalf of itself and Southern Oracle
Music, LLC (ASCAP)
© 2019 Tanya Tucker Music (BMI)
All Rights Reserved. Used by Permission of Universal Music Publishing.

"High Ridin' Heroes" by David Lynn Jones
©1987. Mighty Nice Music (BMI) / Skunk Deville (BMI)—
Administered by Bluewater Music Services Corp. Used by Permission.
All Rights Reserved.

CHAPTER 20

"Your Song" by Elton John and Bernie Taupin
Written by Elton John and Bernard Taupin
Performed by Elton John
© Universal Songs Of PolyGram Int., Inc. on behalf of Universal/
Dick James Music Ltd. (BMI).
All rights reserved.
Used by permission.

"Blue" by Joni Mitchell
Words and Music by JONI MITCHELL
© 1971 (Renewed) CRAZY CROW MUSIC.
All Rights (Excluding Print) Administered by SONY/ATV MUSIC
PUBLISHING, 8 Music Square West, Nashville, TN 37203
Exclusive Print Rights Administered by ALFRED MUSIC
All Rights Reserved. Used by Permission of ALFRED MUSIC.

PHOTO CREDITS

ABOUT THE AUTHOR

Brandi Carlile is a five-time Grammy Award–winning singer, songwriter, performer, and producer. Since her debut in 2004, she has released six studio albums and was the most nominated female artist at the 2019 Grammy Awards with six nominations, including Album, Record, and Song of the Year.

Founded in 2008 by Carlile, the Looking Out Foundation amplifies the impact of music by empowering those without a voice, with campaigns focused on children living in war zones, prevention and reduction in incarceration and recidivism, racial justice, violence prevention, food insecurity, and more. To date, the foundation has raised over $2 million for grassroots causes.

Beloved by fans, peers, and critics alike, Carlile and her band have performed sold-out concerts across the world. Carlile lives in rural Washington State on a compound with her bandmates and their families, as well as her wife, Catherine, and two daughters, Evangeline and Elijah.